China's "Opening"
to the
Outside World _____

China's "Opening" to the Outside World

The Experiment with Foreign Capitalism

Robert Kleinberg

Westview Press

Boulder, San Francisco, & Oxford

Published in 1990 in the United States of America by Westview Press, Inc., 5500 Central Avenue, Boulder, Colorado 80301, and in the United Kingdom by Westview Press, Inc., 36 Lonsdale Road, Summertown, Oxford OX2 7EW

Library of Congress Cataloging-in-Publication Data
Kleinberg, Robert.
  China's "opening" to the outside world : the experiment with
foreign capitalism.
    p. cm.
  Includes bibliographical references and index.
  ISBN 0-8133-7904-0 (hardcover)—ISBN 0-8133-8089-8 (pbk.)
  1. China—Economic policy—1976-   . 2. Shen-chen Special Economic
Zone (Shen-chen shih, China).   3. Investments, Foreign—China.
4. China—Commercial policy.   5. China—Foreign economic relations.
I. Title.
HC427.92.K55   1990
338.951′27—dc20   90-12477
                                                           CIP

Printed and bound in the United States of America

The paper used in this publication meets the requirements
of the American National Standard for Permanence of Paper
for Printed Library Materials Z39.48-1984.

10   9   8   7   6   5   4   3   2   1

Contents

Tables

Abbreviations Used in Notes

FBIS   U.S. Government, Foreign Broadcast Information Service, *Daily Report, People's Republic of China*

FEER   *Far Eastern Economic Review*

JPRS   U.S. Joint Publications Research Service, *Translations on the People's Republic of China* (Washington, D.C.: U.S. Government Printing Office)

SCP   U.S. Department of Commerce, *Survey of People's Republic of China Press* (Hong Kong: U.S. Consulate General)

SWB   British Broadcasting Corporation, *Summary of World Broadcasts, Part 3, The Far East* (Reading, England)

Preface

The purpose and scope of this book will, I hope, very shortly be clear to the reader. Perhaps a word or two would be appropriate first about what this study is *not*. It has not been my intention to theorize about the relationship between foreign economic policy in general and other aspects of domestic politics or foreign relations, because such an effort would require considering similar relationships in other countries and comparing them to those in China, which I was not prepared to attempt. Nor do I apologize for this, because any implications of some general theory of political behavior to China will depend on which of several conflicting interpretations of that country's immediate and unique circumstances one chooses to accept. My aim is to assess the meaning of concrete developments rather than to construct generalizations that a few counterexamples might easily prove fallible.

Although pressing issues are discussed here, this study does not include policy recommendations. To make policy requires an analysis of all the circumstances of the moment, which may include some of the factors I try to explain here, but also many others which fall outside my scope. My goal has been to develop an understanding of an important process at work in China and to try to share that understanding with the reader. Of course, I hope that can contribute to sound policy.

I would like to express my gratitude to a number of individuals without the assistance of whom this study could not have been completed and published. Professors Robert Scalapino, Chalmers Johnson, and Frederic Wakeman, Jr., were very generous with their comments and invaluable help of various kinds. Initial research was done at the library of the Center for Chinese Studies in Berkeley, and I want to thank Annie Chang of the library staff for advice and assistance.

During my one and a half years in China, my understanding of this book's topic and its broader context benefited from many conversations with friends and classmates at Beijing University and other institutions. I regret that it is not possible to thank these individuals by name here, but that does not diminish my appreciation for their help. I owe a special debt to the hosts who welcomed me to live with their families and to dispense with some of the special privileges that normally isolate foreign visitors from the daily realities of life as it is lived by most Chinese.

The University of Kansas kindly supported part of the necessary updating and revision with a summer New Faculty Grant (3752-20-0038).

An anonymous peer reviewer for Westview Press did an outstanding and thorough job of working through the manuscript and pointing out many flaws, large and small. The contribution made by that review is deeply appreciated.

Susan McEachern, Senior Acquisitions Editor at Westview, was supportive, patient, and sensitive to the problems faced by an author trying to produce his first book.

I am indebted for the assistance of Marjorie Kleinberg, Joanne Sedricks, and Virginia Postoak, who typed successive drafts of the manuscript. All three were extremely efficient in producing results of high quality despite having to work from my often messy notes and revisions. Pam Ritchey supervised the laserprinting process with care and professionalism.

Further, I would like to thank my old friend Mr. Nick Karpov, who encouraged me to continue with this endeavor through thick and thin.

Above all, I have been sustained in my work by the exemplary courage and understanding of my dear wife, Angela.

I alone am responsible for this book's contents.

Robert Kleinberg

1

Introduction

> We never permit the use of foreign capital to develop our
> domestic resources as the Soviet revisionists do, never run
> undertakings in concert with other countries and also never
> accept foreign loans. China has neither domestic nor
> external debts.
> --*People's Daily*, Beijing, Jan. 2, 1977[1]

> Ours is an independent and sovereign socialist state. We
> have never allowed, nor will we ever allow, foreign capital
> to invest in our country. We have never joined capitalist
> countries in exploring our natural resources; nor will we
> explore other countries' resources. We never did, nor will
> we ever, embark on joint ventures with foreign capitalists.
> --*Red Flag*, Beijing, March, 1977[2]

Two years after the death of Chairman Mao, the People's Republic
of China began a policy of "opening up to the outside world." Instead of
dividing the world into socialists and capitalists, or exploiters and exploited, China now engages in trade and investment relations with every kind
of country to increase its national productive capacity. But the fact that its
new economic relations are predominantly with capitalist nations does not
mean that China now accepts the reasoning of liberal free trade or capitalist ownership. The opening up policy instead is a return, in economics, to
the most potent factor in the creation of new China itself--nationalism.
    For China, opening up means the adoption by the state of new
methods to promote national economic strength, methods that replace
class warfare and deny the likelihood of global class conflict. The state
now encourages the involvement of foreign partners in China's economy,
at a price and subject to government laws and polices. China offers special concessions to those who bring capital and technology, knowing that

1

capitalist nations have the most to provide. Such measures have facilitated rapid growth and led to some local economic success stories. Some of these successes, however, have had destabilizing effects that challenged the government to devise new methods of control. To manage the balance between local initiative and central intervention during economic reform has proven an impossibly complicated task for the state.

Despite that problem, China's opening up is a development likely to be emulated by other countries ruled by Communist Parties--even where those Parties have not been overthrown in favor of pluralism, as happened in Eastern Europe just prior to publication of this book. Each of the state socialist countries is hampered by the sluggish growth pattern of state-run economies. Each will therefore have a strong interest in China's largely successful experiment with modifying socialism to allow foreign capitalist participation. If China succeeds in securing large amounts of capital and technology, speeding up national growth, yet protecting Party rule and state control of industrial production, it may well influence even the more hardline Communist countries. They will have a huge, unavoidable example of how to increase national economic strength while maintaining Party privileges and political rule. Eastern Europe and the Soviet Union will have an even greater interest in emulating China's foreign economic reforms, now that they are turing away from old-line orthodoxy.

Besides being socialist, China belongs to another group: the world's poor nations. For them, the opening of China will be of the greatest interest as well. If China's opening up succeeds, it will refute Lenin's theory (most of which he borrowed from an English reformer, Hobson) that the poor undeveloped nations of the world are the victims of exploitation by the rich, necessarily culminating in conflict and war among the exploiters. The Chinese hope to show that they can, far from being exploited, manage foreign capitalism for national profit within their socialist borders. China now has the richest capitalist states competing to invest in a domestic market from which they cannot repatriate profits; to offer technology and equipment at the lowest price; to make loans at below-market rates of interest; and to welcome Chinese state-produced exports into their own markets while China rigorously restricts its imports. These accomplishments offer hope to other poor countries that attempt similar strategies. True, China is unusual among them; its huge population is a constant temptation to foreign businessmen who have goods to sell (although they have learned that the domestic market remains limited in its purchasing power). Other developing countries that cannot offer such temptations, however, may well find their own sources of national bargaining power, combined with lures of markets and resources, and reassess their relations with international business.

For Western countries, China's policy will contribute to the widespread concern about the trade policies of newly industrializing countries. Chinese trade protectionism will arouse frustration in the West and diminish confidence in the universality of liberal free-trade principles.

In an era when even close allies, such as the United States and Japan, encounter constant friction about alleged and threatened international trade barriers; when Western Europe's Common Market poses the threat of becoming a jointly protectionist bloc; and when the U.S. uses trade restrictions to add muscle in East-West quarrels, the successful use of a protectionist import substitution policy by the world's largest nation is hardly auspicious for a liberal trading order.

China's opening will be decisive to the success of its national development. It will have worldwide effects. What kind of opening is it and what does this reveal about the Chinese state?

A Hypothesis About the Opening Up Policy

The *duiwai kaifang zhengce*, "policy of opening up to the outside," refers to a set of Chinese foreign economic policies after 1978 that invite and control outside participation in national development. The Chinese reject the term "open door" (*menhu kaifang*), which conveys the very different relations that existed in the imperialist era. That was a term Americans invented.

A Chinese dictionary defines *kaifang* as to "lift a ban, restriction, etc." or "open to traffic or public use." It has an additional meaning: "come into bloom."[3] The translation "opening" or "opening up" is not far off. Since the term is neutral about the extent or kind of opening, there is no objection to the Chinese usage.

China's opening has included several policies. This study focuses on three of the most important: policies that concern foreign investment, international trade, and Special Economic Zones. These are crucial parts of a set of reforms that also included accepting foreign aid and concessionary loans; sending thousands of graduate students abroad to study; letting foreigners travel quite freely in China; and allowing the Chinese people, through the state controlled mass media, to see and learn somewhat more (though still far from a full, objective picture) of the outside world. Regarding these policies and their guiding principles, three broad sources of information are available to Western scholars. First, Chinese publications (some available in translation) contain discussions of policies by Party officials and scholars. From these one can determine the range of acceptable debate, possible future directions of policy, and current guiding ideas. However, except in a few cases, it is far more difficult to ascertain which officials stand where in Party debates about the opening up policy. Second, the Chinese government publicizes many policies affecting foreigners, including laws, rules, plans and economic priorities. A diminishing number of regulations and policies affecting foreigners in China have remained "internal" or secret, subject to Party regulations that prohibit Chinese scholars making them available to foreign colleagues. Third, more economic statistics are becoming available annually. Although some Chinese experts do not consider them wholly reliable because they depend on official local reports with no independent verification, published statistics are useful for comparative purposes. Publication of some sensitive statistics has been delayed. For example, until the mid-1980s it was difficult to find out how much foreign exchange the various provinces earned, because this revealed too much about interprovincial imbalances and central-provincial relations. Although this situation is improving, there are still gaps in available information from any of the above sources, and a study of China's opening up policies should draw on all three types of materials.

To collect facts, however, is not sufficient for understanding the significance of China's opening policy. That requires an investigation of its purposes, scope, and development.

A pioneering work in international political economy by Robert Gilpin[4] is extraordinarily useful for comprehending Chinese policies. Gilpin's book discusses world economic trends and their influence on the foreign economic policies of nations. He observes that as America's relative economic stature diminishes, the international trading order is under increasing challenge from economic nationalism, or neomercantilism. The more each nation moves toward protectionism or other forms of state interference with international trade and investment, the more incentive other nations have to do the same.

It is what the world economic structure encourages in individual states that provides more than a clue about Chinese policy. The People's Republic, determined to raise its economic position in the world, looks at the rapidly developing states of East Asia and finds that all of them (the single exception being British Hong Kong) have relied on extensive direct state interference in foreign trade and investment matters. In such an environment it should not be surprising that China, too, has become a neomercantilist state.

To embrace economic nationalism is to leave other principles behind. Liberals lose their faith in reduced trade and investment barriers, and find convenient exceptions. Marxist China's ideology, too, withers. Marxism can justify alignment with the Soviet Union and dependence on its aid (China's opening of the 1950s). It can, when amended, justify national self-reliance, trade with poor countries, and promoting global revolution (Mao in the 1960s). But when two-thirds of all trade is with capitalists, and they provide virtually all outside investment in national development--when China no longer promotes revolution in Asia, but invests for profit in Australia[5]--then Marxism declines from ideology to slogans of excuse. As an American observer remarks, "Chinese Communist political leaders have shorn socialism of its socialist meaning."[6] What becomes of the inevitable worldwide conflicts between rich and poor classes, the inevitable crises of capitalism, the unification of the oppressed until they overthrow bourgeois capitalism? All of these move into the ever-receding future. China now sees more attractive practical opportunities.

The opportunities the Chinese are turning to grasp are not those of an international system of growing laissez-faire harmony, but of competitive calculation and political action to promote state interests. If China now trades for equal advantage with socialist and capitalist states, it misleads some Westerners, who hope that expanded international trade is a prelude to or even a cause of domestic liberalization. But China accepts neither the premises of international liberalism (that international economic competition can be harmonious and universally beneficial, when divorced from politics), nor its policies (encouraging trade and financial interdependence), nor its predictions (that the benefits of international economic relations will reduce the predominance of state power).

A study of China's opening policies will not only reveal their neomercantilist character, but can provide a model of state reaction to evolving international economic conditions. This study will analyze several of China's economic opening up policies and then compare them. Each of these policies has consisted of an initial solicitation of outside involvement, codified in new laws, followed by central government attempts to control the results. This becomes complicated because some of the economic results of policies are unanticipated ones, and because there are no precedents for a reforming Communist state to follow in response. Nevertheless, a comparison of several different policies will show a pattern: after the initial relaxation of controls, and the growth period that follows, there is always a reassertion of central control to promote the state's perceived interests--before the cycle starts again with another loosening up.

Misconceptions About China's Economic Opening

A clear analysis of China's opening up since 1978 should avoid certain misconceptions. The most widespread misunderstanding about China, especially in the United States prior to June, 1989, has been that it is moving inexorably towards liberalization. This view rests on the assumption that various reforms enacted by Deng Xiaoping's government drive each other forward with increasing momentum.

One of the most persuasive statements of this argument summarized as follows:

> China is now in the process of becoming a more open society. Decentralizing, quasi-market reforms, if they continue, are bound to produce a more liberal political and social climate in China.... The intellectual and legal revolutions, as well as the 'open door' policy, will also stimulate a more liberal trend within China.[7]

Put briefly, the argument runs like this: when China starts to produce and import more consumer goods, it raises popular economic expectations. That broadens public support for foreign trade to get imported goods, which in turn necessitates efficient production of exports. That in turn requires pushing agricultural and urban reforms that restore competition and private incentives. Political support for these reforms comes from thousands of highly-trained students returning from the United States, an open, free market society; and from younger leaders who, better educated than the old guard, are more cosmopolitan and open-minded. Finally, new laws enacted by a less ideological leadership encourage a stable social environment, and lay a basis for cultural and political liberalization. The new policies (as the writer quoted above put it) will create a "strong positive bond" between China and the West based on a "liberal trend within China and China's need for much greater Western participation in its modernization program."[8]

This kind of analysis assumes a clear causal connection among several Chinese policies: internal economic reforms, cultural and legal liberalization, and the foreign economic opening. To group them together can create the impression of a predominant liberal trend. But in fact, the nature of these reforms and the relations among them are considerably more complicated than such an interpretation suggests. Chinese economic reforms often work in contradiction to each other, as (for example) when domestic price reforms raise costs of production and hinder expansion of the country's exports (a problem discussed in a subsequent chapter). And the reforms are far from universally popular with Chinese, among whom they arouse fears of inflation and undependable standards of living.

Chinese commentators, public and private, on China's opening up and other reforms take a realistic view. They usually refrain from asserting that China is moving towards Western-style liberalism. A typical Chinese summary emphasizes that the purpose of expanded economic and technological exchanges is "to promote socialist modernization."[9] Chinese commentators emphasize the practical nature of the reforms, such as the elaboration of a body of foreign investment law. To Chinese this is simply a necessary means of attracting foreign capital, rather than a step towards a society of laws over men. Chinese spokesmen have also made clear the limits of reform. The expansion of foreign contacts and trade has proceeded together with Deng Xiaoping's criticisms of "corrosion by bourgeois ideology from abroad" and his affirmations that "Party leadership and the socialist system...must be improved, but that doesn't mean we can have bourgeois liberalization or anarchy."[10] Deng's intentions in opening China were pragmatic, not liberal.

As for other Chinese, there is little evidence that they see all the various reform measures as logically linked, mutually supporting, and beneficial. Chinese workers, with a disposable income equivalent to a few hundred dollars per year or less, are above all concerned about new price increases. Students, who after ten years of reform are still generally assigned lifetime jobs on graduation, often feel dependent on others who make the vital decisions affecting their lives. Educated Chinese know well that their cultural life and access to independent sources of information remain subject to the unsteady growth of tolerance and broadmindedness in the top leadership of the Communist Party. Any of these groups would be justified in wondering what the liberalization proclaimed by American commentators refers to.

This is not to assert that these commentators are entirely wrong. It is true that the opening in foreign economic policy has coincided with the remarkable decollectivization of agriculture, allowance of some private economic activity, some cultural and ideological relaxation, as well as a new legal system. These are all related in that Deng put them all into effect. And there are other connections. Foreign investment does depend in part on a stable legal order. Foreign trade does require and encourage specialized production for export, including efficient agricultural production made possible by elimination of "people's communes." More sophisticated economic management will rely on increasing numbers of foreign-educated technocrats. Many of the changes are linked--but are they mutually supporting in a way that will drive them all in the same liberal direction regardless of the stated intentions of Chinese leaders?

For many Chinese who study contemporary problems, the ideological certainties of the past (which would condemn today's regime as capitalist and revisionist) have given way to a more modest scholarly specialization that avoids sweeping judgments about the direction of history. In our study of changing policy in a complex country, we would do well to emulate the empiricist methods of many Chinese scholars, and similarly refrain from presuming that reforms must have some outcome that the reformers themselves are unaware of. That does not mean, of course, that we should follow the example of some Chinese scholars who, in their publications, avoid political issues or take government slogans at face value (for examples of these problems, see any of the major Chinese language sources cited in the footnotes).

The Historical Dimension of China's Opening Up

Another caution to make at the outset is to remember that the policies we are concerned with comprise the latest in a long series of Chinese attempts to learn selectively from foreign countries. In fact, since the 1840s, Chinese have talked and written about how to draw a line between Western technique or function (*yong*) and Chinese moral essence (*ti*). This distinction was conceived by nineteenth century conservatives who realized that China must master Western technology, but who wanted to preserve uniquely Chinese moral values.[11]

This problem was elucidated in the formidable life research work of Joseph Levenson. He contended convincingly that drawing such a distinction between Western technique and Chinese moral essence failed, because the study of Western science transformed the entire Chinese world of ideas, including those about Chinese culture itself. It was just as impossible to stop the influence of Western science on all Chinese thinking as it was to diminish the influence of modernization on Confucian society.[12] Nonetheless, as Levenson also pointed out, the failure of the *ti-yong* distinction as a philosophical principle or as a practical guideline did not prevent the idea from remaining popular in China. Echoes of it have been heard throughout the twentieth century, up to present-day calls to preserve Chinese moral standards from Western influences even as the country opens up to foreign technology and management methods.

The distinction between Chinese essence (or morals) and Western technology was maintained even during the rule of Mao, by the Chairman himself. In a famous speech on "ten great relationships" in April, 1956, Mao firmly supported selective absorption of foreign technologies and methods of operation:

> We must firmly reject and criticize all the decadent bour-
> geois systems, ideologies and ways of life of foreign coun-
> tries. But this should in no way prevent us from learning
> the advanced sciences and technologies of capitalist coun-
> tries and whatever is scientific in the management of their
> enterprises. In the industrially developed countries they
> run their enterprises with fewer people and greater effi-
> ciency and they know how to do business. This should be
> learned well in accordance with our own principles in order
> to improve our work.[13]

In the same speech Mao argued that because China was underdeveloped and backward ("poor and blank"), it was amenable to new economic techniques and forms of organization ("good for writing on"). Such claims required faith in the ability of China's leaders and people to pick and choose from advanced science, technology, and management without depending on foreigners or admitting undesirable influences. The same faith in mass willpower and adaptability led Mao to conceive the collectivist "Great Leap Forward" in national development, a catastrophe that ended in famine.

Mao's optimism about adopting capitalist techniques did not extend to allowing capitalist investment. He was ideologically opposed to this, and East-West tensions prevented the possibility from arising. But Mao did promote an opening up in the 1950s, when China accepted massive technical assistance and capital investment from the Soviet Union, violating any purist concept of self-reliance. Hundreds of key projects in metallurgy, motor vehicles, machinery, coal production, etc., were imported and laid the basis of Chinese economic growth until 1960, when Soviet leader Khruschev abruptly cut off aid. In part thanks to this foreign assistance in building production capacity, China's foreign trade grew rapidly, two-thirds of it in the 1950s with the Soviet Union and East Europe.[14] As a result of the Soviet-assisted growth of production, Chinese light industrial and textile exports increased 240 per cent from 1953 to 1959 to a one-year level of US $947 million.[15] The 1950s provide precedents for China's recent expansion of foreign trade and technology transfer on a much wider scale.

In the haste of many commentators to make the obvious contrast between Mao and Deng Xiaoping, the fact that Deng maintained Mao's emphasis on selective absorption is often overlooked. Deng's embrace of foreign trade and investment always sought to protect state control of key sectors of the economy, to limit the political side effects of economic change, and to restrict allegedly harmful foreign influences on China's culture and morals. The following chapters will discuss in detail some of these limitations. In part, they represent the most recent attempt to maintain some traditional Chinese social characteristics in the face of a concerted effort to modernize and strengthen the nation. It is ironic that the once-revolutionary Communist Party now marshals what remains of its ideological force for this conservative purpose, even while it pursues rapid economic development.

Now that Chinese again accept the need to introduce Western technology and scientific knowledge, they frequently revive the idea of preserving a set of supposedly unique Chinese moral values throughout the modernization process. It is not necessary for them to use the words *ti* and *yong*, nor be intellectually rigorous, to make this obvious. The theme of a unique Chinese moral essence unaffected by Western-style modernization is still popular in China. It resonated in a *People's Daily* editorial of July, 1985, by Zhao Fusan, Vice President of the Chinese Academy of Social Sciences.[16] Zhao defended new fashions among the young in hair style, clothing, dancing, and so on as an "awakening of individualism" of a sort different from that of the West. Zhao argued that contrary to foreign news reports, Chinese youth who wear Western-style clothing are not adopting Western values. Rather, both in the mainland and elsewhere,

> China's ancient culture has a deep-rooted impact on... Chinese who, [even] though they may have changed their lifestyle as in overseas Chinese communities, are still under the dominant influence of Chinese traditional values. The policy of opening China to the outside world will have only a limited effect.[17]

Zhao was not downplaying the importance to China's economy of foreign investment and technology, nor was he opposing them. He was maintaining that some fundamental Chinese values (which like most other such writers he did not specify) would endure, strong and unaffected. Thus,

Zhao expressed greater confidence in the strength of Chinese values than other Party members who thought that in the face of pressures to Westernize it was necessary for the government to intervene against "spiritual pollution" or "bourgeois liberalization." What both Zhao and these Party activists shared was a conviction that some unique Chinese moral essence could and should be preserved in a rapidly modernizing society.

There is evidence that Chinese university students hold a similar conviction. It came in the form of a national poll of over 300 students conducted in early 1985 for the journal *Shehui* (Society).[18] (The authors seem to have been unaware of the need for a large, random sample for the results to be statistically dependable, but the detailed tabulations were still the best available evidence of broad trends.) The poll foreshadowed themes that would arise again in the massive protests of 1989.

Chinese students, according to this poll, shared Zhao's viewpoint that China should use Western knowledge for material development, but should also emphasize unique national morals. When asked what aspects of the West China should study, nearly four-fifths (78.1%) said "science, technology, and development". Only a fifth listed "freedom and democracy" (20%).[19] As for the purpose of modernization, for most (58.3%) it was to raise general standards of living; a mere 6.4% agreed that modernization would provide a "material basis for communism".

Yet while the students surveyed strongly supported modernization for material betterment, they at the same time indicated that traditional Chinese morality would continue its role in their lives. Not only did a plurality (40.1%) describe their favorite reading as *classical* Chinese literature. A solid majority also responded to the question, what Chinese things should be pursued in earnest, with "the emphasis on morality in human relations" (56.0%). The expression for "human relations" they endorsed (*renlun*) is defined in the most widely available Chinese-English dictionary published in Beijing as "human relations (according to feudal ethics)".[20] A substantial majority of intelligent Chinese youth are apparently convinced that while Western learning is necessary for modernization, traditional Chinese values are vital to the moral life of the nation--and that the two are compatible.

The defense of Chinese uniqueness from Westernizing modernization, found philosophically untenable by Levenson and practically impossible in old China, now has widespread acceptance. It colors political rhetoric in China, such as Deng Xiaoping's ubiquitous catchphrase, "socialism with Chinese characteristics". It is not a "practical ideology" that indicates any specific solutions.[21] In general, it encourages confidence that international trade and contact will not jeopardize morally unique China. But it also supports a policy of economic nationalism that creates a framework of limitations on foreign penetration within which "Chinese characteristics" (which Deng never defined) can continue to flourish.

However, policy is a practical matter. The theme discussed here accounts for some general political impulses, but not for specific government actions. Only politics and economics can account for how and when the "opening up to the outside" was carried out.

Main Features of the Opening Up Policy

The opening up policies flourished only after Deng Xiaoping took power from Mao's chosen successor, Hua Guofeng, in the first half of 1978. Deng himself had returned to the top ranks as first Vice-Premier and Army Chief of Staff at the fourth National People's Congress in January, 1975. He disappeared one year later after eulogizing Zhou Enlai, who died January 8, 1976. In April the radical "Gang of Four" dismissed him from all posts after the Zhou memorial rally on April 5 at Tiananmen Square, which was a barely disguised attack on the Gang and its policies. Mao died on September 9 of that year. In early October a coup d'etat joined by Hua, with strong regional military backing, overthrew the Gang and Mao's activist widow Jiang Qing. In March, 1977, Hua agreed to include Deng in the top rulership. At the eleventh Party Congress (July-August 1977), there seemed to be a balance of power between Hua and Deng in the Politburo.[22] In late February, 1978, Vice Premier Deng took charge of the "four modernizations" and was soon raising the slogans "Practice is the sole criterion of truth" and "Seek truth from facts", announcing a new flexibility and pragmatism in policy.

Even under Hua, economic modernization began to take priority over everything else. In February, 1978, at the fifth National People's Congress (first session), Hua unveiled a grandiose ten-year economic development plan with the goal to "approach, equal or outstrip [the industrial production of] most developed capitalist countries."[23] Ambitious plans were presented for agriculture, steel, oil, and science. That December, the Party Central Committee declared its top priority

> to close the large-scale nationwide mass movement to expose and criticize Lin Biao and the Gang of Four and to shift the emphasis of our Party's work and the attention of the whole people of our country to socialist modernization.[24]

A Party leader who had been greatly involved in economic affairs during the formative decade of the 1950s, Chen Yun, joined the ruling Politburo and became head of the Central Commission for Inspection of [Party] Discipline. This gave one more signal that nothing was to block the top priority given to economic development.

Deng was clearly in charge by the time the third plenum of the eleventh Central Committee in December, 1978, issued a communique that China would "actively expand economic cooperation in terms of equality and mutual benefit with other countries."[25] In July, 1979, China passed its first law on Chinese-foreign joint ventures. The following February, reformers Hu Yaobang and Zhao Ziyang were put on the Party Politburo Standing Committee. "Revisionist" Liu Shaoqi, the former chief of state who died from poor treatment in jail in the late 1960s, was post-humously restored to honor. However, Deng Xiaoping apparently associated political diversity with the chaotic Cultural Revolution. He decided to delete supposedly guaranteed constitutional freedoms to "speak out freely, air views fully, engage in great debates, and write big-character posters", and to close the so-called Democracy Wall.[26] The political transition from Mao to Deng was completed when Hua Guofeng resigned and Zhao Ziyang was nominated to succeed him as Premier, at the third plenum of the fifth National People's Congress (August-September, 1980).

The new leaders enacted the opening up to the outside world after 1978 in order to increase China's acquisition of technology and capital from a much wider variety of sources than before. They planned to finance this initiative with foreign aid, preferential loans, foreign investment, and rapidly increased exports. At no point did Chinese leaders contemplate embracing free trade or unrestricted competition between Chinese and foreign enterprises.

China's three most important opening up policies concern foreign investment, foreign trade, and Special Economic Zones. The new concessions to foreign investment after 1979 include a growing but often changing body of laws and policies; a willingness to consider various kinds of investment and special trade agreements; and increased international borrowing, mostly at below market rates. Following the Joint Venture Law of July, 1979, the Chinese government has announced a joint venture income tax law, implementing rules on the Joint Venture Law, new exchange control regulations, and an individual income tax law that applies to foreigners.[27] Subsequent measures like the Patent Law of 1984 further define and protect the rights of foreign investors. The foreign investor can propose several different methods of bringing capital or technology to China, ranging from equity joint ventures, with the balance of ownership usually favoring the Chinese side, to compensation trade, in which the foreign partner brings (e.g.) shoe-making equipment and gets shoes in return. The contracts, becoming steadily more flexible as to arrangements, may also specify a different compensating product. Other types of foreign investment projects include simple processing or assembly of products for fee, joint projects by contract that do not involve shared equity, and cooperative development of natural resources (with both sides drawing profits from net production).

China obtained additional foreign capital by borrowing abroad, on very favorable terms. In the initial years of the opening policy, China obtained an extraordinary set of loans at charitable rates, including 106 billion Japanese yen at 3 per cent (repayable over 30 years), US $1.5 billion for energy development at 6 per cent (15 years)--both of these from Japanese government agencies--US $31.5 million interest-free from Belgium (50 years), and US $450 million in special drawing rights in the International Monetary Fund. By the end of 1980, China had $20 billion in available international credit.[28] Remaining prudent, China did not borrow substantially from private banks, but did issue several interest-bearing bonds abroad.

China's foreign investment policy quickly brought striking successes as well as new problems. By the end of 1981, close to US $2 billion in investment had already come in. All of it was from capitalist countries--the United States, Hong Kong, Japan, and several West European countries, in that order. The distribution of this investment was uneven, with a few coastal cities plus Beijing getting hugely disproportionate shares. Even more disturbing from the Chinese point of view, technology transfer was limited. Most projects were agricultural or service-oriented, or involved unsophisticated technologies. While equity joint ventures developed slowly, most foreign investment projects were labor intensive processing ventures or property developments in Guangdong and Fujian Provinces near Hong Kong.[29] The state would now have to try to find ways to influence the quality and perhaps the distribution of foreign investment, while continuing to solicit new projects. That effort is a major focus of this study.

A second major aspect of China's opening after 1979 was a great increase in foreign trade, most of it with capitalist countries. The government carried this out by modifying its administrative structure so as to allow localities and enterprises greater authority over key trade decisions. This loosening of control encouraged growth of trade because enterprises wanted imported equipment, and localities wanted to export to earn foreign exchange (which they could now keep a larger part of) to buy imports. Chinese individuals were also very eager to buy imported consumer goods, although currency restrictions prevented their doing so except when national foreign exchange earnings were relatively high (as in 1979 and 1984).

Both structural and financial reforms allowed rapid growth in foreign trade. Under the pre-1978 structure, all trade deals had to go through layers of bureaucracy noted mainly for their habitual lethargy, including the state Foreign Trade Corporations. These put numerous hindrances between Chinese enterprises and their foreign trading partners, obstructing both trade and effective communication. After 1978, the Foreign Trade Corporations became more product-specialized, and new professional agencies were created to control foreign exchange, administer foreign investment, and promote foreign trade. The government also adjusted internal rates of currency exchange accounting and repeatedly devalued the Chinese currency in order to promote exports while raising the domestic price of imports.

While expanding trade, the government pursued an import substitution policy, setting up trade barriers to prevent foreign goods competing with Chinese ones on the domestic market. Three main tools have been used to implement the protectionist part of this trade policy. First, quotas of import commodities specified in intergovernmental agreements limit quantities of goods by country of origin. Many of these agreements are barters that involve no foreign exchange expenditure.[30] Second, the government instituted in 1980 a provisional import licensing system run by the Ministry of Foreign Trade. Details were at first kept secret,[31] but later clarified in regulations published in 1984. In general, exceptions to licensing were allowed only for urgently needed production goods, or for set quotas of certain other goods during periods of trade surplus. Third, the government maintains steep customs duties further to discourage import of consumer goods or goods that might be produced domestically. Reduced rates apply to natural raw materials for industry, commodities in temporary short supply, machine parts and instruments. Daily use consumer items face a tariff of up to 200 percent of import value, in addition to quota and license requirements. By these methods the central government has protected state enterprise production from foreign competition.

The other side of the coin is that to sustain surpluses, the state has promoted exports by any available means--including neutral packing that "would not bear Chinese trademarks, would not be marked with 'Made in China' or give any hint of the manufacturer's origin." According to Chinese economists, this practice "can help China in avoiding restrictive or discriminatory measures against her goods."[32] The state has played an active role fostering and subsidizing export industries, and attacking trade barriers of other nations.

Like China's new foreign investment policy, its expansion of foreign trade raised complicated new problems. One was the explosion of pent-up domestic consumer demand released by the relaxation of central control, the result being large trade deficits. Chinese consumers' eagerness to purchase foreign goods was hardly lessened by import quotas and protective tariffs. The next problem was to hold this demand for consumer imports in check through central government interventions, without quashing the incentives to export that the decentralization of authority had created in the first place. This dilemma would put ever increasing strain on the government's managerial capacities. The result was a see-saw pattern of relaxation and tightening of central control that developed its own dynamic independent of growth in the volume of foreign trade.

The third major opening up policy after 1978 was the creation of Special Economic Zones. In the first decade, there were four: Shenzhen, next to Hong Kong; Zhuhai, adjacent to the Portuguese colony of Macao; Xiamen, across the straits from Taiwan; and Shantou, "with close trade ties to Southeast Asia" because its Chinese language dialect is widely spoken there.[33] Tropical Hainan Island became the fifth zone much later. The locations of the Zones underscore their political purpose: to develop confidence in the mainland government's reliability among specifically targeted overseas Chinese communities, by granting and implementing relatively generous investment concessions. The economic goals of the Zones were to introduce advanced technology into a "window" for study by Chinese workers and engineers, and to earn foreign exchange through export production. The Zones would in time become a model for development of other coastal areas. Each of the four Zones was previously undeveloped, with poor infrastructure and shortages of skilled and semi-skilled labor.[34] Measures to attract investment to these areas included reduced tax rates, flexible labor contracts and wage terms, acceptance of some wholly foreign-owned investments, and expanded local authority to approve foreign investment projects.

The Special Zone policy had dramatic local results. They were most noticeable in Shenzhen, since the other Zones were very small in size, two to six square kilometers. Some $250 million (US) in foreign investment came to Shenzhen within the first four years, 90 per cent of it from Hong Kong.[35] New buildings sprouted and tens of thousands of jobs were created. But Shenzhen's development proved costly to the state, both in the massive infrastructure subsidies it required and the profit-seeking participation of interior Chinese enterprises it inspired. Nor did Shenzhen succeed in contributing to national development through export earnings or technology transfer, its original justifications.

Many newly established enterprises, instead of exporting, sold or traded goods in Shenzhen itself, which came to be regarded by interior Chinese as a big shopping center. An even larger proportion of foreign investment projects avoided Chinese regulations--such as duties imposed on goods "imported" from Shenzhen[36]--and sold goods inside China. Shenzhen, with its cheap contract labor, readiness to engage in processing operations, and hunger for foreign investment to build a local tax base, became a convenient processing center and bridge to the domestic Chinese market for Hong Kong entrepreneurs.

The Special Economic Zone policy presented the government with unforeseen dilemmas as awkward as those created by other aspects of opening up. Here was a flourishing new city, one of China's most modern, built in just a few years over what had been a backward rural commune. Here was a striking illustration of China's capacity to transform itself with foreign investment. Yet this bold experiment also proved to be a costly drain of capital and skilled labor which added little to China's strength as an international economic competitor. To realize its objective of making the Special Economic Zones serve national economic development, the central government had to tighten control over activities in Shenzhen--but to do so jeopardized the very sources of the city's stunning growth. A subsequent chapter will analyze the government's attempt to find a middle way through this dilemma.

All of the policies to be studied here reflect the economic nationalist goals of Chinese policy. They all have involved rapid growth in

China's levels of economic exchange with other countries, with the state playing an indispensable role, overseeing the process and intervening to reassert its objectives when economic results have proved unsatisfactory. The first step towards a full analysis of this process is to examine more closely the central government's objectives in initiating these policies. We turn to that subject now.

Notes

1. SCP 1977-02, 187.

2. Cited by Terry Cannon in Stephen Feuchtwang and Athar Hussain, eds., *The Chinese Economic Reforms* (London: Croom, Helm, 1983), 295-6.

3. *A Chinese-English Dictionary* (Beijing: Shangwu Yinshuguan, 1978), 380.

4. Robert Gilpin, *U.S. Power and the Multinational Corporation* (New York: Basic Books, 1975).

5. *The Economist*, Nov. 9, 1985, 80.

6. Maurice J. Meisner, "The Chinese Rediscovery of Karl Marx: Some Reflections on Post-Maoist Chinese Marxism," *Bulletin of Concerned Asian Scholars* XVII: 3 (July 1985), 16.

7. Donald S. Zagoria, "China's Quiet Revolution," *Foreign Affairs* LXII: 4 (Spring 1984), 903. This is one of the best of numerous articles that have followed a similar line of reasoning.

8. *Ibid.*, 904.

9. Wang Linsheng and Chen Yujie in Yu Guangyuan, ed., *China's Socialist Modernization* (Beijing: Foreign Languages Press, 1984), 691.

10. Deng Xiaoping, *Selected Works* (Beijing, 1984), 368-9.

11. Joseph R. Levenson, *Confucian China and Its Modern Fate* (Berkeley: University of California Press, 1968), I, 59-69.

12. *Ibid.*, 63-75.

13. Mao Tsetung, *Selected Works*, Vol. V (Beijing, 1977), 305.

14. Teng Weizao in Xu Dixin, ed., *China's Search for Economic Growth* (Beijing: New World Press, 1982), 169-170.

15. Ma Hong and Sun Shangqing, eds., *Zhongguo Jingji Wenti Yanjiu* (Beijing: Renmin Chubanshe, 1983), 468.

16. Translated in *China Daily*, Aug. 2, 1985, 4.

17. *Ibid.*

18. *Shehui* No. 1, 1985, 8-11, 31.

19. *Ibid.*, 11.

20. *Ibid.*, 10,11; *A Chinese-English Dictionary*, 572.

21. See Karl Mannheim, *Ideology and Utopia*, trans. Louis Wirth and Edward Shils (New York: Harcourt Brace, 1936), 55-70.

22. Immanual C. Y. Hsu, *The Rise of Modern China*, third edn. (New York: Oxford University Press, 1983), 782ff.

23. *Ibid.*, 835.

24. A. Doak Barnett, *China's Economy in Global Perspective* (Washington: Brookings, 1981), 66.

25. *Beijing Review*, Dec. 29, 1978, 6-16.

26. Hsu, *The Rise of Modern China*, 799ff.

27. Wang and Chen in Yu, ed., *China's Socialist Modernization*, 695.

28. *Ibid.*, 696-7.

29. Samuel P.S. Ho and Ralph W. Huenemann, *China's Open Door Policy, The Quest for Foreign Technology and Capital* (Vancouver: Univ. of British Columbia Press, 1984), 57-66.

30. Jamie P. Horsely, "The Regulation of China's Foreign Trade," in Michael J. Moser, ed., *Foreign Trade, Investment and the Law in the PRC* (Hong Kong: Oxford University Press, 1984), 13.

31. *Ibid.*, 16.

32. Wang and Chen in Yu, ed., *China's Socialist Modernization*, 691-2.

33. *Ibid.*, 704.

34. Ho and Huenemann, *China's Open Door*, 67-69.

35. *Ibid.*, 67.

36. Wang and Chen in Yu, ed., *China's Socialist Modernization*, 703.

2

The Ideological Principles
of China's Opening Up Policies

How has theory fallen behind realities? The fault lies in
using Marx and Lenin as a 'panacea' for every illness,
something fixed and unchangeable. This is to use a dog-
matic, empty theoretical attitude that Marx, Lenin, and
Comrade Mao Zedong in their prime years opposed, to
treat their theories. Today's realities of reform and building the four modernizations were never experienced by
Marx and Lenin, so they of course cannot have discussed
them; Comrade Mao Zedong also never experienced
them, and besides, not infrequently in his later years
Comrade Mao Zedong's policies were wrong, and only
after order was brought out of chaos did a new situation
emerge...

--World Economic Herald (Shanghai)
December 31, 1984, p. 2

The world's largest Marxist state has changed its aims since the
death of the "Great Helmsman" in 1976. Its "friends all over the world"
are no longer revolutionary comrades, but business partners competing
with each other for China's favor. The People's Republic has not only
cultivated trade relations with nations spanning the ideological spectrum.
It has also welcomed foreign capitalist participation in its economy, subject to state controls.

Despite the new emphasis by the government on economic growth
and profits, national leaders always reaffirm that China will remain a
socialist state. But they seldom trumpet their old claim that they are on
the path to communism. That goal is now relegated to the indefinite
future. As to how long the present kind of socialism will last, one Chinese wrote, "We are not fortune tellers, so we cannot guess."[1] While
Chinese officials and commentators insist they are adhering to the "real"

Marx, their new policies reject historical determinism, downplay class solidarity and deny the likelihood of class conflict--which is the essence of Marxism.

Has China, despite its rhetoric, rejected its ideological inheritance from Marx? Will the economic doctrines underlying Chinese policies replace state socialism with market forces and welfare state capitalism? Do they, as Chinese officials claim, describe a coherent, viable reform program for raising national wealth and strength?

To begin to answer those questions, this chapter offers a distillation of common assumptions about foreign economic policy, as expressed in hundreds of articles published on the subject in China as the "opening up" developed during the decade after 1978. Of course, there have been numerous changes of emphasis and even public disagreements among Chinese commentators (some of which I will discuss in Chapter Four). Harry Harding has categorized these differences as separating "moderate reformers" from "radical reformers."[2] As these terms suggest, a common denominator of support for reform transcends most of the Chinese political spectrum. This chapter identifies assumptions held in common by most Chinese commentators. Of course, the apparent agreement is magnified because Party officials and published authors have no choice but to voice support for whatever line is currently set by national leaders. But even allowing for cautious conformity, there is overwhelming evidence of agreement about some of the basic principles that should guide foreign economic policy reforms. Most of the assumptions to be described here are shared by both "moderates" and "radicals," despite their sometimes wide differences about the pace and priorities of the reform program--and these principles remain widely held even after the shattering events of June, 1989.

Framework of Analysis

To clarify Chinese assumptions about foreign economic policies since 1978, I have drawn on Robert Gilpin's description of three coherent conceptions of international economic behavior and foreign economic policy.[3]

Liberals, as Gilpin uses the term, are those analysts of the international economy who dream of international laissez-faire politics, ever-expanding, specialized production, and trade that promotes universal welfare. They believe that the advantages of free trade policies can gradually become apparent to every nation from successful examples. Nation-states and their policies will in this view diminish in importance, in favor of flows of trade, labor and investment among firms and households trading on the principle of comparative advantage. Politics, such liberals think, is and should be separate from economics.

In sharp contrast, Marxists believe that all history consists of class struggle. At each stage of historical development, a nation's socioeconomic structure shapes its political relations. At any stage of history, the state serves the interests of the dominant social class; in capitalist society the state serves as the "executive committee" of the bourgeoisie.[4] Capitalists in rich countries seek to use foreign trade and investment to obtain cheap labor and raw materials, and to extract profits from poor countries. They press their national governments to represent their interests in the conflict for economic stakes. National economic policies thus serve class interests, and international trade exploits the global poor, who (until they grasp their position, pursue economic self-reliance, and eventually transform the world economic system) lack political means to defend themselves.

Gilpin calls the third conception of international political economy economic nationalism, or mercantilism. According to this point of view, liberal free trade is in decline, to be replaced by economic competition and conflict among nation-states. National, not class, interests determine state policies. The global conflict is not between rich countries that are trying to exploit poor ones, but among all nations. Each has increasing reason to use state power to regulate and influence trade and investment to national advantage. Like Marxism, mercantilism foresees intense international competition; but it asserts that any nation can advance its interests using political power, and can find capabilities to regulate capitalist multinational corporations. The poor can compete and avoid being victims.

Has China replaced Marxism with economic nationalism? Such a possibility is suggested by its abandonment of class struggle, in favor of growth-oriented reforms. Deng Xiaoping's embrace of foreign investment and greatly enlarged trade, made possible by normalization of relations with the Western capitalist countries during the 1970s, always had limitations intended to prevent China ever again becoming overdependent on a foreign partner. The government has tried to protect domestic industries from competition; and by segregation of Chinese citizens from foreigners,[5] to regulate direct personal contacts. Economic measures of control include nonconvertibility of the national currency; duties, import licensing, and discriminatory pricing against imports; and ownership and profit repatriation restrictions on foreign joint ventures. These policies are discussed at length in subsequent chapters.

The best way to understand the intentions behind China's opening up and its limitations is to examine how official and semi-official Chinese commentators have explained them, especially during the crucial years after the opening up reforms were initiated.

On the Nature of International Economic Relations

      Published Chinese analysis of the opening policies during the decade after 1978 describes an international system of competitive states using economic policies to serve national, not class, interests. It consistently affirms that the world economic system, though competitive, gives China opportunities to develop its wealth by obtaining foreign exchange to purchase technology, promoting exports, and restricting imports. Many commentators also emphasize potential dangers from opening up that necessitate state control. More broadly, many perceive foreign economic policy as a part of international political relations. Some of these points can be drawn from their descriptions of the world situation; others can be inferred from what they say about China itself.

      Most Chinese theorists of the opening policies and their limitations see both as a necessary response to world conditions. A typical writer in the official *Beijing Review* described growing worldwide government interference with transnational production, markets, and finances. Conditions that spawned the world economic boom of the 1950s and 1960s--cheap resources and labor, growing markets in Europe and Japan, low tariffs and stable exchange rates--are "now disappearing." International organizations like the IMF and GATT are often "impotent" to stop national protectionism and exchange rate fluctuations. (This observation has not deterred China from making a major effort to gain admission to the GATT, where it would have another forum in which to denounce developed-country protectionism.) Economic cycles add further pressures, and

> Since international economic problems are growing, each country is forced to intervene in an attempt to change the structure of the world economy in a way most favorable to its domestic economy.[6]

Governments (according to the same Chinese commentator) subsidize industries that do well internationally, and limit ones "fated to be defeated in the world competition." Because of competition using advanced production technologies, "international economic relations are characterized by increased friction and fierce competition."

      Chinese analysts nearly always observe that the increasingly competitive world environment has led most nations to engage in trade protectionism. As trade frictions have grown in recent years, they argue, developing countries have turned away from export-oriented strategies and toward import substitution (i. e. protection of major developing industries). To make the best of this situation, China must do the same, most maintain. Chinese analysts see the urgency of such policies as all the more acute given the "new protectionism" of the 1980s (as one called it) involving across-the-board restrictions on all kinds of products imposed by non-tariff barriers.[7] The most vociferous Chinese complaints are reserved for protectionist measures adopted by the United States. American protectionism (in frequently published Chinese descriptions) includes such harmful measures as quotas, tariffs, and anti-dumping laws.[8] Chinese assert that these policies threaten the international trading order and harm the interests of all nations. As they see it, among the results of protectionism by Western nations are currency, trade, and tariff wars of increasing intensity. World economic conditions therefore encourage every nation both to trade for needed goods and technology, and to regulate international economic activity:

> International competition differs [from open competition] because there are sovereign governments in the world economy. The governments will inevitably interfere in international competition, either by supporting their exports or adopting controls on imports. Thus international competition is not truly open competition... This characteristic of international competition allows countries, big or small, strong or weak, to win benefits and avoid harm in foreign economic activities.[9]

The Chinese government recognizes that, as *People's Daily* said in late 1982, "No country in today's world can develop at a relatively high speed without maintaining contacts with other countries."[10] Chinese economists accept the logic of specializing national production and choosing a set of trade partners based solely on economic criteria in order to raise export earnings. Most even accept that for China to supply mainly labor-intensive products "accords with the objective tendency in economic development"[11] because of the country's abundant labor supply.

At the other side of the spectrum, commentators who are critical of the new opening up policies emphasize dangers of economic exploitation or social corruption that could result from expanded foreign trade or contact. According to them, capitalism is still at the root of some foreigners' attempts to exploit China.[12] The reasons include overproduction and a need to dump excess goods, attempts to profit from selling outmoded technology, collusion on price or output, and insistence on supernormal profit rates in developing countries.[13] Some concerns about foreign investment take an apparently Marxist bent: that foreign partners in binational joint ventures may try to "monopolize or control our domestic market"; foreign competition could undercut the development of Chinese export products; foreigners "extort" huge sums for technology licenses; rich country firms will export heavily polluting production plants to poor countries.[14]

Some Chinese continue to see foreign capitalists as antagonists who are deceptive, corrupting, and dangerous.[15] In June, 1988 *People's Daily* issued a more practical warning: localities on China's coast "are

competing with one another to attract foreign investment....Various localities must not go their own way and compete with each other in offering
lower prices...the present situation might undermine the unified policy of
the state..."[16] Offering incentives, this authoritative commentary went
on, is all very well; but Chinese cities should realize that undercutting
each other only plays into the hands of foreign businessmen.

Among those critical of the risks of the foreign presence, economic dangers are always posed as threats to the Chinese nation--not to any
class--and are often accompanied by warnings of undesirable social influences from foreigners. Articles often warn against "blind" imports that
duplicate each other and jeopardize national foreign exchange reserves.[17]
Less frequent but still regular are reminders that nineteenth-century impe-
rialists "used the bad things they offered us to help them pillage China
materially and spiritually."[18] Today, the problem is corruption by foreign
(including Hong Kong) wealth, especially in the Special Economic Zones,
where officials get special (but not terribly effective) training to ward off
bourgeois influences.[19]

Dangers to China from international economic forces are, many
Chinese fear, exacerbated by the country's own vulnerabilities. These
largely stem from weaknesses in attitude. One common complaint is that
many individuals prefer foreign-made goods to domestic ones, even if
quality is equal.[20] A Canton newspaper complained in 1982: "At present,
some people have blind faith in foreign goods...Even a screw has to be
imported. Some imported items are...junk discarded by foreign businessmen, yet our comrades still treat them as treasures."[21] *People's Daily* in
January, 1983, denounced "the mentality and behavior of worshipping and
fawning upon foreign people..."[22] The Party has constantly sought to
curb popular psychological vulnerability to foreigners and their goods.

An even greater perceived threat to China is copying of foreign
lifestyles. Criticisms of this have two premises: first, that "decadent
bourgeois ideas and ways of life [in the 1979 words of *Guangming Daily*]
lead people to degeneration, crime, and despair."[23] Second, that China
can accept Western technology and management methods, but reject the
"great mass of useless, even harmful, things that exist side-by-side with
the truly valuable things under these filthy social systems."[24] According
to Chinese news dispatches, foreign influences are especially severe near
Hong Kong, "with youths and girls wearing outlandish clothes and growing their hair long."[25]

Many Chinese journalists and economists, by omitting such dangers of foreign influence from their commentaries, indicate their disa-
greement with these criticisms. The point here is not that fear of foreign
intrusion is universal (it is not), but rather the character of that concern
which is so often expressed. The defensiveness about foreign influence is
a response not only to foreign wealth, but to the seductive appeal of foreign fashions, materialism, and sexiness. This has taken its strongest form
in warnings that describe an attack by an unspecified "enemy" on Chinese

moral integrity, using everything from bad checks to beautiful women.[26] The moral demand is to resist influences which, whatever their origin, are never mentioned as a threat to any other nation besides China, or to any social class. The issue raised is a clash of national influences, not a class struggle.

The proposed remedies to these alleged threats to Chinese integrity and control are not Marxist--even if the threats themselves are in part identified with capitalism. All of the remedies called for involve the use of state power with no reference to class. For example, to prevent exploitation by foreign investors, the Chinese government has a majority stake in most joint ventures.[27] This reveals the real concern: the objection is not to profit-oriented hiring of wage labor on fixed-term contracts, but to foreign controlled activity on Chinese soil. Chinese insistence on "mutual benefit" from foreign investment reveals confidence that national sovereignty and state controls will prevent exploitation by foreign capitalists, a situation "sharply different from the old 'open door' policy of the imperialist era."[28]

In foreign trade, the new policy (Chinese economists emphasize) is not "an unprincipled opening of our doors to allow...the flooding of our market with foreign goods, leaving us at the beck and call of foreign businessmen."[29] China has the means to prevent intrusion of foreign economic forces; while US barriers against Chinese textiles are "obstinate" and "selfish," it is "completely legitimate" as well as desirable for China to practice protectionist import substitution in order to develop industries that can compete against those of advanced countries.[30]

When Chinese writers use historical analogies in oblique reference to foreign economic policy (a venerable stylistic habit when discussing political issues), they affirm the nation's ability to strengthen itself, overcome vulnerabilities, and regulate foreign influence. *People's Daily* in 1980 praised nineteenth century self-strengtheners who obtained foreign technology for China and stimulated "progressive" capitalism in a feudal country.[31] Despite allusions to Marxist stages of development, the issue was really described in terms of the Chinese nation versus ravaging foreigners. A similar article in 1982 praised opium-fighter Lin Zexu,

> a pioneer in the resistance to foreign aggression... [who put forward] the anti-aggressive and patriotic concept of learning the superior technology of the barbarians in order to control them, which was of far-reaching significance.[32]

One of Lin Zexu's nineteenth-century cannons for fighting foreign barbarians has been placed on a hill overlooking a new port facility at Shenzhen Special Economic Zone.

China's present self-strengthening with foreign trade and investment has political significance, according to Chinese writers. Some asserted at the outset of the opening up reforms that selling exports and earning foreign exchange raises the nation's prestige.[33] Others have said that political relations with various countries, such as EEC members,[34] will be enhanced by trade relations. Yet another related theme is that Special Economic Zones will (in the words of *Fujian Daily*) "have an important significance in winning Taiwan back to the motherland."[35] The Zones serve the political function of reassuring overseas Chinese about the mainland's relations with capitalists.

Numerous Chinese articles supply Marxist-sounding justifications of the new policies. *Red Flag* magazine (prior to its termination in 1988) cited Marx in arguing that that the growth of foreign trade is an inevitable historical trend.[36] Another journal cited the *Communist Manifesto* that in the historical stage after capitalism, the world's economies become interdependent; and praised the younger Stalin for recognizing this and defending foreign trade.[37] Marx and Stalin were cited to justify opening policies: Marx foresaw interdependence and Stalin practiced some trade.

For the rest, Marx was wrong, or, as Chinese began to put it, incomplete. Marx, after all, "had no opportunity to witness foreign trade in any country during his lifetime, and could not write any monograph on this subject."[38] *People's Daily* proclaimed the inadequacy of Marx's solutions to contemporary problems in a famous editorial on December 7, 1984. This broadened a point originally made by Mao in 1937, that since Marx had lived in the period of laissez-faire capitalism, he was not aware of the "laws" of the imperialist era.[39]

Since the Communist Party now considers Marxism incomplete, it can find almost any policy that promotes China's development compatible with Marx. In part it is a matter of using correct vocabulary: foreign trade is "exchange of commodity value," efficient export production "saves social labor,"[40] market forces are the "commodity economy," and so on. In part it is acceptance of a necessary, temporary evil: a prominent Canton social scientist wrote in 1980:

> When private investors outside China enter...their aim is to gain profit. There must be exploitation; this point was clear to us long ago. To realize the four modernizations and develop the socialist economy, we shall tolerate a certain degree of exploitation.[41]

The Party will accept "exploitation" by foreigners not just because it is a temporary situation, but also because it is sure of its political control. Any law passed in socialist China "where the people are the masters," will necessarily be "socialist in nature."[42] This justifies Special Economic Zones, where most capital investment and substantial equity control is by Hong Kong capitalists. Although "national capitalism" prevails now, runs a typical conclusion, "as time passes, the socialist economic component will gradually increase."[43] Elsewhere in the country, foreign investment is also justified as "national capitalism" since it is under Chinese laws and Chinese equity control.[44]

A further reason the Party does not fear capitalists is that it can exploit their divisions. One theoretician wrote in 1985,

> [China can] take full advantage of technological competition among nations...[We shouldn't] have a foreign policy that 'leans to one side,' but [should] bring in whatever country's technology is most advanced, most appropriate, has the cheapest price, and is most advantageous.[45]

As the opening up policy progressed, it became increasingly apparent to China that to have several trade partners competing against each other would be advantageous. Chinese commentators also began to emphasize the beneficial function of international competition:

> The economic relations of the world market also help redistribute wealth among the competitors. In competition, one may obtain what one previously lacked. For example, a producer with no advanced technology or management talents will manage to improve. Otherwise, the producer will be mercilessly cast aside.[46]

All states are under pressure to compete, but can benefit (Chinese are convinced) if they do so successfully. By gradually building their national stock of productive technology and capital even the underdeveloped can catch up with advanced countries.[47]

Post-Mao Chinese comment paints global economic relations as first and mainly international, not inter-class. According to these views, the economic competition for productive resources is among all nations, rich and poor. The risks, to the whole country, come from foreign economic and social influences. This requires state restrictions to protect national interests. On these points, most Chinese commentary expresses a nationalist, not a Marxist, vision.

On the Goals of Foreign Economic Policy

Chinese views about the goals of foreign economic policy in general are implicit in what officials and economists say about Chinese policy. Even before the opening up began, the Ministry of Foreign Trade announced it would import technology to "make foreign things serve China and achieve greater, faster, better, and more economical results in building socialism."[48] The new rulers condemned the "gang of four" for opposing foreign trade and crippling China's economic growth.[49]

        In brief, China's own policies are intended to raise technological
levels of production, and thus increase productivity and national economic
output. As imported technology upgrades the productive process, it is
supposed to improve the quality of export production,[50] earn foreign
exchange which the state can use to buy more equipment and technology,
and so on. State control of foreign exchange earnings is a necessary part
of this benign cycle, as seen in Beijing.
        Chinese recognize that to accumulate foreign exchange, their
economy must adjust to international market pressures. To raise efficiency of export production, they acknowledge, each region must specialize
production in its sector of greatest strength, and the entire country should
promote labor-intensive industries.[51] Chinese economists of the 1980s
have issued few warnings about becoming a cheap labor force for capitalists. They are confident that the protection of state sovereignty and laws
is sufficient guarantee of the welfare of Chinese workers.
        Some Chinese in the early 1980s turned to foreign models to
support their case for using controlled opening policies to get foreign
technology. An economics journal in 1982 cited Japanese development as
proof that importing advanced technology is a "universal...short cut to
economic development."[52] The same article described a model failure:
the Shah's Iran, which imported too much, too suddenly. The contrast
revealed Chinese awareness that uncontrolled growth even of imports
could threaten political stability. This provides an additional reason for
maintaining restrictions on the extent of opening up.
        In discussions of foreign models, many Chinese commentators on
economic affairs placed diminishing emphasis on the differences between
capitalism and socialism. *People's Daily* in January, 1983, asserted that
three kinds of nations had achieved faster growth through active participation in international trade.[53] It cited successes of Japan and Germany
(capitalist); Singapore and Brazil (developing); and Romania and Yugo-
slavia (socialist). This unmistakeably implied that a country's growth
rate, not its economic system, is what matters most. Capitalist Singapore
and Brazil were admirable models because of their trade achievements.
        China's leading economics weekly knocked ideological distinc-
tions down even further in 1984 (the year Marx was formally declared
incomplete in *People's Daily*) by conceding that development strategies of
Singapore, South Korea, Hong Kong, and Taiwan had "proved
successful."[54] It described their strategy as long-term importing of
equipment, starting with simple assembly components, but gradually
upgrading to entire, complex production processes. It asserted that China
could do the same even better. The authors were not advocating capitalism, but rather saying that socialist China could adopt a strategy capitalist
countries had developed. By 1987, frank Chinese discussions of the
achievements of East Asian capitalist states became commonplace. These
discussions frequently concentrated on successful aspects of government
intervention, such as Japan's decades-long selective protectionism to

support infant industries, or foreign exchange controls in South Korea and Taiwan.[55] In this way, Chinese commentary highlighted the similarities between China and its East Asian competitors.

These outspoken remarks by Chinese economists promoting adoption of trade strategies from capitalist countries revealed confidence that China could gain from trading with richer countries based on comparative advantage, without compromising socialism. They credited foreign trade activity with fostering efficient production in all sectors, raising technological levels, "making the people's lives more colorful" with goods sold in free markets, increasing foreign exchange earnings, and creating jobs.[56] On the negative side, all the problems about foreign trade cited in a 1983 *People's Daily* assessment concerned the state's amassing of foreign exchange: localities spending too much, firms duplicating purchases, importing too many large sets of equipment, and so on.[57]

Chinese concerns about foreign trade center on accumulation of national capital, rather than defense of any class interest against inequality, because the goal of socialism has become simply to increase national wealth. In the end, the superiority of socialism "must be revealed", says Deng Xiaoping, "in the rate of economic growth and in economic efficiency."[58] Technological products of capitalism useful to socialism, he also asserted, have "no class character"[59] since they raise the entire country's wealth.

The purpose of accepting foreign investment, as foreign trade, is to promote rapid national economic development by allowing China to master new technologies. The most immediate priority is technical upgrading of existing factories.[60] The long-term goal is to catch up with developed countries in economic strength,[61] and thus to diminish future dependence on outside involvement.[62] China's policy intentions refute Marxist claims that foreign investment by capitalist multinational corporations fosters growing exploitive dependency. Many Chinese theorists believe that by importing capital and technology, a poor country can "stimulate indigenous management and entrepreneurship" and continually diminish its dependence.[63]

Besides securing technology for economic development, published Chinese commentary professes a commitment to equity. Official publications have conceded that to reduce glaring inequalities among China's regions "is a problem of economic and social development strategy that must be solved."[64] The most serious inequality is between the coastal provinces, where nearly all foreign investment has been made, and the underdeveloped interior. But there remain gaps between city and countryside, and widening differentials of income and privilege in the cities.

To address these inequalities, Chinese officials make a trickle-down assumption, contrary to their earlier insistence on egalitarian self-reliance, that as the state accumulates foreign exchange from trade, and uses it to buy productive capital and technology, the whole nation will benefit. For example, despite regional imbalances, Chinese commentators know that the government cannot force geographical redistribution of joint ventures. It can only regulate the proportion of foreign equity control in particular projects and restrict penetration of the domestic market.[65] The problem of domestic equality is not forgotten, but is subordinated to the prime goal of Deng's socialism: to raise national wealth.

For Chinese commentators, the purpose of foreign economic policy is to secure the productive resources necessary to make the whole nation wealthier. The resources China feels itself most sorely lacking are advanced technology and equipment. In bargaining and trading to obtain these resources, Chinese know they can draw usefully on the experiences of capitalist states. Their own government still upholds socialism; but that has been redefined to mean promotion of economic growth with enough equity to preserve political stability.

The Role of the State

Most Chinese writers see the state as a promoter of genuine national interest. They are slipping toward a mercantilist viewpoint: since politics is first of all between nations competing for resources, state power should be used to get ahead in international competition. The state (in this view) is not a prime agent of political class conflict, completing the socialist revolution as Lenin would have it.[66] It may or may not be dominated by one class. In either case the state serves nationalistic purposes, because the major contests in the world are national rivalries.

This economic nationalism is implicit in many articles about the opening policies that depict the state as a benign controlling agent and promoter of modernization. One writer in *People's Daily*, using nineteenth-century analogies, described the state's role as "guidance, promotion, and stimulation" of new enterprises using imported technology.[67] The state must oversee the negotiation with foreign firms of technology transfer, "an important method by which a backward country can catch up with advanced countries..."[68]

State action to secure technology without draining foreign exchange reserves is facilitated by competition among capitalists, and by an equidistant foreign policy that encourages competitive bidding among China's economic suitors--whether capitalist, socialist, or developing.[69] Because the more optimistic Chinese economists assume that capitalist countries in particular have "plentiful idle funds",[70] they believe the state simply needs to adopt regulations to channel and restrain the inflow of capital, as though building dykes on the Yellow River. These optimists believe that so long as foreign investors are guaranteed legal protection of their capital, they will probably invest. However, such a sanguine view is not shared by other Chinese economists, who recognize that too many unfavorable restrictions will result in diminishing foreign investment.

This issue has been debated in China since the early 1980s (see Chapters Three and Five). Chinese economists who want to emphasize the need for restrictions point out that even the capitalist developing states of East Asia limit foreign investment that is primarily intended to penetrate the domestic market.[71] China should do the same, they imply.

In Chinese theory and practice of foreign trade, the state also plays a role of benign intervention. Beijing's leading specialized journal pointed out: "Protectionist policy...does not conflict with an opening up policy."[72] The state according to many Chinese economists has a dual responsibility: promoting exports to earn foreign exchange, and restricting imports of goods China can produce. They argue that this can expand the nation's capital base, and accelerate China's--or any country's--rate of economic development.[73] Few question the government's import substitution policy. One writer even proposed that China should follow what he misunderstood Japan to be doing, and sponsor trade associations to coordinate and uphold export prices.[74] More recently, studies of Japanese trade policy have become more sophisticated, concentrating on the government's past selective use of tariffs and other controls to foster developing industries.[75]

In the Special Economic Zones, too, the central government is seen as the prime regulator and protector of the national interest. By regulating economic relations between the Special Zones and the country's interior, Chinese economists assume, the state can ensure that investment in the Special Zones spreads benefits through wider regions rather than fostering "independent kingdoms."[76] Thus on the one hand, the Zones are intended as "hubs" for widening foreign-Chinese economic contacts.[77] On the other, a new customs barrier has been established between the Zones and the interior, to protect the domestic market from exploitation by foreign capital.

A critical minority of Chinese commentators on the opening policies has asserted from time to time that to protect the nation from harmful outside influences, the state should control imports of ideas, too. For example, Professor Wu Dakun of People's University, criticizing the book *Megatrends* in 1985, suggested to the National People's Congress that Western theories should not be "blindly" imported.[78] As for foreign news reports, Party leader Hu Yaobang (himself associated with relatively "liberal" views and later forced to resign) in 1985 emphasized that journalism must remain under Party control:

> While it is necessary to learn [the] advanced technology [of] reporting, editing, and transmitting information in capitalist countries and advanced management methods, the fundamental principle of bourgeois journalism cannot be adopted, because the social systems are different [sic]. ...It is natural that [journalistic] voices are the same on the political orientation and fundamental policies of the

Party because the Party and government represent the
people and share the same interests.[79]

Hu, laying down the Party line, reiterated the assumption underlying most
of the discussion of the opening policies: the identity of state, Party, and
the "people's" interests.
    What conclusion does all this suggest? To summarize, Marxism
and nationalism overlap when they support a poor country's efforts to get
resources for itself. But they differ over the priority in foreign economic
relations. Nationalism puts one country's interest ahead of any class
interests. On issues of substance that involve use of state power, Chinese
opening policy theorists take the nationalist line.
    Does China still believe in Communism? That rhetorical goal has
been subordinated to securing the technological basis for successful
competition in the international marketplace. To specialize production in
sectors where exports are strongest, a Chinese economist put it, "prepares
the material conditions for the highly unified world economy of communism in the world's future."[80] How far in the future? According to Deng
Xiaoping, China's opening policies will not change until 2050 A.D., and
will "be difficult to change" until 2100.[81] That hardly suggests any
urgent desire to return to orthodox Marxism. As for the next generation,
young Chinese manifest little interest or belief in Communism. The national interest, as the state defines it, has superceded attention to issues of
social transformation that Marxism raises.

Means of Attaining Objectives

    The fundamental practical difference between two conceptions of
economic relations is that neo-Marxist dependency theory suggests that
poor states are vulnerable to exploitation by rich ones; whereas mercantilism suggests that a poor nation like China can use state restrictions and
controls on international economic relations to its benefit. Marxists see
international trade as a means by which capitalist firms get control of
economic resources, and foreign investment as a method capitalists use to
exploit cheap labor. Rich states encourage such activity. Poor states lack
the political strength to control the results. By contrast with this pessimis-
tic analysis, mercantilists assert that any nation, by means of interventionist state regulation of flows of trade and investment, can gain wealth in the
international competition.
    Both theories reject laissez-faire relaxation of trade restrictions.
They differ about whether a poor nation's political efforts can be truly
effective.
    In this respect, too, Chinese commentary since 1978 consistently
expresses mercantilist assumptions. Official or authoritative explanations
of policies that China has adopted are readily available. Despite differ-

ences on certain issues, published analysis assumes active state control of foreign economic involvement, and expresses confidence that the state's role, if properly carried out, will work international economic factors to China's benefit. This is evident in discussions of both foreign trade and foreign investment.

Although foreign trade work has been partly decentralized, overall substantive guidance remains under state control.[82] The state always reserves to itself the right "according to national advantage, to grant or retract an enterprise's foreign trade management rights."[83] Thus, promises that enterprises will be able to conduct foreign trade on their own are limited from the start.

The government intends to use its guidance powers over enterprises to continue its import substitution policy. This is as it should be, most Chinese commentators think. Import substitution, they maintain, will foster growth in a broad base of domestic industries, and protect them from the danger of bankruptcy under the pressure of foreign competition.[84] Some economists argue further that all import products that affect "national livelihood" or for which domestic demand is particularly insatiable should be subject to direct state control.[85]

Beijing authorities use protectionist tariffs, import quotas, licensing, currency restrictions, and negotiated trade agreements. Chinese economists justify such measures as necessary until the country reaches a "high level of economic development"; only then will China be able to replace import substitution with a fully outward orientation.[86] These tools are supplemented by new local specialized import control organs.[87] Such controls are not always resented by Chinese trading enterprises, which are both restricted and protected by them. Some local and provincial exporting enterprises that experimented with autonomous financial responsibility soon opted to return under the wing of direct state control, and the assurance of continued subsidies.[88]

The state's widely supported activism extends to export-related matters. In addition to export licensing, the central government subsidizes or restrains sectors of production in order to support export production and sales. Economists have urged Beijing to retain the right to approve major export items, because competition among exporters could be self-destructive by lowering prices and earnings.[89] Chinese do not all assume that competition leads to greater efficiency. Well-organized state control raises efficiency without a need for duplication of effort by competing enterprises, many think.[90] This conviction has been reinforced by some of the results of domestic economic reforms that have encouraged rapid growth of production. Such growth has caused demand for raw materials and other primary products to rise sharply, in turn leading to shortages of the latter (since the mechanism of higher prices leading to enlarged supply is still working imperfectly). Because of this, Chinese economists emphasize the need for continued state control of the supply, prices, and consumption of primary products to assure stable supplies for all production, including exports.[91]

Many Chinese assume it to be the state's duty to plan export composition. In July, 1978, *People's Daily* called for raising technology-based exports in proportion to agricultural goods.[92] In late 1980 it urged the government to increase machinery exports.[93] In 1981 the same paper called for more exports of natural resources.[94] Another national paper had in June, 1979, proposed restricting exports of "important goods and materials needed for the national economy and the people's livelihood," and exporting light industrial products that "bring quick results, handsome profits, and a large amount of foreign exchange."[95] A Canton paper in 1982 advocated "vigorous" expansion of processed exports, and study of Japan's heavy industrial and chemical exports.[96] Former Minister of Foreign Trade Chen Muhua emphasized high-quality consumer goods exports.[97] More recent analysts have stressed the government's role in diversifying China's export markets, especially through new bilateral trade agreements with countries in the Soviet bloc;[98] and by actively promoting development of new products in order to broaden the range of exports.[99] What all shared was the assumption that while enterprises were being strongly encouraged to export more, the composition of exports and export partners should be planned by the state.

It is true that by the mid-1980s, the government began letting market forces influence the composition of production for export. But central authorities intended to remain heavily involved: after conducting market studies, they were (at least in theory) to guide research, production and sales in accordance with the findings.[100] Market forces would thus be filtered through state directives. As was made officially clear from the outset, the reforms delegated to localities "only the right to operate foreign trade. The right of formulating policy and the right of planning in foreign trade...have all along been concentrated in the central government."[101] Although productive enterprises are to take a leading role in developing and selling exports, central authorities are left the power to set prices on many exports, plan regional production, limit opening of trade ports, and restrict competition among export producers.[102] The government's hope has been to combine flexibility of local initiative with firm and stable central control. The upheavals that threatened centralized authority during the late 1960s are still a haunting specter to Chinese;[103] this makes it difficult to allow and encourage local initiative. Decentralization and state control over foreign trade must find an awkward and unsteady compromise.

According to a comprehensive survey of the government's trade plans published in 1987, the emerging system will have two basic characteristics.[104] Enterprises will be increasingly responsible for their profits and losses in exporting individual products, which it is hoped will encourage them to operate more efficiently. But at the same time, the report states, the government will continue to play a very active managing role:

limiting the list of products handled by each Foreign Trade Corporation; restricting export goods to be shipped out through each of China's ports; regulating the use of foreign exchange surpluses earned by enterprises; holding down prices of domestic production inputs of export goods; and interfering to make sure that the output of enterprises is exported to meet the foreign trade assignment handed down to each province, rather than being sold to other, wealthier Chinese provinces.

To turn to foreign investment, despite substantial decentralization in approvals and administration of small- and medium-sized foreign investment projects, most Chinese analysts want to keep key levers of control and guidance in state hands. Provincial officials can decide to which foreign investments they will grant financial concessions, yet they have been criticized for approving too many joint ventures that compete with Chinese factories for raw materials.[105] *People's Daily* demanded in 1982 that compensation and processing ventures (two major foreign investment categories) be discouraged nationally, if they do not bring in new technology and earn hard foreign currency.[106] (That suggestion, however, was never implemented.) Another type of restriction was proposed by a Chinese economist in 1987. In order to prevent competition among localities seeking to offer concessions to foreign investors (went the published suggestion), every city or investment center should concentrate on a few major production items only. This would reduce duplication and self-destructive competition.[107] Who would allocate these production items among Chinese cities? The central government would do so, was the implicit assumption.

State control is one thing, foreign control is another. Chinese economists are explicit about why limits on foreign equity control are needed. Among concerns about Chinese-foreign joint ventures are that capitalists want especially high profits in poor countries; that foreigners will dominate management of joint ventures; that they charge exorbitant fees for technology licenses; that foreign investors will use joint ventures to dominate the domestic Chinese market; and that they dump polluting industries in developing countries. Yet each of the risks has its remedy: China can control capitalists to its advantage by holding a majority equity stake, by technology assessment, tough bargaining, and by requiring eventual transfer of all assets to the Chinese side.[108] And if too many localities are rushing to engage in similar technology transfer contracts, then (goes a typical suggestion) the central government can set up a transministerial coordinating agency to supervise all contracts that entail technology transfer.[109]

These suggested remedies reveal confidence in China's political capabilities. The Chinese handbook on joint ventures cited earlier said about foreign businessmen who try to "monopolize" the China market:

We must do all-around analysis, we mustn't be too strict. Our broad domestic market, by giving preferential treat-

ment in certain sectors, can encourage more foreign investment [with] more advanced technologies or those
[China is] lacking, and encourage domestic enterprises
conscientiously to raise the quality and technological level
of their products.[110]

By holding out the China market as an inducement, this source argued, the
government can get satisfactory terms and avert monopoly domination.

Those Chinese economists most willing to grant further concessions to foreign capital advocate allowing wholly foreign-owned ventures
to operate freely in China. (Around one hundred had opened there by the
mid-1980s.) They cite these advantages for China: no need to invest
capital or take risks; local labor forces get exposure to advanced technology and management; local governments can pass all kinds of taxes on
such firms; foreign ventures create jobs; and they stimulate complemen-
tary services and industries.[111] Even these writers, advocating "protection and preference"[112] for private foreign corporations, do not say Marx
was wrong. They are confident that Chinese foreign investment laws will
protect worker interests under capitalist firms. The Chinese government,
however, is unwilling to admit large numbers of foreign-controlled enterprises and sacrifice its equity control. Furthermore, the central government seeks (as *People's Daily* explained) to shape the structure and development of foreign investment by regulating its "micro-climate": the
supply of human and material resources to joint ventures; development of
industrial, commercial, and residential facilities, and construction of infrastructure.[113]

None of this suggests the Chinese state only tries to restrain foreign investment. On the contrary, it encourages as much investment as
possible, subject to its rules. But the state retains overall control and
Chinese commentary assumes this will remain so. The state will not
wither away as in the Marxism of Marx, or diminish in importance as in
laissez-faire theories of economic liberals. Rather, the activist state as
Chinese describe it, using central controls to build up national stocks of
capital and raise productive capacity, firmly refutes any idea that a poor
nation must suffer dependency and exploitation.

The Relations Between Economics and Politics

The above suggests that even in their theories, the Chinese are
making limited movement toward laissez-faire liberalism: they believe
the intimate relations between politics and economics will continue.
Although they constantly denounce American trade protectionism, their
theories do not advocate letting state power give way to harmonious,
specialized international production and free trade among autonomous
firms. Nor do they believe other nations will do so. Although they antic-

ipate benefits from international trade and specialization, they foresee intense competition among nation-states, protecting their home markets while penetrating others'. The premises underlying the opening policies are not those of economic liberalism.

Yet there remains an issue that is at the core of theories of development and of international political economy. What relations do Chinese see between political power and existing economic structures of production and trade? Do they still believe with Marx that the economic structures at a given stage of development determine political relations? Expanded to global scale, this means that nations' economic relations determine or limit capacities of national governments to protect their interests. Or do Chinese believe, as do neomercantilists, that political actions of rulers can intervene to influence the international economic distribution of productive capacity? Political choices and actions could then determine or negate some economic outcomes, even for a poor nation trading with the rich.

There is one very Marxist aspect to much recent Chinese analysis of economic problems. As Maurice Meisner has pointed out,[114] numerous theorists are emphasizing a strict interpretation of objective laws of economic development. They think such laws govern development of socialist society, not just capitalism, and can be precisely determined. They reject any Maoist doctrine of "permanent revolution" that ignores these rules.[115]

The main point of these pronouncements is to caution against rash policies. Progress toward socialism is inevitable, but the fundamental stages in development of the economic structure cannot be rushed. Historical development "cannot be altered by the will of man."[116] This comes straight from Marx's insistence that structural change cannot occur until social conditions are fully ripe.[117] Economic structures strictly limit political capacities.

Some of the commentary about foreign economic policy takes a similar line: China must accommodate international economic realities. As in the domestic sphere, "Objective economic laws are inviolable and [those] who violate them will be punished,"[118] so international trade follows "an inevitable trend of economic and social development in all countries."[119] The constraints on China remarked on by Chinese commentators include dependence on foreign technology to speed up development; international market prices that affect export sales; growing protectionism of other nations; "impotence" of international economic organizations that might represent the interests of poorer nations; greed of foreign businessmen; and not least, the structure of domestic production.

The constraints Chinese writers describe all have clear policy implications. China's relative backwardness means that it must get foreign technology. International market competition means that China must raise export quality. Protectionism of other nations means that China cannot afford to open its domestic market without negotiation. National policy seems to have to bend to international economic influences.

Yet as much as Chinese acknowledge the effect of economic conditions on their government's political choices, they are deeply confident that China has the political resources to turn international conditions to national advantage. For example, they maintain that by owning a controlling stake in joint ventures, the government prevents exploitation: it can hire and fire competitive wage-workers, strive for profits, run an enterprise with capitalist management methods--all for the benefit of "socialism."

In foreign trade, Chinese writers also see advantages to an under-developed country, provided state policies are carried out competently. Import substitution (they argue) assists growth of a balanced base of domestic industries. Government subsidies help exports penetrate foreign markets. State planning develops a structure of industries suited to efficient export production. State management preserves foreign exchange balance.

The evidence shows that Chinese have confidence in their nation's political capacities to protect and develop its interests in international economic competition. Most writers believe state policies will promote China's long-term "self-reliance," now redefined to mean diminished dependence on foreign control--not rejection of all direct foreign investment.

When discussing the relations between politics and economics, published Chinese commentators express self-confidence about political measures that seems to contradict their stark economic realism. By their description, each aspect of China's economic situation that impels it to open up also provides opportunities for state-led growth both in absolute terms and relative to competitors. The apparent contradiction is resolved when one remembers why Chinese emphasize Marxist "objective laws of development." It is not out of reborn reverence for a theoretical system they consider out of date. It is rather out of conviction that the reform policies must remain realistic about economic prospects.

Conclusions

Despite the Marxist phrases of justification that often accompany new policy initiatives, Chinese officials and analysts explaining China's foreign economic policy since 1978 have expressed overwhelmingly neomercantilist, not Marxist, views. They perceive international economic relations as a competition among all nations determined to use political means to promote their interests, and having capabilities to do so. They assert that the goals of foreign economic policy are to secure capital and technology to raise the productivity and wealth of the entire nation. They describe an activist, interventionist state promoting a unified national interest.

Only on the abstract issue of the relations between politics and economics do Chinese commentators pay real attention to Marxist ideas. But their allusions to objective laws of development are as much calls for realistic policy as they are prophecies of eventual social change. Recognition of objective conditions that affect political choices does not diminish Chinese confidence that an admittedly backward nation can participate to its advantage in international trade and accept foreign investment. By using state regulation and bargaining power to make progress relative to advanced nations, Chinese believe they can help bring about a redistribution of global economic strength.

This area on which broad consensus existed in China during the 1980s does not consist of specific policy prescriptions, but general concepts that have defined some of the parameters of reform. The reader might think this consensus has been lost after the violent turmoil in June, 1989 severely polarized Chinese politics. Perhaps "consensus" is no longer an appropriate word for anything in China, yet these principles are likely to survive the post-Deng power struggles no matter who emerges on top. The principles outlined above are deeply rooted in the nationalism all Chinese share. Even those Chinese semi-official scholars who now oppose hardline repression and hope for a return to rapid reform have over the past decade consistently maintained their faith in the capacity of government interventionism--if rightly managed--and in the protectionist aspects of Chinese socialism. As for the student-led protest movement so brutally suppressed in 1989, it only reaffirmed a passionate nationalism as the inspiration for its calls for "democracy."

Chinese ideas about the opening policies not only would refute Leninist dependency theories, they also reject Lenin's theory of the state itself. Dependency theories extend Marx's views of class struggle to the global level and decry political weaknesses of poor nations. The many and various Chinese commentators cited in this chapter take an utterly different view, affirming national political capabilities and denying a need for class struggle. As for the state, to Lenin it was just a manifestation of irreconcilable class divisions.[120] The bourgeois state oppresses the workers, and after socialist revolution the working class uses state power along with its own to "suppress the bourgeoisie and crush its resistance."[121] The uses of state power outlined by Chinese theorists have nothing to do with class antagonisms. The state in Chinese socialism is a benign agent of the national interest, and a necessary one, whose interventionist powers used on behalf of all citizens must not wither away. That belief is shared by Chinese who otherwise differ about the desirable speed and details of the reform program.

Chinese rejection of the Leninist view of the state, and adoption on substantive issues of an economic nationalist outlook, constitute one more step in the disintegration of Marxism that began with Lenin and continued with Mao.[122] As each generation of Marxist leaders adjusts orthodoxy to contemporary needs, some of its original elements are lost. Mao made peasants the revolutionary actors and in practice downplayed the urban proletariat. Today's Chinese leaders talk about making the whole country wealthy and avoid class conflict altogether, while their policies widen the inequalities of wealth and power in China, both by region and between levels of workers. As Mao once adjusted Marxist doctrine to the realities of a peasant society, so today's theorists of cooperation with capitalists are responding to international realities that give China incentives to accelerate development by acquiring advanced technology through trade and foreign investment. They are calling into question the Leninist theory that imperialism must characterize relations between capitalist and poor nations--a theory that from the beginning was an ideological pillar of Chinese Communism.

In the following chapters, we turn to some of the practical results of these ideas.

Notes

1. Sun Shuping, cited by Maurice Meisner in "The Chinese Rediscovery of Karl Marx: Some Reflections on Post-Maoist Chinese Marxism," *Bulletin of Concerned Asian Scholars* XVIII:3 (July, 1985), 11.

2. Harry Harding, *China's Second Revolution* (Washington, DC: Brookings, 1987), 77-83ff.

3. Robert Gilpin, *U.S. Power and the Multinational Corporation* (New York: Basic Books, 1975), 26-43 and 215-262.

4. Marx and Engels, *Communist Manifesto*, in Robert C. Tucker, ed., *The Marx-Engels Reader* (New York: Norton, 1972), 337.

5. All foreigners living in China are familiar with their segregation from ordinary Chinese, who are often barred from foreigners'tourist hotels. At Beijing University in 1984-5 and 1986-7, written regulations required all Chinese guests to register in and to leave by 8:00 P.M. But foreigners could come and go freely at all hours. See Beijing University, "Liuxuesheng Zhufang Xuzhi" (mimeo), 3.

6. *Beijing Review*, April 1, 1985, 18-22.

7. *Jingji Yanjiu*, No. 8, 1987, 39-42; and *Shijie Jingji*, No. 12, 1986, 8-12.

8. On American protectionism, see *Guoji Maoyi*, No. 6, 1987, 10-13. On the effects of protectionism in general, see *Jiangxi Caijing Xueyuan Xuebao*, No. 5, 1986, 65-66; and *Shijie Jingji*, No. 1, 1987, 40-41.

9. *Beijing Review*, April 1, 1985, 22.

10. *Renmin Ribao*, Dec. 31, 1982; trans. FBIS, Jan. 4, 1983, K21-23.

11. *Guoji Maoyi Wenti* No. 3, 1981; trans. JPRS 79742, Dec. 24, 1981, 117. Also *Shijie Jingji Daobao*, June 29, 1981; trans. JPRS 78743, Aug. 13, 1981, 54-63. See also Shu-yun Ma, "Recent Changes in China's Pure Trade Theory," *The China Quarterly* 106 (June, 1986), 291-305; and Zhang Yangui, "The Economic Environment and China's Model for the Utilization of Foreign Capital," in Teng Weizao and N.T. Wang, eds., *Transnational Corporations and China's Open-Door Policy* (Lexington, MA: Lexington Books, 1988), 187-189.

12. *Guoji Maoyi Wenti* No. 3, 1980; trans. JPRS 76913, Dec. 2, 1980, 32-35.

13. Wang Yihe and others, *Zhongwai Hezi Jingying Qiye* (Shanghai: Social Sciences Academy Press, 1984), 88-93; and Chen Yin-fang, "Transnational Corporations and World Development: An Evolutionary View," in Teng and Wang, eds., *Transnational Corporations*, 41.

14. *Ibid.* Also *Guoji Maoyi*, No. 3, 1987, 9-11.

15. *Shanghai Shifan Daxue Xuebao*, No. 4, 1986, 10-11.

16. *Renmin Ribao*, June 25, 1988, 1; trans. FBIS, CHI-88-126, 44.

17. *Renmin Ribao.*, May 8, 1979; trans. FBIS May 15, 1979, L 2-4.

18. *Gongren Ribao*, May 28, 1979; trans. FBIS, May 30, 1979, L10-11.

19. *Yangcheng Wanbao*, May 26, 1982; trans. JPRS 81269, July 13, 1982, 28-31.

20. *Renmin Ribao*, April 5, 1985, 2. Also *Guoji Shangbao*, April 16, 1987, 3.

21. *Nanfang Ribao*, Apr. 19, 1982; trans. FBIS, Apr. 28, 1982, p. 1.

22. *Renmin Ribao*, Jan. 4, 1983, 5; trans. FBIS, Jan. 7, 1983, K3-8.

23. *Guangming Ribao*, April 19, 1979; trans. FBIS, May 9, 1979, L 10-12.

24. *Guangming Ribao.*, May 2, 1979; trans. FBIS, May 9, 1979, L 13-14.

25. Canton dispatch, SWB FE/7073, July 9, 1982, C/3-4.

26. *Renmin Ribao*, July 6, 1982; trans. JPRS 81777, Sept. 15, 1982, 35-7.

27. Wang Yihe, *Zhongwai Hezi*, 92.

28. *China Reconstructs* XXXIII: 9 (Sept., 1984), 2.

29. *Ibid.*

30. *Jingji Ribao*, Jan. 22, 1983; trans. JPRS 83018, March 7, 1983, 69; see also Wang Zhenxian, "Transnational Corporations and China's Economic Development," in Teng and Wang, eds., *Transnational Corporations*, 193; and Zhang Yangui, "The Economic Environment and China's Model for the Utilization of Foreign Capital," in *Ibid.*, 187.

31. *Renmin Ribao*, July 14, 1980; trans. SWB FE/6487, Aug. 2, 1980, BII/3-6.

32. *Guangming Ribao*, Oct. 6, 1982; trans. SWB FE/7166, Oct. 26, 1982, BII/S.

33. *Renmin Ribao*, Dec. 4, 1978; trans. FBIS, Dec. 6, 1978, E3-6. Also *Renmin Ribao*, Jan. 31, 1979; trans. FBIS, Feb. 9, 1979, E22.

34. *Da Gong Bao*, Dec. 21, 1978; trans. FBIS, Dec. 21, 1978, N1.

35. *Fujian Ribao*, Sept. 26, 1982; trans. JPRS 82457, Dec. 14, 1982, 79-81. See also Deng Xiaoping, *Selected Works* (Beijing, 1984), 225.

36. *Hongqi*, Apr. 16, 1982, 2-10; trans. FBIS, May 11, 1982, K4-16.

37. Cha Ruqiang in *Weilai Yu Fazhan* No. 20 (Feb. 15, 1985),10-11.

38. *Guoji Maoyi*, March, 1982; trans. JPRS 81994, Oct. 15, 1982, 110-112.

39. Mao Tsetung, "On Practice," in *Selected Works*, Vol. I (Beijing, 1975), 299.

40. *Renmin Ribao*, Sept. 7, 1981; trans. SWB FE/6826, Sept. 12, 1981, C/4-7.

41. JPRS 75423, April 2, 1980, 46-54.

42. *Renmin Ribao*, Aug. 6, 1982; trans SWB FE/7103, Aug. 13, 1982, BII/3-4.

43. Liang Xiang, then mayor of Shenzhen, in *Jingji Ribao*, June 7, 1983; trans. JPRS 84746, Nov. 14, 1983, 51-54.

44. *Nanfang Ribao*, Oct. 26, 1981; trans. JPRS 79807, Jan. 6, 1982, 63-4.

45. Qin Guanghan, "Yanhai Duiwai Kaifang Chengshi Jingji Fazhan Zhanlue Shentao," *Kaifang Chengshi Yu Jingji Kaifaqu Yanjiu* (April, 1985: Jinan and Canton Universities), 14.

46. *Beijing Review*, April 1, 1985, 14.

47. E.g. Rong Yiren, quoted in *Da Gong Bao*, May 7, 1982; trans. FBIS, May 11, 1982, W2-3.

48. FBIS, July 27, 1977, E1-2.

49. *Renmin Ribao*, May 5, 1979; trans. FBIS, May 7, 1979, L9.

50. *Renmin Ribao*, Sept. 7, 1981; trans. SWB FE/6826, Sept. 12, 1981, C/4-7.

51. *Guoji Maoyi Wenti* No. 3, 1981; trans. JPRS 79742, Dec. 24, 1981, 117.

52. *Caijing Wenti Yanjiu*, July, 1982; trans. JPRS 82364, Dec. 2, 1982, 57-69.

53. *Renmin Ribao*, Jan. 4, 1983, 5; trans. FBIS, Jan. 7, 1983, K3-8.

54. *Shijie Jingji Daobao*, Sept. 10, 1984, 2.

55. *Jingji yu Guanli Yanjiu*, No. 3, 1987, 62-64; *Guoji Maoyi*, No. 11, 1987, 25-27.

56. *Jingji Guanli*, March 5, 1983; trans. JPRS 83486, May 18, 1983, 49-56.

57. *Renmin Ribao*, Jan. 4, 1983, 5; trans. FBIS, Jan. 7, 1983, K3-8.

58. Deng Xiaoping, *Selected Works* (Beijing, 1984), 236.

59. *Ibid.*, 333.

60. Xinhua, May 20, 1983; trans. FBIS, May 24, 1983, K10-11.

61. Peng Xianghu, Oct. 4, 1982; trans. SWB FE/7151, Oct. 8, 1982, BII/1-2.

62. *Yangcheng Wanbao*, June 1, 1983; trans. JPRS 84156, Aug. 19, 1983, 84-7.

63. Teng Maotong, March 11, 1982; trans. FBIS, March 11, 1982, K3-4.

64. He Zhukang in *Renmin Ribao*, Sept. 23, 1984, 5.

65. Wang Yihe, *Zhongwai Hezi Jingying Qiye*, 154-156.

66. V. I. Lenin, *State and Revolution* (New York: International Publishers, 1932), 7-20.

67. *Renmin Ribao*, July 14, 1980; trans. SWB FE/6487, Aug. 2, 1980, BII/3-6.

68. *Ibid.* See also *Guangming Ribao*, April 19, 1979; trans. FBIS, May 9, 1979, L10-12.

69. For an excellent treatment of China's increasingly pragmatic relations with the Third World, see Samuel S. Kim,"China and the Third World: In Search of a Neorealist World Policy," in Kim, ed.,*China and the World* (Boulder and London: Westview, 1984), 178-211.

70. *Jiefangjun Bao*, July 21, 1979; trans. FBIS, July 23, 1979, L17-21.

71. *Guoji Maoyi*, No. 11, 1987, 25-7.

72. Wang Yaotian in *Guoji Maoyi*, Aug., 1982; trans. JPRS 82457, Dec. 14, 1982, 53.

73. *Caimao Jingji*, Nov. 15, 1982; trans. JPRS 82724, Jan 25, 1983, 49;*Hongqi*, April 15, 1982; trans. FBIS, April 19, 1982, K3-5. Also *Hongqi*, Oct. 8, 1977; trans. FBIS, Oct. 20, 1977, E1-8.

74. *Fujian Ribao*, Feb. 9, 1982; trans JPRS 81013, June 9, 1982, 80-82.

75. *Jingji yu Guanli Yanjiu*, No. 3, 1987, 62-64.

76. *Ibid.*, 41. Also *Guoji Maoyi Wenti*, No. 4, 1987, 4-8.

77. *Fujian Luntan*, April 20, 1982, trans. JPRS 81634, Aug. 26, 1982, 47-50.

78. *Renmin Ribao*, April 8, 1985, 2.

79. *China Daily*, April 15, 1985, 1.

80. Cha Ruqiang in *Weilai yu Fazhan* 20 (Feb. 15, 1985), 10-11.

81. *Renmin Ribao*, Oct. 12, 1984, 1.

82. See Chapter Four.

83. *Guoji Maoyi Wenti*, No. 5, 1987, 18-19.

84. *Jingji Yanjiu*, No. 8, 1987, 35-44.

85. *Zhongguo Jingji Tizhi Gaige*, No. 4, 1987, 31-32; and *Guoji Maoyi Wenti*, No. 5, 1987, 18-19.

86. Zhang Yangui, "The Economic Environment," 188.

87. Qin Guanghan in *Weilai yu Fazhan*, Feb. 15, 1985, 17.

88. *Guoji Shangbao*, Jan. 10, 1987, 3.

89. Zhou Huamin in *Caimao Jingji* No. 4, Aug. 20, 1981; trans. JPRS 80435, March 30, 1982, 25-31.

90. *Guoji Maoyi Wenti*, No. 5, 1987, 18-19. The government also wishes to prevent "duplication" in scientific research. See *Nature*, Vol. 318 (Nov. 21, 1985), 206.

91. *Nankai Jingji Yanjiu*, No. 5, 1987, 1-7.

92. *Renmin Ribao*, July 8, 1978; trans. FBIS, July 12, 1978, E7-10.

93. *Renmin Ribao*, Dec. 9, 1980; trans. FBIS, Jan 14, 1981, L12-14.

94. *Renmin Ribao*, Nov. 24, 1981; trans. FBIS, Dec. 1, 1981, K22-24.

95. *Guangming Ribao*, May 26, 1979; trans. FBIS, June 7, 1979, L7-9.

96. *Guangming Ribao*, Aug. 19, 1982; trans. JPRS 82068, Oct. 25, 1982, 59-61.

97. *Renmin Ribao*, Sept. 20, 1982; trans. FBIS, Sept. 23, 1982, K3.

98. *Jingjixue Qingbao*, No. 1, 1987, 38.

99. *Guoji Maoyi Wenti*, No. 5, 1987, 5-10.

100. *Renmin Ribao*, Dec. 9, 1980; trans. FBIS, Jan. 14, 1981, L12-14.

101. *Da Gong Bao*, June 19, 1981; trans. FBIS, June 25, 1981, W6-8.

102. See Liu Mingxin and others in *Caimao Jingji* No. 6 (June 15, 1982); trans. JPRS 81938, Oct. 6, 1982, 64-71.

103. Beijing dispatch, Sept. 2-3, 1982; trans. JPRS 81938, Oct. 6, 1982, 59-63.

104. *Guoji Maoyi Wenti*, No. 4, 1987, 1-3.

105. *Renmin Ribao*, Aug. 20, 1982; trans. FBIS, Aug. 27, 1982, K18-20.

106. *Ibid.*

107. *Jingji Yanjiu*, No. 8, 1987, 39-42.

108. Wang Yihe, *Zhongwai Hezi Jingying Qiye*, 88-93.

109. *Guoji Maoyi Wenti*, No. 4, 1987, 4-8.

110. Wang Yihe, *Zhongwai Hezi Jingying Qiye*, 92-3.

111. *Shijie Jingji Daobao*, April 22, 1985, 11.

112. *Ibid.*

113. *Renmin Ribao*, April 28, 1985, 2.

114. Maurice Meisner, "Chinese Rediscovery," 7-9.

115. *Ibid.*

116. *Ibid.*, 8.

117. Marx and Engels, *Communist Manifesto*, in Tucker, ed., *The Marx-Engels Reader*, 344.

118. Xue Muqiao, quoted in Meisner, "Chinese Rediscovery," 7. See also the article cited in note 16.

119. *Tianjin Ribao*, May 18, 1982; trans. JPRS 81523, April 12, 1982, 30-32.

120. V.I. Lenin, *State and Revolution*, 8.

121. *Ibid.*, 37.

122. Benjamin I. Schwartz, *Chinese Communism and the Rise of Mao* (Cambridge: Harvard University Press, 1979), 189-204.

3

Opening Up and Local Development in Shenzhen Special Economic Zone

> The export of capital greatly affects and accelerates the development of capitalism in those countries to which it is exported.
>
> --Lenin, *Imperialism*

When the People's Republic of China decided in 1979 to invite capitalist participation in its long-term development, it allowed new forces to enter its economy, and new political dilemmas to challenge the state. The three most important aspects of China's new "opening up to the outside world"--a welcoming of foreign investment, a greater export and foreign trade orientation, and special zones for capitalist-led development--all added to China's inequalities among groups and regions. But what was more alarming to a state governed by the economic nationalist presuppositions described in the previous chapter was that the new policies also hampered centralized control over the dynamics of growth. After twenty years of political movements and economic stagnation, Beijing abruptly reconsidered its relations with foreign capital, and especially with rapidly growing British Hong Kong.

For Beijing in 1979, economic and political motives coincided. By setting aside territory for the expansion of Hong Kong's economy into China's neighboring Shenzhen municipality, it hoped to attract companies using advanced technology and capitalist management, which could then be studied and adapted for use elsewhere. The state could, it was thought, work a limited local opening to national advantage by accumulating capital and productive technology. At the same time, a capitalist development zone next to flourishing Hong Kong would reduce the yawning disparity of wealth at the Chinese border. It could reassure Hong Kong about China's intentions to permit continued capitalism after the return of that colony to the motherland. And it could, by showing that Beijing tolerates economic diversity, help persuade Taiwan to join a peaceful process of reunification that would supplant armed "liberation." The entire project expressed Beijing's self-confidence in its economic and political managerial capabilities.

The four Special Economic Zones, of which Shenzhen has been the most successful and important, served Beijing's top economic and political priorities. But as this study of development in the largest of the four original Zones will show, they did not serve each of those aims equally well. Shenzhen demonstrated well the non-Marxist, nationalist political principle of Deng Xiaoping, "one country, two systems". It was not as effective in its economic function as a "window" through which China could observe the technological and managerial means of capitalist growth. In fact, while Beijing was advertising Shenzhen's marvelous construction, it was also learning by the mid-1980s that this local success story, measured by its intended contribution to national development, was a failure.

Due to the peculiar economic balance of forces that entered Shenzhen from China and Hong Kong, it became--instead of an export base using the latest production methods--a sophisticated, rapidly growing *import* processing zone, providing cheap land and labor to Hong Kong entrepreneurs eager to penetrate China's protected internal markets. The considerable subsidies Beijing poured into Shenzhen to lay a basis for its development helped build a structure that drained hard currency from Chinese firms and consumers. Instead of earning foreign exchange for the state, Shenzhen punched a hole in the financial protection of China's domestic currency system. Instead of introducing high technology, Shenzhen opened hotels, shops, restaurants, and low-tech assembly plants.

Yet by other standards Shenzhen has been a success: that is, by capitalist standards. It created tens of thousands of jobs, built housing for as many families, developed China's most modern city out of a backward rural commune, diminished the glaring inequality at China's Hong Kong border, supplied goods to China's consumers, and became a model of efficiency--a new object of emulation campaigns--all without posing any direct threat to the Communist Party's monopolistic rule.

The opening of Shenzhen Special Economic Zone, then, produced a local success that was not what Beijing intended. That most of Shenzhen was capitalist did not surprise anyone and disappointed few. But that it was draining trained manpower, scarce capital, and hard currency from inside China was contrary to plan. And that all of this had a dynamic of its own by which rapid development followed local market demands rather than state control, challenged the basic precepts of the opening up policy. Beijing now had a new problem: how to keep Shenzhen growing, but at the same time limit uncontrolled local development which was draining national resources to benefit one small area in a far from socialist manner.

This chapter, based on data published in China, delineates what opened up in Shenzhen and why. It explains the reasoning that led to the creation of China's Special Economic Zones, and the hopes of central government officials that the Zones would benefit the entire nation. It then outlines the preferential policies for foreign capital investment that were adopted in the largest of the original Zones, at Shenzhen. Finally, it evaluates the first five years of results from opening up Shenzhen: the dramatic effects on local development, which were nonetheless inadequate from the state's point of view.

Why Special Economic Zones?

The inner details of Beijing's political decision-making during the 1980s remained closed to outside observers. However, it is possible to piece together a set of acknowledged reasons why the central government decided to establish Special Economic Zones beginning in 1979. The reasons are, in brief, the declining relative performance of the Chinese economy for over twenty years; the economic opportunities available to China, if it followed successful East Asian states in allowing foreign investment, concentrated in zones with extra concessions; and the political benefits from generous treatment of foreign capitalists, especially over-seas Chinese, under the slogan "one country, two systems".

During the two decades prior to 1978, Chinese socialism failed to improve either productivity or real average incomes.[1] This prolonged stagnation was incompatible with China's announced new priority of the mid-1970s and after, the "four modernizations." It contrasted with the economic successes, during the same period, of other East Asian states.

The failure to raise living standards had another result with human and political consequences: the flight of emigrants across the China-Hong Kong border. This continued even after Chinese living standards started to improve in 1979, despite the Hong Kong government's cooperation with Beijing in repatriating illegal refugees. From 1976 to 1981, 480,000 people moved from China to Hong Kong, most illegally--not counting those caught crossing the border.[2] The mayor of Shenzhen admitted in 1983: "We were not able to stop people from leaving, regardless of what measures of confinement were taken."[3] The same remains true today. This embarrassing situation could only hinder voluntary reunification with Taiwan--which, Deng Xiaoping declared, would also depend on the mainland's economic progress in general.[4]

Under Deng's leadership, the Chinese government approved a Joint Venture Law in 1979 and began welcoming certain kinds of foreign investment. It expanded foreign trade with capitalist countries, with the goal of accumulating foreign exchange through export production com-bined with protectionist quotas, import licenses, and comprehensive tar-iffs. The newly flexible official ideology could also justify liberalizing foreign investment rules in a few small, experimental zones, to the point that capitalist investment would soon predominate there.

Not only broad changes in China's aims, but also measures taken by other Asian states encouraged the new special zone policy. A number of China's Asian competitors had established export processing zones with liberal incentives to outside investors: India, Sri Lanka, Thailand, Malaysia, the Philippines, Taiwan and South Korea. These zones have been small, located near seaports or international airports, and in some cases remote from large cities so as to promote development in new regions.[5] Some of the zones--especially in Taiwan and South Korea[6]--have earned substantial foreign exchange through export sales, and created tens of thousands of jobs. Although China is not as export-oriented as some of these other states, it has the same need to earn foreign exchange and obtain production technology.

Consistent with the neomercantilist ideas summarized in the previous chapter, the Chinese government believed that the benefits of export sales from its Zones, and of exposure of Chinese workers and managers to new technologies, could "have a tremendous effect on changing the entire pattern of our foreign economic relations."[7] Though small, the Zones were intended to serve national, not merely local, development.[8] They would use preferential customs treatment, relative investment freedom, and somewhat flexible labor hiring terms to attract foreign investors. Factories, it was hoped, could benefit from preferential treatment and convenient locations to export goods cheaply. Potential profits would encourage foreign capitalists to bring in the best equipment and sophisticated management. This in turn would raise production of high quality exportable goods and earn foreign exchange with which both the locality and the state could purchase more equipment. Chinese workers would gain exposure to modern industrial techniques in small, planned communities where the economic and social effects of the new methods could be watched. In this way, the entire nation could benefit from the opening up of only a tiny part of it--while access to the interior market would (as conceived) remain heavily restricted by the state.

Above all, the Chinese Zones were intended to obtain advanced technology and management methods to be studied and then introduced elsewhere. What engineers and workers could learn in these experimental Zones and apply throughout the country after rotation back would fully compensate for some inevitable local "exploitation."[9] A Chinese journal left no doubt about the perceived nature of management in the Zones' joint ventures:

> As far as the foreign business management in China is concerned, the enterprise is run and managed by the foreign concern while the labor force is sold by us to them...it...[is] capitalist in nature.[10]

But the workers, though under capitalist management, would learn how to handle the latest equipment, and would absorb a "scientific method of cooperation."[11] What they learned, and what specialists learned about advanced technology could be applied nationally. In these ways Shenzhen was supposed to help China, its managers and workers, keep abreast of technological developments abroad.

Besides national economic benefits from local exposure to advanced technology, China had political purposes in promoting Special Economic Zones. One concerns Hong Kong. *People's Daily* declared in 1985:

> In mapping out strategic plans [for Shenzhen SEZ], we must take into account the important factor of resuming sovereignty over Hong Kong by 1997. We must make every effort to minimize the gap in...social and economic development by the end of this century...Shenzhen should strive to reach the medium level and even surpass Hong Kong in some aspects of development.[12]

China wanted to limit the constant loss of people to Hong Kong caused by the glaring contrast at the border.[13] The refugee problem affects national prestige. And after 1997, Chinese soldiers, not British, will be making arrests of those trying to enter Hong Kong.

The Chinese government also intended the Special Economic Zones to advance its political relations with the Chinese people of Hong Kong and Taiwan. China's successful management of Hong Kong after 1997 may help persuade Taiwan to consider negotiation. In the same way, Shenzhen's administration of capitalist-led development inside socialist China will raise Hong Kong's confidence in its own future. Therefore, Beijing believes, successful development in the Zones (including Xiamen, facing the Taiwan straits) "will have an important significance in winning Taiwan back to the motherland."[14] It would help persuade Chinese in Hong Kong and Taiwan that "one country, two systems" is viable, and thereby add to the prestige and negotiating strength of the Beijing government.

The location of the Zones, besides the convenience of all four being small harbors on the seacoast, indicates their political significance: Shenzhen, next to Hong Kong; Zhuhai, next to Macao; Xiamen, across from Taiwan; and Shantou "with close trade ties to Southeast Asia"[15] because overseas Chinese there speak a similar dialect. Each is close to one of the Chinese communities Beijing wants to court, which have capital that could make an important contribution to China's modernization.

Prior to establishment, the four Zones were undeveloped. None of the four had an industrial base, although Xiamen city had a population of 300,000. Shantou had only traditional handicrafts, Shenzhen and Zhuhai were rural communes.[16] To utilize foreign investment, all four Zones needed major development of industrial infrastructure (energy, transportation, communications).

Establishment of the four Zones meant allowing the devolution of certain decisions to local authorities, as well as granting concessions to foreign investors. Guangdong and Fujian Provinces have been allowed greater authority to set high wage levels, approve foreign investments under certain dollar limits, control imports and exports subject to foreign exchange limits, and to regulate the Special Zones. Foreign investment in the Zones takes forms similar to that elsewhere in China: equity and cooperative joint ventures, compensation trade (the foreign provider of capital and technology is paid off in goods produced), processing and assembly for fee, and (less commonly approved) wholly-owned foreign ventures. But extra concessions have been made by the Zones to foreign investors in tax treatment, employment regulations, permissible wage differentials, and administrative treatment.

The Zones did attract considerable outside investment, but until 1984 it was overwhelmingly concentrated in Shenzhen. In fact, in the first three years of opening up Shenzhen alone received one half of all direct investment in China, whereas the other three Zones together received only about seven per cent of it.[17] By the end of 1984, Chinese figures indicate that of total foreign investment of US $840 million in the four Zones, $580 million had come to Shenzhen.[18] It was also the largest of the original Zones:[19]

Shenzhen -   327.0 square kilometers

Zhuhai   -   6.7   "   "

Shantou   -   1.6   "   "

Xiamen   -   2.5   "   "

Only in 1985 was a planned expansion carried out, of Zhuhai to 15.6; Shantou to 52.6; and Xiamen to 131 square kilometers.[20] Besides its dominant size and achievement during the first six years of the Zones' operation, Shenzhen's location next to Hong Kong is a "strategic position" Chinese consider "impossible to exaggerate."[21] Shenzhen is the crossing point for the rapidly growing economic trade between Hong Kong and China.

Of the original four Zones, Shenzhen has been by far the most important in size, location, and achievements, and the one which represents their best prospects. For these reasons, the following analysis concentrates on the development of the Shenzhen Zone (hereafter "the Zone").

Major Features of Shenzhen Special Economic Zone

By designating Shenzhen as a Special Economic Zone (SEZ), the Chinese government provided territory for the expansion of one of Asia's most thriving economies. Hong Kong, with a population of five million and a per capita GNP of US $4,000 in 1980,[22] was suffering from a space shortage, high land values, and rising labor costs. Shenzhen--which in 1978 had 20,000 people and total industrial output of less than $10,000[23]--offered neighboring Hong Kong low land rents as well as a new government commitment to provide cheap labor and subsidize essential infrastructure. Hong Kong is a large consumer market; it has worldwide commercial relations and one of the world's largest container ports. The Shenzhen Zone is thus well placed for export production. But from the vantage point of Hong Kong, Shenzhen is better qualified to produce goods for the undersupplied market inside China.

In July, 1979, the Chinese State Council authorized Guangdong and Fujian Provinces to take special measures to develop their foreign economic contacts. The Shekou area within Shenzhen, across a bay from Hong Kong's New Territories, was designated as an Industrial District under development by the China Merchants Steam Navigation Co. of Hong Kong, which is controlled by Beijing's Ministry of Transportation. Over the next six months, Shantou, Shenzhen, and Zhuhai were established by the central government as foreign investment-led Special Economic Zones. The fourth Zone, part of Xiamen municipality, was designated in October, 1980.

Local officials in Shenzhen never fail to stress the importance of support for their experiment inside the Communist Party Central Committee. With the approval of Deng Xiaoping, that body issued documents that approved creation of the Zone on May 16, 1980, and repeatedly affirmed support in subsequent years.[24] The existence of these documents indicates that Beijing's top leaders were anticipating some opposition from Party officials to the unprecedented new programs. To underscore his personal interest, Deng Xiaoping himself visited the SEZs in the first two months of 1984. He left behind unmemorable but supportive sentences written in his own calligraphy, which were reproduced prominently in locally published promotional materials.

With central government support, the legal structure of the Shenzhen Zone unfolded gradually. It was intended to reassure foreign investors on various points and give them incentives. Provincial regulations issued in 1980 covered equity ratios, contract periods, taxes, visa applications, wages, foreign exchange control, and arbitration. Five more sets of Provincial rules which took effect January 1, 1982, covered details of entry and exit procedures, labor hiring, land usage, business registration, and Zone administration. New investor incentives were issued by Shenzhen on October 4, 1982.[25] Yet further rules were issued by Guangdong

Province in January, 1984, covering contract rights of all parties in foreign economic cooperation; methods of technology transfer; and patent rights.

The major legal concessions to foreigners in the Shenzhen Zone can be summarized as follows (full English texts of published laws are readily available[26]):

--Foreign investment may take a variety of forms. In principle it can involve any sector of the local economy from agriculture to tourism and property development. The Zone welcomes all forms of foreign investment acceptable elsewhere in China, including wholly foreign owned firms. The Provincial SEZ law of 1980 grants such firms the same concessions given other foreign investors.[27] (This regulation was soon extended to fourteen coastal cities, that is, to most municipalities that get significant foreign investment in China.[28]) Some legal questions--such as the structure and composition of joint venture management--are not covered in the SEZ legislation but must be referred to the national Joint Venture Law and subsequent regulations. The Shekou Industrial District within Shenzhen has generally similar investment regulations, except that Shekou explicitly discourages processing agreements.

--Net income of all enterprises is taxed at a 15 per cent flat rate in the Zones, less than in most of the rest of China. There are extra tax reductions of 20 to 50 per cent on projects valued above US $5 million, or which introduce advanced technology. Some projects also get a one to three year tax exemption, at municipal authorities' discretion.[29] Internal regulations specify the length of these special tax holidays; industrial production gets three years.[30] Since 1983, long-term joint ventures (with contracts longer than ten years) have also been given a two-year tax break.[31] Individual income tax rates in the Zones are 3 to 30 per cent, below the national rates of 5 to 45 per cent.[32] Foreign investment ventures can import productive equipment there duty-free.

"In this respect," a city government summary of tax concessions to foreign investors puts it, "we are more preferential than South Korea, Taiwan, and Singapore."[33]

--Land fees, compared with those inside China, are supposed to be preferential. Local authorities have discretion to grant temporary exemptions or to lower fees up to 50 per cent further in certain cases.[34] Special preference is for projects that bring in advanced technology, with the length of fee exemption to be bargained against the level of technology. Shenzhen intends to keep its land use fees much lower than those in Hong Kong.[35]

There are, however, extra charges for power, water, sewer, and telecommunications facilities--which the foreign investor is required to pay for under Article 21 of the Zone regulations. When these costs are included, land rents in Shenzhen compare less favorably with those elsewhere in China.

--Enterprises in the Zones may hire employees on contracts that specify form of remuneration, wages, length of employment, and working conditions. The enterprises decide on wage scales and are encouraged to include a "floating wage" that increases wage disparities and raises individual and group performance incentives. The floating wage can in part be tied to an individual worker's productivity. Firms in the Zones can fire workers who are redundant or violate rules. Workers can resign (a right they often in practice lack elsewhere in China). Wages in foreign enterprises are higher than elsewhere in China but far lower than those in Hong Kong.[36]

On a number of points Shenzhen's labor regulations have been more flexible than national ones. National rules require labor contracts between each enterprise in which foreigners are involved, and workers' trade organizations; Shenzhen contracts are with individual workers. In Shenzhen, unlike the interior, joint venture wage levels are not set in direct proportion to those of state enterprises. Shenzhen firms also have greater flexibility on probation periods, disciplinary measures such as wage reductions, and redundancy dismissals. However, as elsewhere, local government labor bureaus must approve all labor contracts and "examine" discipline or dismissal measures. In practice, most Chinese-foreign joint ventures depend on the municipal labor bureau to find employees, due to the limited pool of trained labor and the household registration system, which prevents workers from migrating to the Zone without permission.[37]

--Central ministry, provincial, and other interior Chinese enterprises may (with Guangdong Province SEZ Administration permission) establish projects in Shenzhen. Thus there are interior-Shenzhen, as well as Chinese-foreign, joint ventures. The purpose of letting interior enterprises participate is to develop a structure for transfer of foreign technology and skills, acquired by joint ventures in the Zone, to China's interior.

--Provision of infrastructure is financed by a combination of state subsidies and local taxes on foreign investment. State-subsidized infrastructure in Shenzhen initially included paved roads, a deep sea lane with a 600 meter freight pier, a 15-kilometer water pipeline, new electricity supplies of one million kilowatts per year, gas supplies, microwave stations, transmission lines, reclamation to expand coastal development areas, sewage systems and storm drainage. Foreign investors are required to install public utility links at their facilities.[38]

--The Shenzhen municipal government cooperated with Hong Kong authorities to simplify approval of visas to cross the Hong Kong border.[39] This applied to Hong Kong entrepreneurs, but not to Shenzhen Chinese, who are generally forbidden to make even temporary visits to the British colony.

--Provincial authorities indicated that the Shenzhen Zone would be a testing ground for relaxation of some economic controls. Price controls would give "extensive" play to market forces,[40] meaning that controls would be upheld only on essential utilities and basic food staples.[41] Foreign exchange controls were also reviewed. From 1981 on there was extensive discussion (see below) of creating a special currency for Shenzhen to dampen black market speculation. Such a currency, linked to the freely convertible Hong Kong dollar, would be a face-saving way of allowing the latter to dominate local finance.[42] However, after prolonged planning, it was never issued.

To complement the legal framework of the Shenzhen Zone, Guangdong Province developed a special governmental structure intended to reduce bureaucratic delays in approving foreign investment projects. In 1980 it set up a Provincial SEZ Administration to examine projects for approval, and an SEZ Development Company to promote and develop joint ventures. Supportive services in Shenzhen are also supposed to be especially efficient.[43]

However, bureaucratic streamlining has been hampered by the Zone having not one but four administrations: the Provincial SEZ Administration; the Shenzhen City government (the SEZ is less than half of Shenzhen Municipality); for Shekou Industrial District in the Zone, the China Merchants' Steam Navigation Co. of Hong Kong, controlled by Beijing's Ministry of Transportation; and for Shahe Industrial District in the Zone, the Provincial Committee on Overseas Chinese Affairs.[44] This confusing situation is the result of (1) the fact that the two Industrial Districts were set up before the larger Zone's establishment, and their separate administrations were never subsequently dismantled; and (2) despite talk of decentralized authority, Guangdong Province wants to retain direct oversight of the Shenzhen Zone (which, remember, is only part of a municipality). Administrative reform has produced redundant structures, including eight municipal government commissions, numerous departments, and branch agencies of Provincial and central organs. Despite numerous reorganizations,[45] overlapping authority remains, especially between Provincial and municipal units.[46]

The special administrative arrangements include important local rights to approve foreign investment projects. Local authorities (in the Zone Administration, and the special units that run Shenzhen's industrial districts) have been allowed to give the go-ahead without central approval to deals of less than HK \$30 million (for light industry) or HK \$50 million (heavy industry).[47]

Central and provincial authorities, realizing the deleterious effects of inadequate infrastructure, also allowed Shenzhen Municipality to retain all of its foreign exchange earnings for basic construction.[48] This supplemented large but insufficient central contributions.

Start-up project capital came from foreign investment, as well as loans in both renminbi and hard foreign currency from the People's Bank of China to numerous Shenzhen enterprises.[49] The People's Bank was authorized to set special rates of interest in the Zone, which could be relatively responsive to international market pressures. Fourteen foreign banks were also allowed to set up offices in Shenzhen, though their role generally remained limited to information gathering and client advising.[50]

The Shenzhen Zone has opened up legal preferences, a streamlined administrative structure, and supportive infrastructure to foreign investors. More important than any specific concession has been the unambiguous priority local government has given to rapid development. This means not only improving the physical investment environment, but promising to cut red tape in approvals and provision of production supplies.

Local Development After 1979

The Shenzhen Zone drew on foreign investment to build a new city, create thousands of jobs, develop extensive local industry, and stimulate regional agriculture. Shenzhen, in 1978 a small undeveloped rural commune, by 1984 was the site of 46 per cent of enterprises using foreign capital and 22 per cent of all foreign investment in China.[51] In comparison with the other centers of foreign investment--Beijing, Shanghai, and Canton--Shenzhen therefore had far higher per capita investment, allowing probably the most rapid economic growth of any municipality in the country.

By the end of 1984, total actual foreign investment in Shenzhen stood at US $580 million, and was growing rapidly.[52] Some 90 per cent of this came from Hong Kong, with Singapore, the US, and Japan trailing far behind.[53]

One must caution that Chinese experts consider statistics from Shenzhen useful for comparative purposes but not exact.[54] One source of confusion, besides the desire of local officials to produce glowing statistical reports, is the publicity given planned or "pledged" foreign investment instead of the actual amount. By August, 1981, actual investment was only 36 per cent of that pledged.[55] By mid-1985, the proportion dropped to about one quarter of US $2.6 billion supposedly pledged.[56]

Still, the rapid growth of real foreign investment in Shenzhen was remarkable. It was concentrated mostly in thousands of small-scale processing and assembly projects, and "cooperative joint ventures" between Chinese and Hong Kong enterprises.[57] The preponderance of such ventures, which were clearly there to take advantage of cheap Chinese labor, would be the first tipoff of suspicions in Beijing about the level of technology being introduced into China through Shenzhen. Sympathetic Chinese economic studies stressed the apparent decline of low-tech "compensation trade,"[58] but there was no evidence that other types of ventures brought in more advanced technology.

The inflow of foreign capital to Shenzhen was matched by substantial national subsidies for development of local infrastructure. Chinese sources vary widely on their extent. Some local officials insist that all infrastructure has been paid for out of local revenue sources.[59] By contrast, a study team from Nankai University estimated that sources of "investment" in Shenzhen (the economists did not specify infrastructure or project investment) could be divided into three equal parts: local financial appropriations; bank loans (unspecified--must be Chinese); and foreign investment together with internal Chinese enterprise capital.[60] A third Chinese source indicated that from 1979 through 1983, tax receipts amounted to 17 per cent of the total value of basic local construction,[61] although the authors hoped taxes would bear more of the burden in the future. In any case, the government certainly shouldered the cost of 25,000 Army (PLA) engineers and construction workers ordered to the Zone to help build basic infrastructure.[62]

Table 3-1

Shenzhen: Sources of "Capital Construction" Investment

	1979 to 1984	1979 to 1986
Foreign Capital	31.0%	20.0%
Shenzhen municipal allocations and local enterprise investment	18.7%	27.0%
Shenzhen-interior joint ventures	3.0%	12.0%
Bank loans (Chinese)	29.3%	30.0%
Direct state investment	8.7%	3.0%
Other (including state-funded special projects	----	8.0%
Provincial allocations	1.4%	----

NOTES: First column does not add to 100 because of categories omitted by data source. Central ministry contributions may be understated.

SOURCES: 1984 figures: Fang Sheng, ed., *Shenzhen Tequ Jingji Kaocha* (1984), 17. 1986 figures: *Beijing Review*, Feb. 24, 1986.

Two other Chinese studies provide the breakdown of "capital construction" investment sources in Shenzhen shown in Table 3-1. Capital input from interior sources has been massive. The 1986 source gives a (probably exaggerated) figure of US $840 million of actual foreign investment. Based on the proportions in Table 1, Chinese capital investment in Shenzhen would then have been over US $2 billion. The "window on the outside world" was an expensive creation indeed.

The national subsidies to Shenzhen far exceeded local hard currency income, which reached an annual level of US $78 million in 1983.[63] This came from export sales, tax revenues on foreign investment ventures, and local sales to foreigners. Yet another source of potential investment capital is to issue shares for private investors, a method which has been tried in Shenzhen but lacks clear legal support and regulations.[64]

A much more substantial injection of capital, skilled manpower, and relatively advanced equipment came from interior Chinese state and provincial enterprises, and joint ventures they formed with Shenzhen's own firms. By 1982, no fewer than 179 such enterprises (of which 46 were state-owned) were employing 48,581 people in Shenzhen and earning profits there of RMB 176.5 million.[65] These Chinese enterprises can profit in Shenzhen, but their investments take job- and wealth-creating capital away from needier parts of the country. They invest in Shenzhen despite generally being denied the tax preferences granted to Chinese-foreign joint ventures.[66]

From development stimulated by foreign and domestic investment, Shenzhen's tax revenues and economic activity both grew at phenomenal rates. City revenues in 1983, for example, were 81.5 per cent higher than in the previous year. Retail sales more than doubled.[67] Local foreign currency earnings surpassed an annual level of $100 million per year.

Shenzhen boomed. Local population jumped from 30,000 to over 360,000 in five years to 1985. Average income, at least in nominal terms, rose to approximately twice the level in major Chinese cities.[68] By 1982, Shenzhen had 15 new buildings of more than 18 stories, and by 1984, 63 more were under construction.[69] And in such areas as telecommunications capabilities, Shenzhen would become China's most modern city.

Chinese articles proudly cited the growth of industrial output in Shenzhen from RMB 60 million in 1979 to 1.8 billion in 1984, and 2.4 billion in 1985.[70] A dramatic development indeed--yet even a self-congratulatory article had to concede that only eleven per cent of foreign investment projects undertaken in 1984 were technology-intensive (a proportion said to be increasing).[71] Foreign investors were attracted by cheap labor, but were not bringing the advanced equipment Shenzhen was supposed to secure for the benefit of the whole nation.

How much foreign investment was going into industrial projects at all--high tech or otherwise? A Chinese source put the industrial proportion of foreign investment rather high,[72] as shown in Table 3-2. Accept these figures and assume that 43.6 per cent of the total were industrial projects, and that (see previous paragraph) 11 per cent of those projects involved high technology; then only some 4.8 per cent of total foreign investment did so. Bearing in mind that foreign investment was itself perhaps a third of local capital investment, the proportion of capital input going to high-technology industrial development amounted to less than two per cent.

Table 3-2

Actual Foreign Investment in Shenzhen -- Initial Years

	Total Proportion of Foreign Investment		
	1979-1983	(1983 only)	1979-1983
Industrial	HK $1.29 bn	HK $473 m	43.6%
Property Development	789 m	386 m	26.5%
Tourist Facilities	151 m	17 m	5.1%
Commercial, Service	225 m	142 m	7.5%
Transportation	37 m	21 m	1.2%
Agriculture	45 m	17 m	1.5%
Other	435 m	76 m	14.6%

SOURCE: Gu Shutang, ed., *Shenzhen Jingji Tequ Diaocha he Jingji Kaifaqu Yanjiu* (1984), 51.

On the other hand, property development (hotels, restaurants, and resorts) and commercial facilities accounted for a substantial proportion of foreign investment, and contributed neither technology nor export sales. They did, however, benefit the locality with jobs, construction, cash earnings, and tax revenues.

The population boom along with local construction and income from intensive development of assembly industries also greatly stimulated agriculture in the neighboring areas of Bao'an County. In 1983, for example, its rural areas' total income reportedly grew by 43 per cent,[73] spurred on by peasants' participation in part-time processing arrangements, as well as cash cropping. Instead of local self-reliance, the explicit policy goal in agriculture after 1979 was to cash in on growing demand in Hong Kong and Shenzhen markets by raising or growing pigs, chickens, fish, lichees, fruits and vegetables.[74] This was summed up in the Zone's agricultural slogan: "Emphasize serving the Zone, at the same time serve exports."[75] Cash crop output went up spectacularly, and export sales of agricultural products from Bao'an County in 1983 were 3.7 times higher than in 1978.[76]

Of course, the Zone also greatly expanded economic opportunities for its urban dwellers. Not only did the employed population multiply tenfold[77] but "young people awaiting jobs [i.e. unemployed] are practically nonexistent."[78] The number and quality of jobs created compares favorably with other Asian export processing zones, ranging from Kandla in India, which generated only 1,400 jobs from 1965 to 1978, to Taiwan's three zones which peaked at 80,000 jobs before declining slightly after 1981.[79] Further, Shenzhen avoided a problem of export processing zones in Taiwan, Sri Lanka, South Korea, and the Philippines. The zones in these states have a disproportionate number of young female workers, from 75 to 85 per cent, with high mobility and rapid labor turnover.[80] This creates an unstable social base for ongoing development. Although visitors to Shenzhen see assembly rooms with only female workers, the labor force as a whole has remained roughly balanced between the sexes.

Real standards of living rose sharply too. One Chinese source claims that urban wages in Shenzhen rose by 133 per cent from 1978 to 1984, reaching an average of RMB 1,571 per year (some $600) in 1983.[81] The mayor of Shenzhen claimed that per capita income reached $1,000 in 1984,[82] which gives an idea of the statistical discrepancies brought in by local officials. He probably took this figure from joint ventures and wholly foreign owned enterprises, which at that time were paying around HK $800 (US $100) per month, 30 per cent of which was deducted for social welfare benefits and insurance.[83] Only a minority of Shenzhen workers have been employed in such enterprises. A more sober 1984 estimate of workers' wages in the Zone gave a figure of RMB 131 (about US $50) per month, still almost three times the 1978 level.[84]

It may seem odd that exact per capita income figures for Shenzhen are not available (probably varying widely even in internal Chinese sources); the explanation lies in profit levels that determine the large "floating" wage component. Chinese sources have published a table that describes 1984 wage grades in Shenzhen's Shekou Industrial District.[85] It shows 15 grades of wage levels from apprentice (RMB 30 per month less than US $10) to common worker (RMB 35-44) to Party and management committee members (RMB 140-158). (These sources leave out the numerical distribution of these wage grades among workers.) While salary numbers have now risen, these figures indicate the approximate relative distribution of rewards within enterprises. In addition to the basic salary, a substantial portion of each worker's wages in the Zones includes a "floating" bonus,[86] dependent on his position and his group's performance (measured by productivity or income), which fluctuates annually. A typical Shenzhen firm pays bonuses of 30 and 60 per cent of wages if profits exceed RMB 50,000 and 100,000 respectively, and cuts wages up to 8 per cent if planned profits are not attained.[87] Shenzhen did establish strong group incentives.

In discussing wages and incomes one should concentrate on real, not nominal levels. Some data on this have been provided by the Shanghai *World Economic Herald*[88] (see Table 3-3). This source described Shenzhen living costs as 50 per cent higher than in Shanghai; but wages were higher as well. Inflation had an initial boost after 1979, reflecting sharply growing demand for both goods and manpower. But real wages moved ahead of prices in the inflationary spiral. While these data suggest that real living standards rose, they do not reliably indicate the magnitude of increase. The source fails to state whether floating wages are included in the wage levels, or to explain the basis or content of statistical categories (especially the fourth).

Despite statistical fuzziness, there seems little doubt that in Shenzhen per capita living standards, including purchases of major consumer goods, rose dramatically.[89] When one recalls that the population grew tenfold in six years, the per capita rise in income is even more remarkable. And thanks to the building boom, average residential floorspace per capita rose from two to nine square meters in four years ending 1983.[90] To the daily life of local residents who benefit from them, these results of development in Shenzhen are of great significance.

The local boom did sustain growth in productive capacity. After services, most project investment went to light industry. The proportion of heavy industry in manufacturing production was only seven per cent in 1981, as compared with 51.3 per cent nationally.[91] This is explained by the preference of foreign investors for processing and assembly projects to take advantage of cheap labor costs, and by Shenzhen's inadequate transportation facilities. In the early 1980s, China was anyway attempting to switch its national emphasis to light industrial development, so municipal and Zone authorities did not initially object to the type of industrial projects that market forces were bringing to Shenzhen. Major growth areas have been electronics assembly, textiles, furniture, and food processing.[92]

Where did the material inputs for this production come from? Table 3-4 presents data on the first five years of Shenzhen's development. A growing amount of raw materials and inputs for construction and industrial assembly was imported, causing a drain of hard currency. As the following section will show, export sales that might compensate for this drain were disappointing.

Table 3-3

Annual Inflation of Wages and Prices, Shenzhen, First Five Years

	1979	1980	1981	1982	1983	1984
Avg. state enterprise monthly wages	45.1%	36.0%	5.5%	14.2%	15.0%	27.5%
Commercial retail price index	17.1%	13.7%	7.8%	7.7%	2.1%	(-1.4%)
Local cost of living	13.2%	20.4%	7.9%	(-3.4%)	2.1%	(-2.1%)
Local retail prices	28.4%	67.9%	72.9%	63.6%	115.0%	17.5%

SOURCE: *Shijie Jingji Daobao*, Dec. 10, 1984.

Table 3-4

Shenzhen: Sources of Key Production Inputs, 1983
(Total Value RMB 306 million)

Supplied from interior of China	RMB	33 million =	10.9%
Imported	RMB	178 million =	58.0%
Cooperative barter (includes export for imports)	RMB	77 million =	25.1%
Local sources	RMB	18 million =	6.0%

NOTE: includes steel, cement, wood, minerals, and electrical equipment.

SOURCE: Fang Sheng, ed., *Shenzhen Tequ Jingji Kaocha* (1984), 18.

Another aspect of development in the Shenzhen Zone was its use as a financial laboratory to test new methods of raising investment. This meant not only acceptance of wholly foreign ventures (still unusual elsewhere in China), but also issuing of equity ownership shares by local enterprises. In Shenzhen's first stock ownership experiment, the Sanhe Company was formed in June, 1983 with six local and state Chinese enterprises as initial shareholders, and sold additional shares to Chinese enterprises and foreign investors.[93] The company's plan indicated that foreigners would be offered only "preferred" shares which (if the enterprise's earnings are sufficient) pay investors a set rate of interest. These shares would be a minority of the total issued and would not control management. Control would be in the hands of Chinese enterprises that could buy the "common" shares (a majority of the total issued).[94]

Chinese economists sympathetic to this experiment--which is not creeping capitalism but rather a form of Chinese-foreign joint venture with dispersed foreign participation and assured Chinese control--cite five advantages:[95]

1. it develops a broader range of sources from which to solicit capital;

2. it encourages foreigners to invest freely in various amounts;

3. it supports stable development of the enterprise, because equity shares can be issued in steady increments, and once issued, the company's equity cannot shrink even if shares are resold (see below);

4. it facilitates accumulation of large amounts of capital necessary to accumulate large equipment items;

5. it allows Chinese to study advanced management methods of stock-issuing companies in advanced capitalist countries (commentators ignore the differences between Chinese and capitalist methods of issuing shares).

It is not clear how Chinese economists view price fluctuations that would be inevitable for these shares and bonds. They seem to believe that existing equity will not change in value even after shares are resold[96]--if so, a sure misunderstanding. Opponents of such experiments stress the risks of dispersed ownership on the Chinese side.[97] However, the experiments themselves have remained limited and an extensive secondary market in equities has not developed.

Shenzhen also experimented with unfamiliar social policies, subject to limits. Like the other Special Economic Zones, Shenzhen remains under firm Communist Party control. All key local government positions are filled by Party members,[98] and no politically independent newspapers or broadcasts are permitted. But no one can stop residents watching Hong Kong television broadcasts.

Shenzhen allows its new university to operate much as a business-oriented college as Hong Kong might. University rules differ from those in other Chinese colleges: students can work part-time for hourly wages; they are allowed to set up and run cooperative recreational and social facilities; students can choose and change roommates; foreign students are not segregated from Chinese; students can petition to change majors; they can take courses outside their majors; they find their own jobs on graduation, often based on previous part-time work experience. These are all mundane rights to any Western student, but are unavailable to most Chinese students at major universities.

Shenzhen, then, is more than an economic experiment; it is a social testing ground, too. Limited social reform has a clear connection with economic policies, as in the business-oriented college. The student rights are intended to make graduates more competent and functional in a competitive labor market. Yet the reforms do not constitute political liberalization: there are no extra-Party student political organizations. Here, in a small college with just over 1,000 students, the Party can observe whether undesirable influences creep in when a limited expansion of freedom is granted.

To summarize, can we call Shenzhen's development as a Special Economic Zone a success? The answer depends on one's perspective. The municipality itself was transformed from a small backward farm town serving as transit-point for those fleeing to Hong Kong, into a thriving city of 350,000 people, with rapid growth, no unemployment, and an average standard of living that (while not approaching Hong Kong's) is by far the highest in China. Industrial development has proceeded rapidly, as has infrastructure construction.

With rapid local development came problems. First, only one third of Shenzhen's industrial output in the first half-decade was exported.[99] With cheap labor and state subsidized infrastructure, it became an *import* processing zone--where light industrial plants set up with Hong Kong investment assembled raw materials and largely imported parts to make goods and sell them inside China. Second, the technology brought in by foreign investors was not advanced. Roughly one half of projects with foreign participation brought little technology at all, beyond cash registers. Third, the Zone required massive infrastructure investment by the state. Statistics indicate that China matched foreigners' contributions with its own equally exceptional level of capital investment. Fourth, corruption spread and Shenzhen became an infamous black market center, with open trading in Hong Kong dollars. Finally, at least some Hong Kong fly-by-night operators made insupportable capital commitments to Shenzhen, prompting the Zone to tighten its joint venture contract regulations in 1984.[100]

Aside from the last two, all of the Zone's problems affected the Chinese state more than the locality. The slow growth of export sales hindered China's hoped-for extraction of foreign exchange earnings from Shenzhen, but the sales by Shenzhen firms inside China were highly profitable to local Chinese and joint venture firms (taking their rapid growth as indication). Low-tech projects did not bring in equipment that could transform production elsewhere in the nation--but did gradually develop a sound industrial base that matched Shenzhen's capabilities, as a previously undeveloped area. Infrastructure investment too was a drain on limited national hard currency reserves, but prepared a viable structure for Shenzhen's development. Finally, corruption and speculation indicated the tremendous market pressures entering from Hong Kong's thriving economy, and the opportunities to take advantage of China's price and currency restrictions. But these symptoms hardly lessened Shenzhen's flourishing growth; their cost was to orderly, state-controlled development. Corruption, which usually involved payments for access to the protected domestic market, called into question the capacity of the "one country, two systems" concept to maintain limited capitalist activity under socialist administration. Worst of all, it was an example of lawlessness that could influence the rest of the country.

Most of the negative features of Shenzhen's development, then, concerned its contributions to national development and its relations with the state. An appraisal of Shenzhen's development from the state's point of view makes a sharp contrast to the local prosperity and successes it created, a contrast that Beijing officials would find difficult to ignore. Their reaction, and the subsequent development of Shenzhen, are the subjects of the next chapter.

Notes

1.   David K. Y. Chu, "The Politico-economic Background to the Development of the Special Economic Zones," in Chu and Kwan- yiu Wong, eds., *Modernization in China, The Case of the Shenzhen Special Economic Zone* (Hong Kong: Oxford Univ. Press, 1985), 29-30.

2.   A. J. Youngson in Youngson, ed., *China and Hong Kong, The Economic Nexus* (Hong Kong: Oxford University Press, 1983), 4-5.

3.   Quoted in *Jingji Ribao* (Beijing), June 7, 1983; trans. JPRS 84746, Nov. 14, 1983, 51-4.

4.   Deng Xiaoping, *Selected Works* (Beijing, 1984), 225.

5.   Kwan-yiu Wong and David K. Y. Chu, "Export Processing Zones and Special Economic Zones as Locomotives of Export-led Economic Growth," in Chu and Wong, ed., *Modernization in China*, 2-8.

6.   *Ibid.*, 8-14.

7.   *Fujian Luntan*, April 20, 1982; trans. JPRS 81634, Aug. 26, 1982, 47-50.

8. *Renmin Ribao*, Feb. 1, 1986, 2; trans. FBIS, Feb. 4, 1986, K5-6: "Special Zones serve the whole country, and the whole country supports Special Economic Zones."

9. Guangdong trade official Sun Ru, quoted in *Wen Wei Po*(Hong Kong), March 9, 1980; trans. JPRS 75423, April 2, 1980, 46-54.

10. *Jingji Yanjiu*, Feb. 20, 1983; trans. JPRS 83174, April 1, 1983, 18-29.

11. *Ibid.*

12. *Renmin Ribao*, Aug. 12, 1985; trans. *Far Eastern Economic Review*, Sept. 19, 1985, 63.

13. *China Daily*, Feb. 4, 1986, 3. See also *Fujian Luntan*, April 20, 1982; trans. JPRS 81634, Aug. 26, 1982, 47-50.

14. *Fujian Ribao*, Sept. 26, 1982; trans. JPRS 82457, Dec. 14, 1982, 79-81.

15. Wang Linsheng and Chen Yujie, "Economic Relations with Foreign Countries,"in Yu Guangyuan, ed.,*China's Socialist Modernization* (Beijing: Foreign Languages Press, 1984), 704.

16. Samuel P. S. Ho and Ralph W. Huenemann, *China's Open Door Policy, The Quest for Foreign Technology and Capital* (Vancouver: University of British Columbia Press, 1984), 67.

17. James B. Stepanek, "Direct Investment in China," *China Business Review* IX:5 (Sept., 1982), 21.

18. Gu Mu, SEZ state councillor, quoted in *he Economist*, Sept. 14, 1985, 79.

19. Clyde D. Stoltenberg, "China's Special Economic Zones," *Asian Survey* XXIV:6 (June, 1984), 642-3. Also *Shenzhen Tequ Bao*, May 3, 1985, 1.

20. *Shenzhen Tequ Bao, Ibid.*

21. *Jingji Yanjiu*, Feb. 20, 1983; trans. JPRS 83174, April 1, 1983, 26.

22. Yen-Tak Ng and David K. Y. Chu in Chu and Wong, eds., *Modernization in China*, 42-3.

23. Cai Renqun, cited in *Ibid.*

24. Shenzhen City Government, "Shenzhen Jingji Tequ Jiben Qingkuang Jieshao," Feb., 1983, 2-3; and Thomas Chan et.al., "China's Special Economic Zones: Ideology, Policy, and Practice," in Y.C. Jao and K.C. Leung, eds., *China's Special Economic Zones* (Hong Kong: Oxford University Press, 1986), 88.

25. China International Economic Consultants, *The China Investment Guide* (London: Longman, 1984), 513-545.

26. *Ibid.*

27. SEZ Regulations of Aug. 26, 1980, Ch. I, Articles 1 and 4; China International Economic Consultants, *The China Investment Guide*, 515.

28. Timothy A. Gelatt, "Legal Aspects of Investing in China's Special Economic Zones: Considerations for U.S. Investors," testimony before U.S. House of Representatives Special Subcommittee on U.S. Trade with China (mimeo), Sept. 12, 1984, 2-3.

29. Shenzhen City Government, "Shenzhen Jiben Qingkuang," 5-6.

30. Michael J. Moser, *Foreign Trade, Investment, and the Law in the PRC* (Hong Kong: Oxford University Press, 1984), 163.

31. Xue Muqiao, ed., *Almanac of China's Economy 1984* (Hong Kong: Modern Cultural Company, 1985), 338.

32. Gelatt, "Legal Aspects," 6-7.

33. Shenzhen City Government, "Shenzhen Jiben Qingkuang," 6.

34. Gelatt, "Legal Aspects," 10.

35. Shenzhen City Government, "Shenzhen Jiben Qingkuang," 6-7.

36. Wong and Chu in *Modernization in China*, 203.

37. Michael J. Moser in Moser, ed., *Foreign Trade*, 157-9.

38. Elson Pow and Michael J. Moser, "Law and Investment in China's Special Investment Areas," in Moser, ed., *Foreign Trade, Investment, and the Law in the PRC,* second ed. (Hong Kong: Oxford University Press, 1987), 222.

39. Shenzhen City Government, "Shenzhen Jiben Qingkuang," 8-9.

40. *Gangao Jingji*, April, 1983; trans. JPRS 84564, Oct. 19, 1983, 55-57.

41. *Shenzhen Tequ Bao*, Dec. 10, 1984, 2.

42. *FEER*, March 21, 1985, 150-1; and May 2, 1985, 56.

43. Shenzhen Municipal Party Committee, ed., *Qianjinzhong de Shenzhen* (Beijing: Red Flag Publishers, 1984), 40.

44. Wong and Chu, *Modernization in China*, 176-179.

45. *Ibid.*, 181-2.

46. *Ibid.*, 184.

47. Wang Shouxin, Shenzhen SEZ Research Center, Shenzhen University; interview, May 8, 1985. Projects with investment value over HK $100 million must be approved by both provincial and State Council authorities: those above HK $30 million (for light industry) or above $50 million (for heavy industry) go to the province and the State Planning Commission. Smaller projects require approval only of the Zone administration. Fang Sheng, ed., *Shenzhen Jingji*, 118.

48. Ho and Huenemann, *China's Open Door*, 67-8.

49. In the two years ending mid-1984, these loans (including those to joint and cooperative joint ventures) totalled RMB 91 million plus U.S. $39 million.

50. Y. C. Jao, "Banking and Currency in the Special Economic Zones: Problems and Prospects," in Jao and Leung, eds., *China's Special Economic Zones*, 161-5.

51. Xue Muqiao, ed., *Almanac of China's Economy*, 1984, 339.

52. *The Economist*, Sept. 14, 1985, 79; and *Beijing Review*, Feb. 24, 1986, 15, 29.

53. Prof. Wang Shouxin, SEZ Research Center, Shenzhen University, interview, May 8, 1985. Figures published in Shenzhen Party Committee, ed., *Qianjinzhong de Shenzhen*, 31.

54. Prof. Wang Shouxin, interview, May 8, 1985 (see previous note).

55. Ho and Huenemann, *China's Open Door*, 66.

56. *The Economist*, Sept. 14, 1985, 79.

57. *Guoji Maoyi* No. 38 (Feb., 1985), 36.

58. First source: Gu Shutang, ed., *Shenzhen Jingji Tequ Diaocha he Jingji Kaifaqu Yanjiu* (Tianjin: Nankai Univ. Press, 1984), 52; second source: Fang Sheng, ed., *Shenzhen Tequ Jingji Kaocha* (Shenzhen Univ. Press, 1984), 21.

59. Jiang Taichang, of Shenzhen Municipal Social Development Commission, interview, May 9, 1985.

60. Gu Shutang, ed., *Shenzhen Yanjiu*, 6.

61. Fang Sheng, ed., *Shenzhen Jingji*, 156.

62. *Shenzhen Tequ Bao*, Sept. 26, 1983; cited in Chu and Wong, *Modernization in China*, 132.

63. Xue Muqiao, ed., *Almanac of China's Economy*, 1984, 522.

64. Gu Shutang, ed., *Shenzhen Yanjiu*, 6-7.

65. Fang Sheng, ed., *Shenzhen Jingji*, 159. The numbers cited did not include some 300 other Shenzhen enterprises with affiliates inside China.

66. For example, first- and second-year income tax exemptions applied to equity joint ventures that will operate at least ten years extend to domestic enterprises only if they are in hardship. They would then be unlikely to have funds to pay anyway. Fang Sheng, ed., *Shenzhen Jingji*, 156-161.

67. Xue Muqiao, ed., *Almanac of China's Economy*, 1984, 522.

68. Jiang Taichang, interview, May 9, 1985 (see note 59).

69. Xue Muqiao, ed., *Almanac of China's Economy*, 1984, 521.

70. *Beijing Review*, Feb. 24, 1986, 15.

71. *Ibid.*

72. Gu Shutang, ed., *Shenzhen Yanjiu*, 51.

73. Xue Muqiao, ed., *Almanac of China's Economy*, 1984, 521.

74. *Ibid.*

75. Shenzhen City Government, "Shenzhen Jiben Qingkuang," 13-14.

76. Xue Muqiao, ed., *Almanac of China's Economy*, 1984, 521.

77. *Beijing Review*, Feb. 24, 1986, 15.

78. Xue Muqiao, ed., *Almanac of China's Economy*, 1984, 523.

79. Chu and Wong in *Modernization in China*, 12.

80. *Ibid.*, 12-13.

81. Xue Muqiao, ed., *Almanac of China's Economy*, 1984, 523.

82. *Beijing Review*, Feb. 24, 1986, 16.

83. Gu Shutang, ed., *Shenzhen Yanjiu*, 4.

84. *Ibid.*, 2.

85. Gu Shutang, ed., *Shenzhen Yanjiu*, 112-113. The same chart is reproduced in Fang Sheng, ed., *Shenzhen Jingji*, 88, but described there as standard wage grades for Shekou enterprises.

86. Gu Shutang, ed., *Shenzhen Yanjiu*, 4.

87. Fang Sheng, ed., *Shenzhen Jingji*, 92-94.

88. *Shijie Jingji Daobao*, Dec. 10, 1984, 1.

89. Xue Muqiao, ed., *Almanac of China's Economy*, 1984, 523.

90. *Ibid.*

91. Chu and Wong in *Modernization in China*, 60.

92. *Ibid*, 61.

93. This and following, Fang Sheng, ed., *Shenzhen Jingji*, 23-26.

94. *Ibid.*

95. *Ibid.*, 24-25.

96. *Ibid.*, 24: when shares change hands, it will not affect the "original investment situation" of the enterprise.

97. See summary in *The Economist*, March 29, 1986, 67.

98. C.Y. Chang, "Bureaucracy and Modernization: A Case Study of the Special Economic Zones in China," in Jao and Leung, eds., *China's Special Economic Zones*, 109.

99. *Beijing Review*, Feb. 24, 1986, 15.

100. Timothy A. Gelatt, "Legal Aspects," 14.

4

Shenzhen's Relations with the National Economy

"Comrade, please speak Mandarin [not Cantonese]."

--sign posted around Shenzhen in 1985

Shenzhen after five years of rapid growth presented a picture of success under China's policies of opening up to the outside world. It was as though Hong Kong's New Territories had spread across the Chinese border. Shenzhen was creating thousands of new jobs, raising the living standards of all its residents, expanding production in all categories, and stimulating the economy of the whole region.

Yet flourishing local growth, from the state's point of view, is not an unmitigated benefit. It could be favorable, from that perspective, if development follows state priorities, if it stimulates and supports growth elsewhere in the country, if it does not generate tensions among regions developing at a different pace. Otherwise, the state could well make a mixed, even a negative appraisal of successful local growth.

From Beijing's perspective, the questions were not merely about Shenzhen's growth rate or its creation of jobs. Equally important were Shenzhen's contribution to wider development, its achievements as a so-called "window" for introducing advanced technology into the more backward interior, its absorption of state subsidies, its market demand for skilled labor and Chinese capital. Further, development in Shenzhen was led by foreign capitalism, rather than by state plan. Its attraction or diversion of resources, however fruitful locally, could diminish the state's capacity to guide development even with the indirect levers preferred after recent decentralizing reforms. What would Beijing see in the results of Shenzhen's experiment with local capitalism under the rubric of state socialism, and how would it react? That is the topic of this chapter, which again draws mainly from Chinese sources.

What Beijing Learned from Shenzhen

Central government leaders knew from the outset that China had to provide Shenzhen extensive subsidies in both infrastructure (transportation, energy, communications facilities, etc.) and project capital investment. In other Asian states, successful development of export processing zones had depended in part on such subsidies.[1] Foreign investors will not be interested in any zone if movement of supplies and products is severely hampered, or if basic communications services are lacking. China devoted substantial resources to construction of roads, electricity, power, communications, water, sewage, and related facilities. Chinese statistics again vary, naming total sums for the first five years of RMB 1,964 million (US $785 million)[2] up to nearly twice that figure:[3] substantial sums for a Zone with 300,000 people.

As for the benefits Shenzhen was supposed to return the country for this generous support, the central government hoped to encourage transfer of technology inward from the Zone (though the time frame for this was never specific). However, Shenzhen was not successful in acquiring advanced technology, and could offer only limited training to workers being rotated from the interior. Chinese enterprises were nonetheless interested in Shenzhen's commerce and trade, which could be profitable. One source claims interior Chinese firms earned RMB 18.7 million in semi-convertible Foreign Exchange Certificates in 1982 alone,[4] with which these firms could purchase imported equipment.

What did Shenzhen gain from these interior Chinese firms? Chinese economists cite four benefits.[5] First, they brought capital injections that alleviated the Zone's need for investment. Second, these firms set up factories that filled gaps in Shenzhen's industrial development. Third, they supplied vital technical and management personnel, as well as up to 150,000 temporary skilled workers to fill manpower needs.[6] Fourth, they supplied products that contributed to Shenzhen's export sales and foreign exchange earnings.

Lured mainly by trade and profit opportunities, large numbers of interior firms came to Shenzhen. By 1983, 298 firms affiliated with enterprises inside China (most not involving foreign capital) had registered to do business there. Most of them were small--87 per cent involving investment of less than RMB 5 million.[7] Yet their total investment was substantial.[8]

The participation of interior Chinese enterprises in Shenzhen attracted the attention of the Shenzhen Municipal Party Committee, which convened a conference in May, 1983, on "summing up experiences" of these interior firms. This conference formulated new regulations which, according to Shenzhen's Vice-Mayor, "clearly pointed out" two principles.[9] First, "the emphasis of the linkage to the interior should be on industrial items." Second, interior firms in Shenzhen would get preferential treatment on land use fees, enterprise income taxes (set at 15%), supply and import of raw materials, and distribution of profits in interior-Shenzhen joint ventures. These rules clearly meant that Shenzhen leaders anticipated a continued need for capital and manpower contributions from the interior (thus the incentives)--but they now recognized that benefits in the form of industrial management or technical expertise must go to the interior in exchange. At that time there were still as many commercial ventures as industrial ones among Chinese project investments in Shenzhen,[10] indicating that Chinese firms went there to trade and shop rather than to absorb new industrial production methods.

The use of Shenzhen as a trading post had curious consequences. Interior firms with branches there preferred to sell in Shenzhen for readily-available hard currency, which involved less difficulty and fewer intermediate organizations than exporting their products. There they could also buy imported equipment and personal goods. Shenzhen became an entrepot for those prevented from going to Hong Kong itself. One result: a high proportion of Chinese visitors to Shenzhen went there to buy and sell export products made in China--many of which had received state export subsidies![11]

China supplied Shenzhen with a large and (costly for other localities) relatively skilled workforce. Before 1979, Shenzhen had fewer than 130 workers with technical training; by 1984, a "considerable" proportion of the 300,000 living there had technical training or experience.[12] Even among the new population of 15,881 officials, the proportion with specialized postsecondary training exceeded 21 per cent (versus less than 9 per cent of the far smaller cadre group in 1978).[13]

Yet Shenzhen was not satisfied with this influx of trained workers, specialists, and officials. As one report noted in 1984, the interior Chinese labor market "is far, far from satisfying the needs of Shenzhen SEZ."[14] The main reason cited by the report was Chinese restrictions on mobility of technically trained workers. A shortage of trained personnel (the report added) discouraged foreign investors from introducing technology to Shenzhen.

Without doubt the state subsidies of Shenzhen's infrastructure, the capital investment by interior firms, and flow of trained manpower to Shenzhen helped stimulate other parts of China. Firms earned profits. They bought better equipment. Their workers had exposure to an incentive-based, labor contract work system. But at what cost? Was a concentrated investment of Chinese capital and labor in one small showcase Zone necessary to accomplish these ends? The investment had been made in hopes of encouraging foreigners to bring in advanced production technology. They were not. As *China Recontructs* reported in 1986:

> Quite a few of the new Shenzhen industrial enterprises
> are only of a simple processing nature and do not involve
> advanced technology. The net value of last year's [1985]

industrial production was only 21 per cent of the gross value, lower than the national average.[15]

A substantial proportion of foreign investment in Shenzhen did go to industrial projects: from 1979 to 1984, 44 per cent. But what sort of industry did that minority of projects involve? A 1984 report by the Municipal Party Committee surveyed 2,214 imported sets of equipment, and found the stark results indicated in Table 4-1.[16] Since most foreign capital brought to Shenzhen came in the form of equipment,[17] the picture of Shenzhen as a technological window for China is dismal indeed--in five years the whole Zone only obtained 147 pieces of advanced equipment!

Table 4-1

Industrial Equipment Brought to Shenzhen, 1979 Through 1983

Total	2,214	=	100%, of which:
Advanced level	147	=	7%
Equivalent to level inside China	512	=	23%
Ordinary (*yiban*)	868	=	39%
Backward (*luohou*)	687	=	31%

SOURCE: Shenzhen Municipal Party Committee, ed., *Qianjinzhong de Shenzhen* (1984), 32.

While Shenzhen municipal government reports written for visiting Chinese officials downplay this failure and speak of successful examples of factory automation,[18] evidence suggests the Party Central Committee in Beijing became aware of the situation by 1982 and ordered Shenzhen to "emphasize obtaining knowledge- and technology-intensive advanced industry."[19] This brought little change.

To explain Shenzhen's failure to attract advanced technology despite massive investment in supporting infrastructure, Chinese economists largely blame foreign investors:

Foreign businessmen more often than not transfer to us equipment that is antiquated, inappropriate, and obsolete;

some of the equipment brought into Shenzhen has already
been abandoned as too old for Hong Kong, or [consists of]
products of the 1940s and 1950s.[20]

Further, the study quoted here goes on, many of the equipment sets are
incomplete, missing key parts, or lacking instruction manuals.

A second reason cited by a Chinese study for the failure to acquire
advanced technology is the management structure of some enterprises,
especially those that conduct processing and assembly operations. In such
ventures, foreign businessmen do not directly participate in management,
and do not have a close connection with the operation of the project;
"therefore" the equipment they do supply is relatively backward.[21] A
better explanation might be: advanced equipment is much more expensive than disused antiques; foreign businessmen want to minimize the
costs they put into labor-intensive processing operations involving an
untested workforce; therefore they see no reason to supply the latest.

The most important reason for Shenzhen's failure to introduce
advanced equipment was the inadequacy of the investment environment
despite intensive infrastructure development. The labor force, as some
Chinese economists indirectly concede, was not prepared to utilize advanced technologies on any wide scale. According to one report, Chinese
enterprises often have "no alternative but to depend on foreign businessmen, and to engage foreign technical personnel." And because of inadequate information and Chinese technical capabilities, foreign businessmen
can sometimes cheat their Chinese partners.[22]

Besides failing to bring in high technology, Shenzhen in its initial
five years fell short of its other assigned goal for serving national development: to earn foreign exchange through export sales. Local foreign
exchange earnings in 1983 rose to US $78.55 million, 13 per cent higher
than the previous year.[23] Fully 70 per cent of Shenzhen's products until
1984 were sold inside China, and the most aggressive domestic sales were
by firms with foreign participation.[24]

The fact that half of Shenzhen's basic raw materials were imported
added a further drain of hard (convertible) currency. Until 1985, a larger
proportion of raw materials was imported to Shenzhen than the proportion
of finished goods that it exported. Other Asian export processing zones
have also depended overwhelmingly on imported raw materials, often
given special duty treatment. Even the successful zones in Taiwan and
Korea, after years of effort to increase local supplies, were importing 54
and 65 per cent of their raw materials in 1979.[25] What made these zones
more profitable than Shenzhen to the host states was their greater success
with export sales. Taiwan allows only two per cent of its zone's sales to
be sold in its domestic market.[26]

Beijing encouraged interior firms to operate in Shenzhen with the
goal of exposing them to foreign technology and management. For that
purpose, workers were rotated between interior and Shenzhen enterprises

(often through interior-Shenzhen joint ventures involving only Chinese capital). Unfortunately for the "window" concept of exposing workers to high technology, most of the interior enterprises pursued commerce and trade rather than industry. Chinese economists have justified this outcome as "one hundred per cent necessary" in light of the shortage of goods and services that was causing local inflation. They also have identified what "attracts the interest of [Chinese] internal investors": relatively low investment required, low risk, and quick financial turnover[27] -- exactly the same features that attract foreign capitalists. The local opportunities for profit led Chinese and foreign capitalist investors to act alike, and discouraged industrial investment by interior firms. This diminished the possibilities for training and rotating Chinese workers, and added impetus to Shenzhen's growth as a Chinese trade and shopping center.

Chinese firms preferred commercial undertakings such as shops and restaurants which earned Hong Kong dollars or Foreign Exchange Certificates (FECs, normally held by foreigners), adding a surcharge for any payments received in ordinary domestic currency. A survey of 61 Shenzhen shops found that 45 or 74 per cent demanded payment in FECs. The domestic currency (renminbi) traded at a steep discount, and

> People coming to Shenzhen have one outstanding feeling: using renminbi you're often unable to buy anything good.[28]

Stores would only sell for renminbi the inferior goods for which they could not obtain hard currency. And to whom did they sell the better, hard currency-priced goods? Ninety per cent of goods sold in Shenzhen were bought by interior Chinese:[29] they were coming to the Zone to purchase Chinese-made goods, obtainable only for convertible currency that required a black-market premium! Such is the thirst for high quality goods inside China.

While the foreign currency-oriented commercial markets held attractions for Chinese firms, they became an accounting nightmare. Firms operating in Shenzhen had to keep books in three different currencies: domestic renminbi, FECs, and Hong Kong dollars. This made it "difficult for management units to grasp the actual situation of each enterprise."[30] Chinese firms could fudge the figures they gave state auditors. They were learning, but not about how to run high-technology industries.

Despite the preference for commercial operations, industrial development proceeded at a rapid pace. As discussed above, it was mostly of a low-technology variety, taking advantage of low labor costs. The development of Shenzhen from nearly zero to an industrial output of RMB 1.8 billion in 1984,[31] would tend to widen regional inequalities in the country as a whole. Even in 1980, four cities with six per cent of China's population produced 28 per cent of national industrial output by value, and 45 per cent of exports.[32] Although Shenzhen's output was of insufficient magnitude to have a major effect on this skewed distribution, by attracting investment from the interior, it drained Chinese capital resources that could have been used on infrastructure in the interior. State investment was subsidizing commercial and light industrial development that was of major benefit only to one locality.

The state lost even more in Shenzhen because of Hong Kong developers who signed contracts for joint investment ventures, then withdrew in response to Hong Kong property market fluctuations. This was a major cause of the shortfall of real as opposed to "pledged" investment--the proportion being as small as one-sixth, according to a 1984 report.[33] It led to announcement of Shenzhen's longest law by far, a 41-article Contract Law especially for the Zone,[34] with provisions designed to prevent damaging pullouts by Hong Kong businessmen.[35]

Even before the Party became concerned about these economic problems of Shenzhen, it worried about the Zone's effects on social morality. Newspapers began to complain early on that upholding morality was "more difficult" in the Zones in light of the bourgeois temptation to "lead a luxurious and extravagant life...." As for officials,

> Since the cadres in the Special Economic Zones have come
> from various parts of the country, it is unavoidable that the
> motives of a small number of them are not pure.[36]

The operation of a quasi-market economy in Shenzhen, with the financial havoc of three currencies, created plenty of opportunities for profiteering. This led the Party in May, 1982, to launch a province-wide "full-scale campaign against corrosion within the Party" to counteract bourgeois influences.[37]

The campaigns did little to stop the festering corruption, which Chinese papers reported in detail. Typical was a story about "maggots of the Special Zone", such as Peng Guoxian, who used his position as deputy director of the municipal "border defense" to waive controls on certain nearby construction work. In payment for this, a construction group built him a four-story house that resembled "a crane standing among chickens".[38] But that was small stuff. By 1986, Shenzhen-interior border guards had in just over a year seized RMB 85 million in contraband and illegally transported goods.[39] One only wonders what they failed to catch. The legal principle that Shenzhen joint ventures could import goods duty free if for their own productive use, and not for domestic resale, proved nearly unenforceable.

On the other hand, numerous Chinese reports acknowledged some beneficial influences on workers and officials in Shenzhen. News reports praised Shenzhen's worker incentives. A 1983 report in *People's Daily* claimed that work efficiency was 150 per cent higher in Shenzhen than elsewhere in China and attributed this to the incentive system,[40] which the paper declared to be just as important as importing foreign capital.

Similarly, Chinese reports praised Shenzhen's use of a responsibility system for managers, who "are not permitted to resort to subterfuges and alibis."[41] The implication was that lessons in "advanced scientific administration" could benefit all of China. Morale among officials and their work efficiency were also reported high, aided by their relatively low average age (of 40, in 1984) and the high proportion with specialized training in cadre schools.[42] Reported instances of efficient work styles helped counteract Shenzhen's negative reputation for fostering corruption.

Beijing began to learn about the problems of Shenzhen by 1983. The Special Zone was drawing out large national subsidies of infrastructure capital, trained manpower, and project investment from Chinese firms. Development was largely following market pressures rather than state plan. This meant concentrating on commercial activity and labor-intensive, low-technology industrial development. Also in response to market demand, both commerce and industrial production were directed at the Chinese market. Further, the loosening of restrictions and the black market opportunities on the boundary between the state-controlled and free market economies encouraged smuggling and corruption. If state subsidies to Shenzhen continued, they would be investing national resources in a small area that was already China's wealthiest, measured per capita. They would be supporting further rapid growth of capitalist-led development at the expense of state-led construction in the interior--the opposite of the original idea that the state would make Shenzhen benefit the entire nation. Yet Beijing must consider the benefits of the Shenzhen policies too, in a flourishing new city that inspired the national slogan "Time is Money--Efficiency is Life". How did the central government assess the situation?

Debates over Special Economic Zone Policy

By now the levels of the problem are becoming clear. From the point of view of local benefits--creation of employment, development of roads, energy facilities and industrial plant, stimulation of agriculture, raising standards of living--Shenzhen Zone achieved in its first five years a remarkable success. But from the point of view of the state, the Zone's net results were ambiguous: intensive development of one politically significant municipality, at a cost of state subsidies that diverted valuable resources from elsewhere. Worse, the benefits that Shenzhen was intended to provide the state--examples of high technology and foreign exchange earnings--fell far short of expectations. No wonder Deng Xiaoping in June, 1985, raised the possibility that the Shenzhen "experiment" might "not succeed."[43]

As authorities in Shenzhen emphasize, Beijing's decisions made the Zone possible, and would determine its future. The issue for Beijing was whether to allow local capitalist-led growth that was efficient and rapid, but was making a rich town richer under growing foreign influence while taking resources away from the state's centrally-administered development. The government's tools were central regulations that determined the extent of local autonomy, and control over state subsidies that could be turned down or shut off.

A debate ensued among Chinese officials, economists, and theorists about the "nature" of the Zone--is it capitalist or socialist? In somewhat veiled argument, the most pro-opening up position calls Shenzhen Zone "socialist." This downplays its differences from the rest of China, and emphasizes that the Party and the state economic sector are fully controlling the Zone. Therefore, by implication, Shenzhen can be fully integrated with the internal economy, instead of being walled off to prevent a drain of cash and state subsidies. And since the Zone itself protects socialism, its concessions could be extended to many other coastal cities in China without threatening state control or Party power.

Those following this line of analysis favor loosening state controls and allowing further decentralization (while insisting that the broad principles of state interventionism outlined in Chapter Two will remain). This does not mean they are political liberals, as their reiterations that the Communist Party must maintain its political monopoly make clear.[44] But they do justify Shenzhen as no threat either to socialism or to Party political control. They embellish their benign diagnosis with phrases from Lenin about "using capitalism to serve socialism."[45]

This school (which in this debate includes prominent economist Yu Guangyuan[46]--asserts that the Zones are "basically socialist" because capitalist activity there is dependent on supplies and support from the state-owned sector. Although the proportion of foreign participation in Shenzhen may grow (the argument runs), foreign equity holdings will after some years all pass over to Chinese ownership.[47] Besides, the socialist economy, through capitalist investment and "socialist workers", is part of the Zone's structure. Finally, the Zone itself is only a small area with special policies, "only a pinprick" on China,[48] and could not threaten the "absolute predominance" of socialism throughout the nation.[49]

Those who take this approach also defend Shenzhen's allowing extensive property developments by Hong Kong investors.[50] Many disagree with the Zone's proclaimed policy (not upheld anyway) of discouraging processing arrangements that do not introduce new technologies. They emphasize advantages of such arrangements: stimulating the local economy, raising incomes, earning foreign exchange, maintaining factory facilities, creating jobs, and "promoting social stability."[51]

In this view, if local benefits are sufficient, the government need not demand that projects contribute more to state-led national development. It should not saddle foreign investors with more regulations in an attempt to readjust the structure of local production. And China should take a relaxed attitude toward wholly-foreign owned firms that earn foreign exchange through export sales, create jobs, avoid potential management conflicts inherent in joint ventures, and bring knowledge of new production and management techniques.[52]

Shenzhen's defenders downplay social influences that alarm some Party officials. As one article reassuringly put it, Party organizations in Shenzhen are fully prepared for the "flies and mosquitoes" that buzz in through the open window.[53] Even *People's Daily* chimed in, assuring readers in May, 1983, that young people in Shenzhen still loved socialism, though they wanted to learn "useful" things from capitalism.[54] A Fujian paper went even farther, actually praising Hong Kong:

> The high efficiency of our Hong Kong compatriots is a major factor in their achieving the speedy development of the Hong Kong economy....The [Chinese] 'slow motion' low efficiency is a decadent tradition and real disaster left to us as a legacy from the old society, a tradition that must be thoroughly eliminated in our socialist modernization drive![55]

At the other extreme of the debate over developments in Shenzhen has been a hardline statist position. This "leftist" view, which calls Shenzhen capitalist and wants to restrict its concessions by area to the Zones at most, has been at odds with Chinese policy: in 1982 the Guangdong Provincial Party Secretary responded to such calls by rejecting fears of "some people" who "worried that [the Zones] will turn into colonies."[56]

The hardliners play up threats to state control, especially from the growth of wholly-foreign owned firms in Shenzhen, which have no inherent connection with Chinese interests.[57] Usually the hardliners question specific concessions or sound warnings about certain effects of opening up, rather than making a broad theoretical attack on the policy itself. To do the latter would put them in conflict with the senior leader, Deng himself. They oppose processing deals because foreign businessmen control production, the output competes with Chinese goods, and very little advanced technology is provided.[58] In 1982 one critical article even demanded a review of joint ventures (usually considered the most desirable type of foreign investment from China's point of view): "In the long run, China must benefit most."[59]

Hardliners see an inevitable "contradiction" between foreign managers trying to penetrate China's domestic market, and their Chinese partners who want to export to earn foreign exchange.[60] They emphasize that the Chinese side should control all joint ventures, and reject the view that a 51 per cent Chinese stake is adequate guarantee of their interests: Chinese Board Chairmen (they point out) may well make excessive concessions to the foreign side; foreigners' accounting may be more persuasive to Boards of Directors than Chinese calculations; and some Chinese Board Chairmen are "leading comrades" who are old, feeble, and poorly informed.[61] Finally, the hardliners warn about undesirable consequences of foreign investment that require tight controls on foreign firms: tax evasion, attempts to dominate the domestic market, export of polluting industries to China, and wage structures that "hurt the interests" of Chinese workers.[62] All of these dangers imply a need for severe restriction of foreign investment.

Even those projects that do supply advanced technology can produce dependency on foreign personnel and foreign-supplied information, resulting from the shortage of trained Chinese technicians. The hardline analysts blame foreign investors for supplying inferior equipment,[63] and do not address the level of skills in the workforce. Their statements highlight the problems of even the "best" deals and cast further doubt in Chinese minds about Shenzhen's concessions. The same is true of their reminders that Shenzhen has already turned labor into a mere commodity like any other traded in the marketplace.[64]

The hardliners criticize Shenzhen's relatively free market in currencies, and its open aversion to the nonconvertible Chinese domestic currency. Some Chinese commentators have seen the open local preference for Hong Kong dollars as a threat to "national dignity," and "a very bad political influence."[65] This led to a further debate on whether a special Shenzhen currency would diminish black marketeering.[66] By 1986 Beijing decided not to issue the special currency. But black market activity was another problem for hardliners to play up, as they did at the Sixth National People's Congress (third plenum) in April, 1985. One delegate denounced the "chaos" of Shenzhen's currency markets as proof that the Zone overemphasized money at the expense of "spirit"--and rejected the conclusion of visitors to Shenzhen who claimed, "'Today's Shenzhen is tomorrow's China.'"[67]

There was an even more potent issue Shenzhen's critics could raise. While market speculators took advantage of differentials between nominal and real currency prices, others with special access to goods or money--Party officials and their relatives--engaged in profitable deals and backdoor arrangements. By 1982 Deng Xiaoping himself was lamenting the "moral degeneration" in the Zones he had created.[68] Blame was put at the door of foreign capitalism, although the true cause was domestic capitalism: the opportunity for instant profit by officials who could facilitate illegal import or trade deals. The correlation between capitalist participation, market forces, and corruption could only underscore the hardliners' contention that Shenzhen was capitalist, in the worst of senses.

Its defenders and critics call Shenzhen socialist or capitalist and stress its successes or its problems. The line approved by central government authorities generally takes a middle ground, admitting Shenzhen's problems, but maintaining that they can be limited by activist state regulation.

Mainstream economists categorize Shenzhen as "state capitalism" or "coexisting capitalism and socialism," or something similar, such as

> A new type of transitional economy under socialist state management that takes national capitalism as its principal part.[69]

Any of these definitions implies a local balance of power between the Chinese state and foreign capitalist interests, a balance which leans toward Chinese advantage thanks to the subordination of all economic activity in the Zone to Chinese law, and the dependence of all joint and foreign ventures on supply "lifelines" from state-run industries.[70] These prevent capitalists from making the Zones a "beachhead" from which to restore imperialism.

Mainstream writers are frank about their admiration for some other Asian export processing zones, especially in Taiwan and the Philippines. They credit Taiwan's zones for turning its trade deficit into a surplus during the early 1970s. Yet they point to problems of special zones elsewhere: low wage levels, failure to acquire high technology, and susceptibility to capitalist cycles and downswings.[71] Such perceptions help justify a two-edged view that Special Economic Zones are good for China, but must be guided properly to avoid drawbacks.

Chinese comparisons of Shenzhen with Taiwan's export processing zones maintain that no matter how numerous the similarities,[72] China's Zones are different because all activity there is subject to the laws of a sovereign socialist state.[73] This, it was hoped, would ensure that the Zones earned a net hard currency surplus.[74] Since it was well known that the zones in Taiwan and South Korea had succeeded in this last respect, Shenzhen's constant drain of hard currency for the first six years was a disappointment. *People's Daily* observed in early 1986:

> ...Special Economic Zones should be more capable of increasing foreign exchange earnings through exports than other regions...for an inward-oriented economy [at Shenzhen] we would not have built Special Economic Zones.

The paper called for "unanimity of understanding" on that point.[75]

On the other hand, mainstream economists suggest that some of the policies they favor in Shenzhen indicate where China may well open up further in the future. For example, Shenzhen began a policy that became a national principle with great fanfare in October, 1984: the separation of Party administration from enterprise management. This means reducing Party interference with daily economic decisions of firms, and letting them concentrate on their own separate accounting, on raising efficiency and productivity. Such a domestic policy facilitates export growth.

In three other areas Chinese economists have also called for loosening restrictions: diminishing hard currency export subsidies to force Chinese enterprises to improve productivity under international market pressure;[76] loosening (to an unspecified degree) national labor restrictions to facilitate worker recruitment by Shenzhen enterprises[77] (though just the opposite happened); and extending sales rights in China's domestic market as a way of attracting more foreign investment. One writer suggested a permit system for letting foreigners sell inside China;[78] another emphasized that those foreign investors most needed by Shenzhen or those who reinvest profits locally should have preference over other joint ventures in getting access to the Chinese domestic market.[79]

Mainstream Chinese economists have also proposed new restrictions. For example, they favored limiting the activities of foreign banks in the Shenzhen Zone to strengthen the competitive position of the Bank of China, until it could develop solid relations with local clients.[80] They also supported limitations on issuing of "stock" by Shenzhen enterprises, to maintain the principle that most "common" (voting) shares be Chinese held and that the Chairman of the Board will always be selected by the largest Chinese stockholder.[81]

The issue in the debates among these three viewpoints was how to respond to economic growth in Shenzhen that created a net drain on the national economy. Added to the failure to secure advanced technology--which was anticipated by Chinese economists familiar with other Asian export processing zones--was the outflow of currency from Chinese consumers that made Shenzhen a smashingly successful *import* processing zone.

The three viewpoints just described suggest Beijing's three policy alternatives in response. First, it could ignore Shenzhen's failure to achieve its initial goals, and accept a local success that built China's most modern city from nothing in a few years. It could allow Shenzhen to continue its flourishing, market-driven development, and accept its influence on economic and social habits elsewhere in the country. It could establish similar concessions to foreign investors elsewhere. However, Beijing's insistence that Shenzhen serve as a "window" to benefit national development prevented full acceptance of such a choice. The "window" had two meanings: that Shenzhen would obtain technologies and goods with which to raise national wealth; and that in contrast to an open door, the size of the area in which concessions were offered would remain limited.

The second choice, corresponding to the views of hardline statists, would be to decide that Shenzhen had failed to reach its goals, that no more Zones would be established and that Shenzhen should undergo a transition back to socialism. Beijing would not choose this route, because to do so would signal potential investors not just in China, but in Hong

Kong and Taiwan, Beijing's unreliability. Such a reassertion of national self-reliance would erode both China's appeal to investors and its political persuasiveness. Also, such a policy would eliminate hope of reforming Shenzhen to make it serve broader national needs.

The third choice was the middle way backed by mainstream economists. This was to keep Shenzhen going but try to redirect the Zone and stop its drain of valuable national resources. Any new restrictions would have to preserve as much as possible the incentives to foreign capitalist participation that allowed Shenzhen to flourish in the first place.

New Measures of State Control

How would the central government react to its discovery that local development led by foreign capitalist investment was absorbing national resources of capital and skilled manpower? Would it clamp down on the source of growth, and reassert state control? Would it try to ensure Chinese dominance of ongoing economic growth? Would it cease direct and indirect subsidies that were underwriting the participation of capitalists? Would it cut its losses by raising an economic barricade between China and Shenzhen Zone, to stop the resource drain?

The most revealing measure Beijing took was to make the boundary between Shenzhen and the Chinese interior into a physical "control line." This was completed in early 1985. On a visit in May of that year I saw barbed wire and electrical fencing, as well as checkpoints beginning to watch for smuggled goods crossing the 86-kilometer boundary. The intention behind this "second line" was to begin shifting the customs boundary between Hong Kong and China to the interior side of Shenzhen.[82] This was tantamount to recognition of Shenzhen's economic integration with Hong Kong--from which it derived nearly half of project investment, along with equipment, experienced management, and skilled manpower. The new physical boundary also meant that Beijing would try to stop the drain of national hard currency and skilled manpower resources into the Zone. Of course, it was built at national expense.

The rationale for this measure was obvious; its implementation far more complicated. Cutting the drain of money and resources would not jeopardize foreign investment levels (the rationale went), so long as Shenzhen's border with Hong Kong continued to diminish in importance. Hong Kong investment indeed continued. But the second line raised questions. Should price controls in Shenzhen be phased out, and prices linked to those in Hong Kong? This would require further isolation of Shenzhen from the interior. Should producers (e.g., farmers) near Shenzhen be able to charge the Zone whatever prices the market would bear for their goods?[83] Should goods sent to China from Shenzhen pay import duties? Now that Shenzhen was symbolically set off from China and linked to Hong Kong, the permissible extent of its economic integration with the interior remained at issue.

The central government also came close to approval of a "Special Zone currency" for Shenzhen through the local branch of the regulatory People's Bank. This would have given Shenzhen a convertible Chinese unit of exchange to replace Hong Kong dollars, open preference for which diminished the black market value of Chinese currency by about half.[84] In March, 1985, Shenzhen officials were saying the new currency would be issued later that year.[85] It would be pegged to a basket of foreign currencies,[86] to discourage the local black market in Hong Kong dollars. The problem would be to stop the new, convertible currency from crossing into China. By early 1986 this appeared impossible, and the plans were first postponed, then scrapped.[87]

People are easier to control than money. The central government was unable to restrict movements of money between Shenzhen and China, but could and did do something about movements of people. Shenzhen's urban population had grown from 27,366 in 1978[88] to nearly 300,000 in 1984. By 1990, planners project a Zone population of 400,000, to double ten years after that. Hong Kong developers are pressing for much higher figures.[89] The influx of workers was not enough to satisfy Shenzhen, however, where extra incentives for newcomers were designed to attract even more.[90]

The central government recognized a brain drain of trained Chinese attracted by Shenzhen's material incentives, and in order to cut perceived losses, issued new labor mobility restrictions, to be enforced by the Shenzhen Zone Labor Department starting April, 1985.[91] Henceforth only workers under contract could move to Shenzhen, and the number of these would be "strictly controlled." Potential incoming workers must take a test to qualify for entry. From 1985, Chinese visitors to Shenzhen were required to obtain a visa with photograph, complete identification, and explanation of purpose. This made it much harder for ordinary Chinese to visit Shenzhen than it is for Hong Kong citizens.

While Beijing restored some central control over Shenzhen's economic relations with the interior, it also acted to limit the Zone's integration with Hong Kong. On the issue of foreign bank branch offices in the Zone, the central government compromised between exclusion and openness, limiting the functions those offices could perform.[92] The purpose, as a Chinese economist noted, was to protect the state bank:

> We must use restrictions on foreign banks to protect the Bank of China. If we restrict the scope of foreign banks' activity in issuing foreign trade letters of credit, we can strengthen the position of the Bank of China in the financial work of the Zone.[93]

On the other hand, some economists pointed to potential benefits to be had from fuller participation by foreign banks, namely: a greater inflow of information about global markets and technologies, attraction of additional investment clientele to Shenzhen, expansion of the range of locally available financial services, broadening the sources of local tax revenue, and strengthening competitive pressure on Chinese banks to improve their management.[94]

Beijing announced the regulations for foreign banks in Shenzhen in April, 1985.[95] According to these regulations, foreign banks would be permitted to issue loans and take deposits in either renminbi or hard currency, handle foreign trade transactions, and even sell stocks (anticipating the future?). However, implementation was slow and at first, foreign banks were only allowed to maintain advisory relations with foreign investment enterprises. Chinese plans did not envision broadening the role of foreign banks until the Bank of China's competitive position was stronger.[96]

While Beijing was deciding how to retain some control over foreign influence on Shenzhen's financial system, the central government put the word out that it expected an improvement in local export sales. By mid-1984 internal reports were bluntly stating that over two-thirds of Shenzhen's production was being sold into China's interior, the opposite of the original plans.[97] That year and early in 1985, numerous Beijing officials were exposed to the problem firsthand. By December, 1985, the Chinese official press was openly discussing the "wave of criticism" of Shenzhen.[98] Every local report from Shenzhen repeated solemn assurances that the Zone was now becoming export-oriented, and thus making the contribution to national development originally hoped for. Local theorists came up with a convenient new explanation, that Shenzhen had only just entered a stage of development in which the Zone could "shift from an 'inward' to an 'outward' strategy."[99] By early, 1986, the mayor of Shenzhen was claiming that export sales had risen to over 33 per cent of the Zone's production.[100] Beijing continued to demand an increase in that proportion.[101] *People's Daily* suggested that to improve its situation, Shenzhen could sell some products to China as import substitutes:

> Special Economic Zones can sell on the domestic market the 'foreign goods' they produce so long as the state needs them. In this way, the state does not have to import these goods.[102]

While pushing an export orientation for Shenzhen, Beijing also began to discourage the Zone from engaging in simple processing and compensation trade which generated merely local employment and profits. This was in reaction to finding that most equipment supplied for assembly operations was backward and outdated.[103] Again, some disagreed, noting that such trade provided local income, economic diversity,[104] training for local workers, jobs, and competitive stimulus to Chinese enterprises.[105]

The low grade of investment, however, became too obvious to ignore. In particular, 65 per cent of medium and large size foreign investment projects in the Zone through the first five years consisted of commercial and other nonindustrial items.[106] Twice as much foreign investment there was devoted to property developments such as resorts and hotels, as to industry.[107] This was perhaps encouraged by the provincial land regulations for the Zone issued in November, 1983, which allowed a secondary market in real estate rights of usage.[108]

Besides addressing purely economic issues, central authorities sought to deal with corruption among local officials. When a controlled price and wage system touches a market system as vigorous as that of Hong Kong, opportunities are created for those with special access in the controlled system. They can secure production supplies, give valuable domestic market information, and help skirt import restrictions--services valued by market system producers. Since even top wages in the controlled system are low by international standards, temptations to profit through collusion with market forces are especially great.[109] Shenzhen's government found merely a rhetorical answer to this problem: namely the claim that it would initiate a "two hands" policy: one hand resolutely continues the opening up policy to obtain foreign capital and technology, while the other hand firmly strikes back at selfishness, corruption and criminal activities.[110] So far, the "two hands" have not managed to gain mastery of the invisible hand.

Before striking out with punitive measures, however, Zone authorities have attempted to anticipate and forestall corruption by giving local officials special training. According to a municipal Party report in 1986, "one third of [Shenzhen] city's annual revenue is spent on expanding the socialist ideological or cultural position [sic]."[111] All higher-ranking officials have attended courses in Party policy, Zone regulations, and "political theory."[112] The Zone has also promoted a crop of younger, better trained officials.[113] National authorities hoped that meritocratic personnel policies combined with extra training and indoctrination would be effective preventive medicine. But for many, the ideological vaccination failed. The problem of smuggling was perhaps the first to be recognized in the Zone,[114] and one of the first to be acted against,[115] with little apparent result.

Local and national authorities also tried to streamline the Zone's cumbersome bureaucracy. "Mother-in-law" agencies had flourished to the point that 36 approvals were required for some import-export deals in the Zone.[116] The State Council's Special Zone Office with Premier Zhao Ziyang nominally in charge,[117] was supposed to address this sort of problem. The tasks of this office were to help top authorities monitor activities and problems in the four Zones; to devise measures for streamlining local administration; and to approve larger foreign investment projects. This office may have been behind a major reorganization that produced substantial cuts in municipal government staffing.[118] In a sharper reassertion of central authority, in August, 1985--one month after Deng Xiaoping publicly expressed his doubts whether Shenzhen would ultimately be successful[119]--its mayor was replaced. The sudden leadership change was a sharp reminder of the Zone's responsibility to meet policy objectives set for it in Beijing.

To summarize briefly, the central government adopted measures to restrict the outflow of national capital, manpower, and money from the interior to Shenzhen. It tried, by discouraging processing contracts, to get foreign investors to bring in a higher grade of technology. It sought to put pressure on Shenzhen firms to export more of their output and thereby raise national hard currency earnings. And it nearly issued a special convertible currency for Shenzhen, deciding not to only when it realized that the Zone's financial system could not be separated from China's.

Yet while it took steps to pressure Shenzhen into an export orientation, the central government did not curtail the major concessions to foreign capitalism that (together with state subsidies) had been the source of Shenzhen's phenomenal local growth. Special tax treatment, joint venture opportunities, and cheap contract labor were all maintained if not enhanced. The activities of foreign banks would gradually expand, after state banks were prepared for the competition. Even more significant, the government took few steps to stop Shenzhen's gradual economic integration with Hong Kong. It did not curtail the growth of Hong Kong-owned ventures in Shenzhen. Knowing that most economic activity in Shenzhen was controlled or substantially influenced by Hong Kong capitalists, Beijing made a tactical compromise: accept the benefits of local development by capitalist investment, but cut the flow of costly state support in the forms of capital, hard currency, and trained labor.

The Late 1980s

In the years after the central government readjusted the rest of the country's relations with Shenzhen Special Economic Zone, there was a period of slower but more stable growth. Beijing continued to send signals that it would no longer subsidize Shenzhen; but neither would it force Shenzhen to turn away from the low-tech and commercial investment on which it depended. Chinese economists and commentators after 1985 showed a sober awareness of Shenzhen's real prospects. One analysis published in 1987 was entitled hopefully: "Shenzhen is Just Now Taking Off--It Certainly Can Take Off."[120]

Shenzhen has continued to suffer from fluctuations in China's national foreign trade and investment policies. A surprising example is the export restrictions instituted by the central government in 1986. Their purpose was to restrict cut-price exporting by Chinese enterprises whose purchasing expenses were being underwritten by the central government. The restrictions established ceilings of export volume for each province, which in the case of Guangdong Province were so low as to force a sharp drop in Shenzhen's exports in several categories (especially perishable agricultural items).[121] This, of course, contradicted Beijing's desire to promote Shenzhen's exports and foster its self-supporting growth.

Central government pressure did finally begin to increase the proportion of Shenzhen's output destined for export sale, but progress came slowly. Even in 1986, Shenzhen's imports by value exceeded its exports by more than half.[122] In 1987, its exports rose sharply, thanks in part to a fall in the value of the Hong Kong dollar (linked to the US dollar), making the area's exports more competitive.[123] Government intervention, however, did not succeed in upgrading investment in Shenzhen from its concentration on assembly, processing, and service ventures.

As national subsidization diminished in the late 1980s, much of Shenzhen's luster disappeared--despite an improved transportation infrastructure that will soon include several new highways built in part with Hong Kong capital, ports with 45 berths, a new airport, and new rail lines within the Zone.[124] Part of the problem is that the Zone has not attained its goal of serving as a model of openness to the outside world. Rather, government restrictions and bureaucratic interference in economic activity continue to abound. They were sharply criticized in a report prepared for China's State Council in 1988.[125] The report noted that state enterprises in Shenzhen despite their proclaimed autonomy continue to depend on direction from higher authorities. It argued that because of their backdoor connections these enterprises dominate some sectors of the local economy, and they concentrate on commercial trading rather than industrial construction. Meanwhile, foreign investment is still hampered by the fact that as of early 1989, according to one account, "setting up a foreign enterprise in Shenzhen still requires approval from more than 30 government departments...."[126]

More of Shenzhen's special privileges have been curtailed by the central government. The Special Economic Zones in January, 1989 lost their right to retain 100 per cent of their hard currency earnings, and are now required (like other coastal areas) to turn over at least 20 per cent of them to Beijing. This measure was intended to curtail the superiority in purchasing power that Chinese businessmen in Shenzhen had built up over their interior comrades--a situation that aroused resentment elsewhere and stimulated provinces and localities all over China to staff their own trading offices in the Zone.[127] In 1988, to take only one example, no fewer than 130 enterprises from the poor interior province of Hunan were operating in Shenzhen. They were blamed by officials at home for depriving Hunan of hard currency income by moving their export operations out to more lucrative Shenzhen.[128] The state's response to such complaints from various provinces was to cut back Shenzhen's privileges, and this combined with the tightening of national fiscal controls led to a sharp drop in foreign investment in Shenzhen after 1987. Actual foreign investment utilized in the four original Zones in that year was as follows:[129]

Shenzhen	US$404 million
Zhuhai	$ 69 million
Shantou	$ 81 million
Xiamen	$ 18 million

Shenzhen still remains more successful than the other original Special Economic Zones, which have all been afflicted by similar problems and are less successful at attracting foreign investment. The Zhuhai Zone began to appear livelier than its neighbor, Portuguese Macao, but was hampered by an even weaker transportation infrastructure than Shenzhen's. The Xiamen Zone belatedly began attracting substantial investment from Taiwan in 1988, but total foreign investment there in the first half of that year was an unspectacular US $15.7 million, and its export income was actually falling.[130] Most foreign investment from Taiwan is going to Southeast Asia, where conditions are more favorable than in China.

Nonetheless, the Chinese central government, impressed with the rate of development in the Special Economic Zones, has extended some of their features to other competing coastal areas. The decision to "open" fourteen coastal cities to foreign investment was made after Deng Xiaoping's approving visit to three of the original Special Economic Zones in early 1984.[131] Preferential treatment for foreign participants (in terms of tax and other concessions) was concentrated in "Economic and Technological Development Zones" located near these fourteen cities. In February, 1985, the central government formally designated four huge new "open zones" extending inland on the Yangzi, Pearl, and Yellow River deltas and in southern Fujian Province, intending to integrate the development of the smaller existing special zones with the neighboring industrial and agricultural hinterlands. Finally, in 1988, Hainan Island was designated the fifth Special Economic Zone. Each of these areas was allowed to offer foreign investors many of the same preferential terms as the four Zones, and to retain some local foreign exchange earnings. Shenzhen has continued to lead the way in policy innovations later adopted in other "open" coastal areas. For example, Shenzhen in 1987 pioneered the auctioning of long term (50 year) land leases to stimulate investment in local property development, a practice which later in the same year was approved by the State Council for several other coastal cities as well.[132]

The opening of new coastal areas reflected a desire to increase the rate of foreign investment in some of the major centers of the domestic economy, rather than allowing it to concentrate in showcase peripheral zones with weak linkages to the interior. This might improve the prospects for assimilation of imported production technology into the domestic economy. The number and size of the new zones has changed repeatedly, as national policy adapts to the economic realities of the country's various regions. The fact that some cities are readier than others to absorb large amounts of new foreign investment prompted the shift in some government pronouncements from fourteen to four coastal cities as the focus of the opening up effort. Among the coastal cities in general, policies vary increasingly as all of them become more autonomous from the central government.

The creation of various "open zones" along China's coast signified that the profitable aspects of the original four Special Economic Zones would now be applied on a wider basis, while some of the subsidies and special prerogatives of the original Zones were cut back. The obvious implication was that in comparison the latter would be less and less "special."

Continuing this trend, in April, 1988 the State Council announced that the number of "open" coastal cities and counties was being expanded from 148 to 284, and would now embrace a population of 160 million (up from 90 million).[133] Most of these were expansions of already existing open areas, notably in the northern coastal provinces of Shandong and Liaoning. The official announcement declared: "This is expected to encourage township enterprises in the area to expand their labor-intensive production for the export market."[134] One month later the Governor of Shandong Province announced that the entire 50,000 square kilometer Shandong Peninsula had been designated as "open." These "open economic zones" would offer foreign investors preferential customs and tax rates and reduced land use fees. City-level officials would henceforth be allowed to approve foreign investment contracts of up to US $30 million.[135]

However, the rapid growth in size of the coastal "open" zones could not mask the constraints imposed on their ability to attract foreign investment by red tape and poor infrastructure, as well as the national fiscal austerity program. As an article in the official press summarized: "...the cutback in domestic investment has denied the development zones the financial resources they principally relied on to continue capital construction projects and new investment. Most of them have now had problems repaying debts--Tianjin has been the only one to repay a major loan of 40 million yuan."[136] In other words, the coastal provinces under the austerity policy simply lacked the resources to match the commitments from foreign investors that they hoped to attract. The austerity became even more severe after the June, 1989 massacres drew international reaction and diminished the government's fiscal resources.

The fifth and newest Special Economic Zone, Hainan Island, is having considerable difficulty attracting interest among foreign investors despite Beijing's propaganda portraying it as a potentially lucrative tropical Shangri-La. Tourism has also been slow to develop. Hainan is hampered by lack of infrastructure, the inconvenience of not having direct land connections, and incomplete laws and regulations. The central government, having learned a lesson in Shenzhen, has no intention of pouring in massive subsidies to develop infrastructure in Hainan. That island's trade is growing (it reached a volume of US$ 770 million in 1988), but a trade surplus has been maintained only by dodgy tricks such as stockpiling imports for resale at a premium to the mainland; arbitrarily accounting many of these imported goods sold to mainland enterprises as "exports;" and softening the terms of the central government's foreign exchange remission requirements.[137] Nearby Guangdong Province was not to be outdone, however. It began to insist that all Hainan trading companies use Guangdong-registered vehicles for transport there, thus infusing a part of Hainan's earnings into Guangdong as well.[138]

Hainan, meanwhile, celebrated its 1987 promotion to the status of full province by selecting some of the same leaders who had been implicated in (and in some cases reprimanded after) a $1 billion-plus corruption scandal in 1984-5, an episode that had caused a national stir but made a great many fortunes in Hainan.[139] Presumably the status of full Province would lead to even greater autonomy for the island in seeking foreign finance and retaining earned foreign exchange, and would create more profitable opportunities for officials and their friends. Hopes that smuggling and commerce would again enliven the local economy inspired a rush of popular migration to the island from several neighboring provinces. However, in the political turmoil of 1989, Hainan's Governor was suddenly fired because of allegedly corrupt dealings involving his wife and son. Since similar charges could as well be levelled against many other Chinese officials, singling him out was taken as a political attack on an individual (Liang Xiang) strongly associated with Shenzhen and Canton who was an advocate of further opening up.[140] However, this was not Liang's first dismissal (he had earlier been replaced as mayor of Shenzhen when Beijing was not satisfied with results there), and both he and Hainan will doubtless recover.

As for Shenzhen, two fundamental problems continue to plague that Zone: bad work habits and corruption. With regard to the former, a Chinese report in mid-1987 cited foreign complaints that Shenzhen's four- and five-star hotels had one-star quality service.[141] More tellingly, the report pointed out that some of Shenzhen's factories by now had facilities and equipment better than some of their Hong Kong counterparts, but their products remained uncompetitive in quality and style. The clear implication was that Shenzhen remains unprepared for any high-tech stage, and still needs to work hard to match Hong Kong (which after all is itself not an advanced technology center). And Shenzhen continues to depend on Hong Kong for most of its foreign investment. The original hope that Shenzhen would be a "window" on advanced technology seems dashed.

Meanwhile, there were new revelations of questionable or illegal business practices by Chinese enterprises in Shenzhen. All had one thing in common: they added to the drain of national capital resources. For example, one report indicated that in the first half of 1985, Shenzhen's export income was US $265 million, of which only $179 million was deposited in banks as required by law. There is no record of what happened to the other $86 million.[142]

Skimming off export income was not the only interesting practice of Shenzhen's Chinese enterprises. New forms of speculation have sprung up. Take the case of Shenzhen's "land development companies," of which there are 33 (one for every 10,000 residents). For whatever reasons, the Shenzhen city government has customarily transferred land to them without charge to develop and then sell use rights to other enterprises or joint ventures. Many land development companies have used improper methods to secure the best land parcels; waited for several years as land values rose; then rented land at exorbitant rates, or engaged in disguised buying and selling. As a result of such activities, municipal land use fees collected in Shenzhen to mid-1987 were less than a third of the amount needed to pay the interest on national land development loans to the city.[143]

Shenzhen continued to have difficulty combatting corruption, which descriptions painted as widespread. A newly established crime reporting center in Shenzhen accused 566 people, including 148 higher-level Party officials and managers, of involvement in crimes (mostly "economic crimes") in the first three months of the center's operation in 1988.[144] In less than three months, 111 cases of corruption and bribery were uncovered in Shenzhen, along with 94 other cases of embezzlement, tax evasion, smuggling, etc. Incidents of dereliciton of duty by law enforcement personnel in Shenzhen reported in those three months cost the state RMB 130 million in losses.[145] Of course, no one knows the total extent of such losses. But these statistics suggest that tax evasion and other illegal practices by Chinese enterprises sap Shenzhen's potential reinvestment capital, just as the Zone is being asked to become more self-reliant.

Conclusions

Among the economic results of China's decision to open up to foreign investment after twenty years of unproductive isolation, no one would deny that Shenzhen's opening has been a local success. But many would join the Chinese "wave of criticism" because of what this small area cost the state, and the currency earnings and technology it failed to provide. Shenzhen illustrates dramatically the tendency for Chinese localities to identify and pursue interests utterly distinct from those perceived by the central government, and for the latter's goals to be undermined by market forces released in the economic reform process. Because its results considered from a national standpoint are controversial, Shenzhen provides a test case of how Beijing will respond when aspects of its economic opening policies turn out differently than intended.

Beijing's responses to developments in Shenzhen were intended to pressure the Zone into paying closer heed to its original objectives of providing national (not merely local) benefits. The alternatives facing Beijing ranged from inaction to a full reimposition of socialism. The central government chose to reassert control over capital, goods and people moving across the Zone's boundary. It redoubled political indoctrination of local officials. It tried to reorient the Zone's production in order to raise its export earnings.

Yet these steps left intact most of the Zone's advantages to capitalist investors. Indeed, Beijing decided to begin extending similar concessions to foreign investment in development zones within fourteen major coastal cities, though implementation did not begin until the mid-1980s. This broadening of the development program reflected a realization that China's existing major industrial centers on the coast were better prepared to attract export-oriented foreign investment than the previously undeveloped and still inexperienced SEZs.

While the opening of a fifth Special Economic Zone on tropical Hainan Island in 1988 cannot be explained in this way, its opening up under particularly liberal terms reflects Beijing's realization that this large backward region with considerable potential for tourism and processing facilities is unlikely to develop without foreign capital. And, like Shenzhen with its "second line," the Hainan Island SEZ with its especially relaxed regulations is set off from the mainland by a distinct boundary--in this case, water. In Beijing's eyes, this probably makes it a "safer" concession to capitalism than some part of the mainland, absurd as that might seem to observers from countries with more highly developed transportation systems.

The central government permitted Shenzhen Zone's close relations with foreign capital and management to remain, despite its inadequate achievements in transfer of technology. But Beijing realized that in its quest to make Shenzhen flourish, it had poured in more capital investment both directly and indirectly than did foreign investors--and it began to clamp down on those subsidies after 1984. The central government did little to discourage Chinese enterprises from throughout the country that followed local profit incentives and pursued commercial and property development ventures in Shenzhen with abandon.

Why did the government allow Shenzhen's dependency on foreign and domestic capitalism to grow, and take only measured steps to curtail state subsidization of the Special Economic Zone experiment? There are two major reasons, neither of which indicates a diminished capacity of the central government to pursue interventionist economic policies when it sees fit. The first reason is that it remains desirable to China's top leadership to continue allowing Shenzhen to make itself wealthy. To reduce central subsidies for the Zone was more politically palatable for Deng Xiaoping and his supporters than backtracking abruptly from a policy with which they are closely identified. The development of Shenzhen demonstrates that China's growth-oriented economic nationalism can compromise on formerly rigid Marxist principles. The doctrine of the opening up policy does not dictate unremitting, universal state control. While it does mean applying restrictions on foreign investment and trade to try to make them serve national advantage, it does not reveal great concern with domestic inequalities of wealth and power that are widened by foreign investment-led growth.

The second reason for Beijing's moderate response to the costs of development in Shenzhen is political nationalism. Reunification with Taiwan and Hong Kong remains one of China's paramount priorities. Beijing has announced that to achieve this goal, it will apply the "one country, two systems" solution to Taiwan as well as to Hong Kong. This is an invitation to Taiwan to observe the treatment of Hong Kong under this formula, both prior to and after 1997. If Taiwan is watching Hong Kong, Hong Kong is watching Shenzhen. The Chinese government is well aware that Shenzhen, dominated by Hong Kong capitalism, will be seen by overseas Chinese as a bellweather of China's openness to their partnership. This gives Beijing political reason to tread cautiously in Shenzhen, as the following passage makes apparent:

> Hong Kong people say that since capitalist enterprises are allowed to exist in Shenzhen, they have no need to worry about the future of Hong Kong. Taiwan compatriots also follow Shenzhen's developments with interest....After her visit to the Special Zone, a Taiwanese correspondent said with emotion, 'How eagerly I want to see an early reunification of Taiwan with the mainland.' She said the existence and development of the economic zone had given her 'confidence in the reunification of the motherland.'[146]

Beijing allowed Shenzhen to keep its largely capitalist structure, while reducing its drain on state resources and reaffirming state socialism in China beyond Shenzhen. National unity and unification took priority over state controls that would destroy a fruitful growth of local capitalism. It was therefore a gesture of nationalism when the Tiananmen parade on the thirty-fifth anniversary of the People's Republic of China in 1984, some distance behind the portraits of Marx, Lenin, and Mao, also included a prominent display of that new slogan from Shenzhen Special Economic Zone:

Time is Money--Efficiency is Life.

Notes

1. David K. Y. Chu and Kwan-yiu Wong, eds., *Modernization in China, The Case of the Shenzhen Special Economic Zone* (Hong Kong: Oxford University Press, 1985), 17-18.

2. *Renmin Ribao*, March 29, 1984; cited in *Ibid.*, 18.

3. Samuel P. S. Ho and Ralph W. Huenemann, *China's Open Door Policy, The Quest for Foreign Technology and Capital* (Vancouver: University of British Columbia Press, 1984), 70-71. The Shenzhen Zone Development Company estimated in 1983 that RMB 2,088 million (at 1981 prices) of outside infrastructure investment would be needed for the Zone's development. This did not include subsidized urban construction estimated at RMB 1,670 million. These amounts were exceeded by around 1984. See Gu Shutang, ed., *Shenzhen Yanjiu*, 38; Fang Sheng, ed., *Shenzhen Jingji*, 119. These sources claim that state subsidies to Shenzhen were tapering off by 1984, a claim which is justifiable only if one ignores indirect subsidies--notably provincial contributions, investment by Chinese state enterprises, and municipal borrowing from Chinese state sources. Reliable figures on these are not available.

4. Gu Shutang, ed., *Shenzhen Jingji Tequ Diaocha he Jingji Kaifaqu Yanjiu* (Tianjin: Nankai University Press, 1984), 74.

5. *Ibid.*, 73-74.

6. *Ibid.*

7. Gu Shutang, ed., *Shenzhen Yanjiu*, 75.

8. Interior Chinese enterprises invested RMB 169 million in Shenzhen by 1983. See *Ibid.*, 71; and Shenzhen Party Committee, ed., *Qianjinzhong de Shenzhen* (Beijing: Red Flag Publishers, 1984), 42.

9. Shenzhen Party Committee, ed., *Qianjinzhong de Shenzhen*, 42-43; Gu Shutang, ed., *Shenzhen Yanjiu*, 76-77.

10. Gu Shutang, ed., *Shenzhen Yanjiu*, 71.

11. *Ibid.*, 139.

12. *Ibid.*, 73.

13. Fang Sheng, ed., *Shenzhen Tequ Jingji Kaocha* (Shenzhen University Press, 1984), 109.

14. Quoted in Gu Shutang, ed., *Shenzhen Yanjiu*, 58.

15. *China Reconstructs*, December, 1985, 26.

16. Shenzhen Party Committee, ed., *Qianjinzhong de Shenzhen*, 32. I have corrected errors in the original source's percentage calculations.

17. *Ibid.*

18. Shenzhen City Government, "Shenzhen Jingji Tequ Jiben Qingkuang Jieshao," (pamphlet, 1983), 11-12.

19. Shenzhen Party Committee, ed., *Qianjinzhong de Shenzhen*, 31.

20. Gu Shutang, ed., *Shenzhen Yanjiu*, 8.

21. *Ibid.*, 54.

22. *Ibid.*, 57.

23. Xue Muqiao, ed., *Almanac of China's Economy, 1984* (Hong Kong: Modern Cultural Company, 1985), 522.

24. Gu Shutang, ed., *Shenzhen Yanjiu*, 78, 81-2.

25. Chu and Wong in *Modernization in China*, 15.

26. *Ibid.*, 16.

27. Gu Shutang, ed., *Shenzhen Yanjiu*, 77.

28. *Ibid.*, 135-137.

29. *Ibid.*, 136.

30. Fang Sheng, *Shenzhen Jingji*, 62.

31. *China Reconstructs*, December, 1985, 25.

32. Ho and Huenemann, *China's Open Door Policy*, 52.

33. Gu Shutang, ed., *Shenzhen Yanjiu*, 6.

34. China International Economic Consultants, *The China Investment Guide* (London: Longman, 1984), 532-8.

35. *Ibid.*, 534. The new law required guarantees from both sides in Chinese-foreign contracts, and specified penalities for nonfulfillment.

36. *Yangcheng Wanbao*, May 26, 1982; trans. JPRS 81269, July 13, 1982, 28-31.

37. *Ming Bao* (Hong Kong), May 28, 1982; trans. FBIS, May 28, 1982, W1.

38. *Yangcheng Wanbao*, Aug. 8, 1982; trans. SWB FE/7103, Aug. 13, 1982, BII/5-6.

39. *Wen Wei Po* (Hong Kong), March 12, 1986; trans. FBIS, March 17, 1986, W 1-2.

40. *Renmin Ribao*, May 6, 1983; trans. JPRS 83595, June 2, 1983, 94-106.

41. *Nanfang Ribao*, June 14, 1982; trans. JPRS 81634, Aug. 26, 1982, 51-4.

42. Gu Shutang, ed., *Shenzhen Yanjiu*, 3.

43. *Renmin Ribao*, June 30, 1985, 1.

44. Shi Xiulin, *Jingji Tequ Wenti Tansuo*; trans. *Chinese Economic Studies*, Winter 1985-86, 35.

45. *Nanfang Ribao*, Oct. 26, 1981; trans. JPRS 79807, Jan. 6, 1982, 63-64.

46. Gu Shutang, ed., *Shenzhen Yanjiu*, 178 fn.

47. Shi Xiulin, *Jingji Tequ Wenti*, 27-33.

48. *Jingji Yanjiu*, Aug. 20, 1981; trans. JPRS 79100, Sept. 30, 1981, 36-42.

49. *Shijie Jingji Daobao*, June 15, 1981; trans. JPRS 78684, Aug. 5, 1981, 29-37. See also Gu Shutang, ed., *Shenzhen Yanjiu*, 178.

50. Interviews with Shenzhen officials, May, 1985.

51. *Nanfang Ribao*, Aug. 26, 1982; trans. JPRS 82457, Dec. 14, 1982, 58-59. See also Shi Xiulin, *Jingji Tequ Wenti*.

52. *Yangcheng Wanbao* (Canton), April 27, 1982; trans. JPRS 81395, July 29, 1982, 62-63. Strong reform proponents have also used the Shenzhen example to promote a loosening of national economic controls. For example, *Jingji Yanjiu* asserted on February 20, 1983 (trans. JPRS 83174, Apr. 1, 1983, 24) that Shenzhen had already shown that production costs, profits, and economic targets in export production "cannot and should not" be planned, but should be left to market forces.

Two economic theorists proposed in February, 1985 the creation elsewhere in China of new types of special zones specifically devoted to export processing, coastal free trade, tourism, natural resources, and even "internal 'overseas student' education zones." They did not explain how these zones would work, but with so many categories, they would be likely to spread throughout China. See *Weilai Yu Fazhan*, Feb. 15, 1985, 21.

53. Xinhua, Nov. 15, 1982; trans. JPRS 82457, Dec. 14, 1982, 85-86.

54. *Renmin Ribao*, May 6, 1983; trans. JPRS 83595, June 2, 1983, 94-106.

55. *Fujian Luntan*, April 20, 1982; trans. JPRS 81634, Aug. 26, 1982, 47-50.

56. *Da Gong Bao* (Hong Kong), June 14, 1982; trans. SWB FE/7064, June 29, 1982, BII/13.

57. Gu Shutang, ed., *Shenzhen Yanjiu*, 179.

58. *Nanfang Ribao*, June 14, 1982; trans. JPRS 81634, Aug. 26, 1982, 51-54.

59. *China Daily*, Sept. 19, 1982; quoted FBIS, Sept. 20, 1982, K15.

60. *Ibid.*

61. Gu Shutang, ed., *Shenzhen Yanjiu*, 66-67.

62. *Ibid.*, 68-80.

63. *Ibid.*, 57.

64. Fang Sheng, ed., *Shenzhen Jingji*, 98.

65. *Ibid.*, 63.

66. *Ibid.*, 64-5.

67. *Renmin Ribao*, April 8, 1985, 2.

68. *Ming Bao* (Hong Kong), May 28, 1982; trans. FBIS, May 28, 1982, W1.

69. Gu Shutang, ed., *Shenzhen Yanjiu*, 182.

70. Wang Muheng and Chen Yongshan, "On the Nature of Asian Export Processing Zones and China's Special Economic Zones," *Zhongguo Jingji Wenti* No. 6 (1980); trans. *Chinese Economic Studies* XIX: 2 (Winter 1985-86), 11-16.

71. *Ibid.*, 8-11.

72. Guangdong Province trade official Sun Ru in 1980, trans. JPRS 75423, April 2, 1980, 46-54.

73. *Nanfang Ribao*, Oct. 26, 1981; trans. JPRS 79807, Jan. 6, 1982, 63-4. Also *Jingji Yanjiu*, Feb. 20, 1983; trans. JPRS 83174, April 1, 1983, 18-29.

74. *China Daily*, July 8, 1985, 2.

75. *Renmin Ribao*, Feb. 1, 1986, 2; trans. FBIS, Feb. 4, 1986, K5.

76. Gu Shutang, ed., *Shenzhen Yanjiu*, 140.

77. *Ibid.*, 58.

78. Fang Sheng, ed., *Shenzhen Jingji*, 131.

79. Gu Shutang, ed., *Shenzhen Yanjiu*, 131.

80. *Ibid.*, 154; and Y.C. Jao, "Banking and Currency in the Special Economic Zones: Problems and Prospects," in Jao and C.K. Leung, eds., *China's Special Economic Zones* (Hong Kong: Oxford University Press, 1986), 160-161.

81. Gu Shutang, ed., *Shenzhen Yanjiu*, 168.

82. Prof. Wang Shouxin, Special Economic Zone Research Center, Shenzhen University; interview, May 8, 1985.

83. Fang Sheng, ed., *Shenzhen Jingji*, 41-42.

84. Gu Shutang, ed., *Shenzhen Yanjiu*, 134, 136.

85. *FEER*, March 21, 1985, 150-151.

86. *FEER*, Dec. 20, 1984, 8.

87. *Shenzhen Tequ Bao*, April 13, 1985, 1. See also *FEER*, May 2, 1985, 56; and Gu Shutang, ed., *Shenzhen Yanjiu*, 60-68. Some details of the Shenzhen currency plan are available in these Chinese sources, and confirm that it would have entailed the financial linkage of Shenzhen to Hong Kong and its separation from the interior of China. These sources reveal that, although at first it would probably have been given a pegged value, it would have been linked to a basket of foreign currencies and gradually allowed to float, as Shenzhen developed a more elaborate foreign currency trading system. On the other hand, serious consideration was given to trying to eliminate domestic renminbi from the Zone altogether, to prevent black market trading for Shenzhen currency. In effect, these measures would let Shenzhen residents buy imports freely with their local currency, while preventing Chinese elsewhere from doing so. Chinese protectionism would be withdrawn from Shenzhen but reinforced outside the zone. The plan could not work, however--no fence would keep the new currency out of China, or renminbi from trading in Shenzhen.

88. David K.Y. Chu in *Modernization in China*, 131-2.

89. *Ibid.*, 133.
90. *Shenzhen Tequ Bao*, Aug. 26, 1982; cited in Chu and Wong, *Modernization in China*, 135.
91. *Shenzhen Tequ Bao*, April 4, 1985, 1.
92. *Ibid.*, May 31, 1982; cited in Chu and Wong, *Modernization in China*, 189. See also Note 80.
93. Gu Shutang, ed., *Shenzhen Yanjiu*, 153-4.
94. *Ibid.*, 151-3. For another pro-foreign bank argument, see also Wu Dakun, "Guanyu Shenzhen Waizi Yinhang Shengge wei Fenhang de Wenti," in Qian Jiaju, ed., *Tequ Jingji Lilun Wenti Lunwenji* (Beijing: Renmin Chubanshe, 1984), 92-101.
95. *China Daily*, April 16, 1985, 2.
96. Fang Sheng, ed., *Shenzhen Jingji*, 84.
97. *Ibid.*, was one such report.
98. E.g. Liu Guoguang, Vice President of the Academy of Social Sciences. See *China Reconstructs*, December, 1985, 25-26.
99. *Ibid.*, 27.
100. *Beijing Review*, Feb. 24, 1986, 15.
101. *Renmin Ribao* overseas edn., Feb. 1, 1986; trans. FBIS, Feb. 4, 1986, K5-6.
102. *Ibid.*, K6.
103. Gu Shutang, ed., *Shenzhen Yanjiu*, 54.
104. *Nanfang Ribao*, June 14, 1982; trans. JPRS 81634, Aug. 26, 1982, 51-4.
105. Fang Sheng, ed., *Shenzhen Jingji*, 25-6.
106. Shenzhen Party Committee, ed., *Qianjinzhong de Shenzhen*, 30.
107. Ho and Huenemann, *China's Open Door*, 70. See also Shenzhen Municipal Party Committee, ed., *Qianjinzhong de Shenzhen*; and *China Reconstructs*, Dec. 1985, 26.
108. Michael J. Moser in Moser, ed., *Foreign Trade, Investment, and the Law in the People's Republic of China* (Hong Kong: Oxford University Press, 1984), 162.
109. *Yangcheng Wanbao* (Canton), May 26, 1982; trans. JPRS 81269, July 13, 1982, 28-31.
110. Shenzhen City Government, "Shenzhen Jiben Qingkuang," 29.
111. Municipal Party Secretary Liang Xiang in *Beijing Review*, Feb. 24, 1986, 18.
112. Fang Sheng, ed., *Shenzhen Jingji*, 115.
113. Gu Shutang, ed., *Shenzhen Yanjiu*, 3. According to this source, by 1984 the proportion of Shenzhen cadres at assistant manager level or higher with university training rose from 65% to 80%, and their average age dropped from 50 to 40.
114. *Shijie Jingji Daobao*, June 21, 1982; trans. JPRS 82068, Oct. 25, 1982, 20-21.

115. Guangdong Provincial Service, Oct. 21, 1982; trans. JPRS 82237, Nov. 16, 1982, 88.

116. Fang Sheng, ed., *Shenzhen Jingji*, 123-4.

117. *Wen Wei Po* (Hong Kong), June 24, 1982; trans. SWB FE/7062, June 26, 1982, BII/1.

118. See Chu and Wong eds.,*Modernization in China*, 180-9.

119. *FEER*, Sept. 19, 1985, 61.

120. *Shijie Jingji Daobao*, June 1, 1987, 15.

121. *Guoji Maoyi Wenti*, No. 4, 1987, 4-8.

122. *China Trade Report*, Dec., 1987, 16.

123. *Shijie Jingji Daobao*, Nov. 16, 1987, 5; see also *FEER*, March 24, 1988, 82.

124. *JETRO China Newsletter* No. 78 (Jan., 1989), 7-13.

125. *FEER*, Dec. 15, 1988, 118.

126. *FEER*, March 2, 1989, 60.

127. *Ibid.*

128. *FEER*, Jan. 12, 1989, 45.

129. *FEER*, March 2, 1989, 60.

130. *Ibid.*, 61.

131. Elson Pow and Michael J. Moser, "Law and Investment in China's Special Investment Areas," in Moser, ed., *Foreign Trade, Investment and the Law in the People's Republic of China*, second edn. (Hong Kong: Oxford University Press, 1987), 233.

132. *FEER*, July 14, 1989, 22-25.

133. *Beijing Review*, April 25, 1988, 46.

134. *Ibid.*

135. *Ibid.*

136. *Beijing Review*, January 2, 1989, 29.

137. *FEER*, May 18, 1989, 58-59. For a post-Beijing massacre report on conditions and prospects in Hainan, see *New York Times*, Dec. 4, 1989, 32.

138. *Ibid.*

139. *FEER*, Sept. 8, 1988, 127.

140. *FEER*, Sept. 28, 1989, 10-11.

141. *Shijie Jingji Daobao*, June 15, 1987, 15.

142. *Guoji Maoyi Wenti*, No. 4, 1987, 5.

143. *Shijie Jingji Daobao*, Oct. 26, 1987, 13.

144. *Liaowang* (overseas edn.), No. 26, 1988, 17-18; trans. FBIS, CHI-88-126, 57-8.

145. *Ibid.*

146. *Beijing Review*, Feb. 24, 1986, 17.

5

The Management of Foreign Trade: Decentralization, Adjustment, and Readjustment

"Decentralization and control are two sides of one coin."

--Huang Wenjun, Spokesman, Ministry of Foreign
of Foreign Economic Relations and Trade, 1986

Among the several dramatic economic reforms initiated by Deng Xiaoping's government since 1979, one that has aroused many hopes in the West (especially among businessmen) is the People's Republic's active pursuit of greatly expanded levels of foreign trade. This policy represents a complete rejection of self-reliance as that principle was understood by Mao Zedong. Both the rapid growth in China's foreign trade and the predominance of capitalist trading partners suggest an utterly new, more flexible and open approach by the Chinese government after 1978. Does this represent a change of goals for China, and an acceptance of free trade? Or is it rather a change of strategy to achieve the long-cherished aim of national self-reliance, now redefined to have a more pragmatic meaning?

An overview of the roots of Chinese foreign trade policy reveals some continuities in both goals and the structure of state control that the Chinese theorists quoted in Chapter Two find necessary. Self-reliance defined broadly to mean building a broad base of key national industries has been a consistent political theme in China since before 1949. What changed was the means. China discovered that its long term goal of industrial self-reliance was actually hindered by depending on Soviet aid and loans in the 1950s and by attempting extreme forms of local self-reliance in the 1960s. The supplementary boost the economy needed from imported equipment, realized Deng Xiaoping in the late 1970s, could be obtained from a variety of competitively courting partners, and paid for by increased exports.

That idea gave rise to China's opening up in foreign trade, resulting in a drastic increase in trade activity that twice went out of control. Such experiences seemed to prove that Deng's idea required renewed state intervention into import and export flows to keep Chinese consumer demand for imports in check, and to maintain a favorable trade balance.

The levers of state control over foreign trade had long been in place, most of them since the 1950s. What happened after 1978 was that indirect control, using structures and methods previously established in different circumstances, replaced some direct central commands. Yet the unsteady use of indirect controls and decentralized administration revealed inexperience and confusion. Unanticipated consequences of China's new foreign trade strategy led to fresh attempts to restore order by fiat. And then, in cyclical fashion, a renewed phase of opening up would begin.

Before proceeding to the details of the opening up in foreign trade reform, this chapter briefly examines the development of trade controls and their economic consequences since the 1950s. This will provide perspective on the dynamics of later reforms which attempted to find a compromise between state control and local initiative. The subsequent discussion will demonstrate that despite many changes in how policy is realized, and despite some unintended consequences of administrative reforms, China has held firmly to its dual goals: economic growth, and development of a broad base of industries under national control. And as under the new policies, foreign trade rises in volume and importance to China, state intervention and management become increasingly crucial.

The Development of China's Foreign Trade: Opening to the Soviet Union in the 1950s

Because of Mao's alignment with the international Communist movement, China's foreign trade from 1949 through the 1950s was overwhelmingly with the Soviet bloc. The unforeseen result was economic dependency on the Soviet Union--and a major setback to China's development when political relations soured by 1960.

Mao's ideology, combined with the outbreak of East-West conflict in the Korean War, produced a political alliance of China with the Soviet Union. As Mao declared in June, 1949: "We belong to the side of the anti-imperialist front headed by the Soviet Union and so we turn only to this side for genuine and friendly help."[1] During the early 1950s, China virtually copied much of the Soviet political structure, and aligned with Moscow in both domestic and foreign policy. China's socialist collectivization of agriculture jumped from stage to stage with growing fervor. Industry was put under centralized control. Abroad, China's participation in the Korean War beginning in 1950 led to an American trade embargo and curtailed trade possibilities with other Western countries.

In addition to aligning itself with other socialist states in economic and foreign policies, China adopted measures to assure full state control of foreign trade. The first step was to take over foreign trade work itself, part of the Communist Party's policy of confiscating capitalist assets. In 1950, China had (by one count) 4,600 private import and export enterprises employing 35,000 people. Their activity still included a third of the nation's international trade. But by 1952, state-run foreign trade activity accounted for some 93 per cent, and by 1955, more than 99 per cent, of the total.[2] This enabled the state to regulate all trade through bilateral purchase and barter agreements, through state-set prices administered by the Foreign Trade Ministry, and by customs tariffs.

The government during this period created a number of institutions involved in foreign trade control. In 1951, a Customs Law enacted import and export duties on 17 general categories of goods, including 936 specific classifications--a system that, with adjustments, remained until 1982.[3] In 1952, the China Council for the Promotion of International Trade was set up to promote economic relations by organizing trade exhibitions and arranging technical exchanges, and to provide legal advice and related services to those involved in foreign trade. The Council was a semiautonomous body under the general supervision of the Ministry of Foreign Trade. In the following year, the Chinese Import and Export Inspection Bureau was created under the Ministry of Foreign Trade to control commodity quality. And in 1957, the semiannual Canton trade fair, which would later play a significant role in promoting China's exports, began.[4]

Early on, the state established controls on import pricing and distribution. Import prices from 1953 on were actually held down, with purchases subsidized to match state-set domestic factory output prices. The inexperience of government trade administrators produced confusion. For example, some Chinese units acting as import agents included handling fees in setting prices, others did not. Equivalent goods from different countries, handled by different importing units, were as a result sometimes assigned different prices--all under "central" control.[5] Nonetheless, imports were centrally restricted by quantity and category to urgent production needs or items China could not produce.

China's opening to foreign (Communist bloc) capital and trade in the 1950s had important economic results. Soviet technical contributions were substantial. Soviet-Chinese joint ventures were set up to exploit resources in the border province of Xinjiang, although these were terminated after Stalin's death in 1953.[6] However, throughout the decade hundreds of key Chinese industrial projects were undertaken with Soviet aid and technology. To support this development, China began to import an overwhelming proportion of capital goods. During the early part of the First Five Year Plan (1953-1957) China still paid for these imports with exports of primary agricultural and mineral products.[7]

Then, successful economic recovery from the civil war and industrial construction under the First Five Year Plan contributed to the beginning of a shift in export composition. Unprocessed agricultural goods fell from 55.7 per cent of exports in 1953 to 40.1 per cent by 1957.[8] The most significant reason for their declining proportion was the growth of light industrial and textile exports, which in the period 1953 through 1959 increased 240 per cent to a one-year level of US $947 million.[9] Such a broadening mix of exports is a generally reliable indicator of diversified production and probable rising per capita incomes in an economy.[10] By the end of the decade, China was exporting a higher proportion of manufactured goods than South Korea, Singapore, or Taiwan at that time.[11]

While this indicated real preliminary progress toward a diversified economic base, it was achieved at a cost of dependency. Two-thirds of growing Chinese foreign trade during the decade was with the Soviet bloc.[12] Equally crucial as a cause of China's vulnerability in trade relations was the quality of trade with the Soviets. Of all China's imports during the 1950s, both from the Soviet Union and as a whole, capital goods (on which basic industrial growth relied) accounted for over 90 per cent. More than 70 per cent of China's exports were primary goods and processed agricultural commodities.[13] China even borrowed from the Soviet Union to cover its trade deficits in seven of ten years. Just how vulnerable all of this made the Chinese became apparent in 1960. In that year, rapidly worsening political relations between erstwhile fraternal allies led Khruschev to pull out all aid and advisers. Bilateral trade dropped sharply. It took Chinese industry decades to recover from this blow--such was the dependency that adherence to international Marxist unity had created.

Although in this period China's trade with Western countries remained very low--lowest of all with the United States, which maintained the trade embargo--China did conduct substantial trade with Hong Kong. In fact, Hong Kong was China's second largest trade partner after the Soviet Union, accounting for nearly 10 per cent of the nation's trade during the decade, in part enabling China to circumvent the American embargo. Trade with Japan continued at a low level (less than 2 per cent of total trade) until 1958, when China broke trade relations completely after an incident in which Japanese youths desecrated a Chinese flag.[14] Politics limited the growth of China's trade with and potential export earnings from both the West and Asia, during this pro-Soviet phase. At the end of the decade only a third of total exports went to the West.

The Development of China's Foreign Trade:
Isolation and Dependence in the 1960s

After the destructive 1960 break with the Soviets, Mao demanded that China follow a policy of strict national self-reliance, and the country did so for twelve years. In overreaction to the shock of Soviet withdrawal, Mao revised Marxist ideology again, to make it consistent with self-reliance, and this strict line continued to hamper development of trade with the West. Furthermore, the United States trade embargo on "Red China" remained in force. Widening of trade would have to await improved political relations.

State control of foreign trade continued during this period, even during what Chinese now call the "years of great chaos" in the late 1960s. In the area of import price controls, the State Council in December, 1963 instituted a new set of regulations which remained in effect from 1964 through 1980.[15] These regulations continued and standardized the earlier policy of pricing most imports according to (subsidized) prices of equivalent domestic goods. This meant that the state held import prices artificially low, in effect subsidizing them too. The central government held the price lever, but did not yet use it as a protectionist device. Import controls remained direct--through bilateral agreements, quotas, and import licenses.

The first effect of Maoist self-reliance policy was a repeated drop in China's volume of foreign trade. Natural disasters, the "Great Leap," and the Soviet pullout had all crippled China's production capacity, and thus its export potential. China now reacted to the slump in its purchasing power by cutting trade levels, rather than allowing a large trade deficit to develop. China was determined not to repeat its deficit-aggravated dependence of the 1950s on the Soviet Union or any other major power.

The distribution of China's diminished trade volume shifted dramatically during the 1960s. The greatest change was in China's trade with the Soviet Union, which by 1970 declined to only one per cent of China's total trade by value.[16] During the twelve years 1960 through 1971, only 24.6 per cent of Chinese trade was with Communist countries.[17]

Trade with Japan and the West began to expand again in the 1960s. In September, 1960, Zhou Enlai laid down "Three Trading Principles" for Sino-Japanese trade that allowed trading with friendly firms, despite political differences between the two governments over Japan's relations with Taiwan. Trade with Hong Kong remained relatively stable; as Hong Kong's major food supplier, China earned a bilateral trade surplus of over $5 billion during the decade.[18] Trade with other Asian countries such as Malaysia and Singapore increased slightly as China imported some consumer goods from them. China had no recorded trade with the US during the 1960s, but its exchanges with the West European countries and Canada began to grow, also due to Chinese imports of consumption goods. These Western countries accounted for one fifth of China's trade, and China ran deficits with all of them.

The Chinese break with the Soviets, and embrace of self-reliance, did not solve China's problem of dependency. A look at the nation's trade composition during the decade will illustrate. In exports, the volume of many textile and light industrial good sales fell by a third or more during the Cultural Revolution,[19] their production hampered by domestic political upheavals. Recovery took more than ten years.

While China's hard currency-earning exports fell during the 1960s, its more limited import purchases had to incorporate a much larger proportion of basic consumption goods (as high as 55 per cent in 1964) including grain.[20] These import needs reflected the consequences of radical economic policies, especially the farm collectivization of the late 1950s, which disrupted agricultural production to the point of causing widespread hunger. One result was that food imports increasingly displaced capital good purchases that might have helped sustain economic growth. Imports of grain, which peaked at 6.2 million tons in 1966, accounted for China's largest bilateral trade deficit in the 1960s--with Canada.[21] Mao's policies and political movements proclaiming self-reliance interfered with the growth of export production, hampered earning of foreign exchange needed to acquire the means of industrial development, and thus actually increased dependency on foreign sources of consumption goods.

It was Premier Zhou Enlai who began the movement toward a new foreign economic policy. In joint communiques with Japan and the US in 1972 and 1973 respectively, Zhou endorsed bilateral trade even though these countries' governments were still extending political recognition to Taiwan. China's trade with the West now began to expand. Beijing had previously insisted such trade would be a violation of its "Five Principles of Peaceful Coexistence" proclaimed in 1955, which called for noninterference in internal affairs (such as the Taiwan question). Now the Principles were bent so that China could get technology from the West. Deng Xiaoping made a contribution to China's policy reversal in an April, 1974 speech to the United Nations, in which he redefined "self-reliance" to accommodate increased foreign trade and aid.[22] All of this met with the vehement opposition of Jiang Qing and the radical "gang of four," who were then playing a major political role in Beijing.

China's foreign trade responded vigorously, if somewhat unsteadily, to Zhou Enlai's new approach. It experienced average annual growth of 23 per cent for seven years. Thanks largely to exports of crude oil and petroleum, the deficit was held even lower than in the 1960s.[23] The "self-reliance" anti-trade politics of the gang of four were losing and the economics of comparative advantage gaining. The issue was decided by the political coup against the gang in October, 1976.

As foreign trade increased rapidly, China diversified its range of partners to include the United States, as President Nixon relaxed the 21-year embargo against China after 1971. Sino-US trade picked up rapidly, accelerating in the excited months following announcement of the short-lived Chinese Ten Year Plan in February, 1978. China imported grain, cotton, machinery, equipment, and crude materials from the US, and exported to it both manufactured goods and raw materials.[24] Japan remained China's largest trade partner continuously starting from 1970, that is, from two years before the Zhou-Tanaka communique gave the trade official approval. After 1974, expanding crude oil exports allowed China (though still running bilateral trade deficits) to increase imports of Japanese machinery, equipment, and steel. Hong Kong maintained its position as China's second largest trade partner and as source of surplus,[25] from foodstuff and petroleum exports and from manufactured exports shipped to the British colony for re-export overseas.[26]

The result of these trends was that by the time China's opening up policy finally started in 1979, capitalist countries already accounted for 87 per cent of the gross value of China's foreign trade.[27]

China also made considerable progress in diversifying its composition of trade with a broader mix of exports, years before Deng's opening up. The share of textile and industrial products in exports grew, made possible by increased manufacturing production.[28] The fact that China's exports in 1979 were some six times higher than in 1970 allowed China to purchase substantial amounts of capital equipment to further expand export production.

In this brief survey of 29 years of the People's Republic's foreign trade, one can see several long-term trends that prefigured the results of the later opening up policies. First, trade tended to grow steadily whenever and wherever it was not impeded by political dogmas or poor foreign relations. It grew in the 1950s, in the early 1970s, and again after the fall of the gang of four in 1976. Second, China has consistently held to an import substitution policy for finished goods, protecting against consumer imports except when economic failures made purchase of some basic survival goods unavoidable (as during some of the "self-reliance" years). Third, China made some progress toward raising its proportion of manufactured exports well before Deng's reforms were under way. Fourth, foreign trade was under direct state control--but the levers of indirect control later preferred by the government, such as tariffs, quotas, and prices were already in place. All of these points foreshadowed the opening up policy after 1979, which sought to attract the widest range of trade partners, to import capital and gradually upgrade the mix of exports, while using central government intervention to protect developing domestic industry.

Decentralization and Control in Chinese Theories
About Opening Up in Foreign Trade

As the above indicates, the composition of China's foreign trade was shifting to reflect a more diverse mix of industrial production well before the opening policies were formally announced in 1979. Further, the levers of state control and regulation of trade activity essential to the post-1979 policy had long been in place. What was new in Deng Xiaoping's policies was the realization that the long term goal of national self-reliance could be more effectively realized by much higher levels of economic exchange, through which China could obtain capital and technology to promote its modernization.

The fundamental premise underlying China's foreign trade reforms and all aspects of the opening up policies is that they do *not* constitute an "open door" to foreign intrusion. The Chinese reject that term "because of [its] historical associations." Under the early twentieth century open door policy, "China figured only as prey," while China today is a sovereign state protected by its laws.[29] Chinese commentators, in keeping with their generally economic nationalist tendencies, stress that the essential difference between the "open door" as historical symbol and current policies is the capacity of the Chinese nation to protect its interests through state regulation of international dealings that cross its borders.

From before the beginning of the opening up policy, Chinese officials and economists made clear that foreign trade would be a supplement and contributor to, not a replacement of, self-reliant industrial development. As *People's Daily* put it in 1981:

> We should not indiscriminately import everything or regard everything 'foreign' as valuable or good. Our consistent policy is to give priority to self-reliance and regard foreign trade as supplementary.[30]

Supplementary, the paper explained, to the industrial foundation being developed by China itself. Economist Teng Weizao noted in 1982 that China's per capita foreign trade still ranked among the lowest in the world; Beijing, he asserted, was now seeking to restore a level of trade appropriate to the country's level of development.[31]

The Chinese accept foreign trade because they have learned that isolationism is counterproductive for a large complex nation.[32] By late 1978, Party theoreticians had already accepted the logic of international specialization, according to which countries with various technological levels have "an objective condition for exchange" which justifies a division of labor between them.[33] It did not take much longer to throw out Mao's concept of regional self-reliance within the country; now, asserted the Beijing journal *International Trade Problems* in 1981, each region should increasingly specialize production in its areas of greatest strength to contribute to national export production. As for the country as a whole, it would be proper for China, at its present stage of development, to specialize in labor-intensive forms of production.[34]

Chinese economists realized in the early 1980s that there remained plenty of room for debate on the contribution foreign trade should make to industrial construction. They remained cautious about the extent to which China should follow other Asian models. On the pro-emulation side, economic reformers at a national conference on the opening up policy in

April, 1985 (which was closed to foreigners) postulated a three-stage opening up process. First, the "preparation stage" in which the country would engage in large-scale exporting to earn foreign exchange, as well as improving the environment for foreign investors. Second, a maturation stage in which introduction of more technologies allows greater satisfaction of domestic consumer needs and more participation in the international market. Third, the "soaring" stage involving extensive structural adjustment to the international market, and expanded exchange of capital, skills, and technology.[35] For Chinese (ex-) Marxists, putting phases of the opening into a historical progression gave them an aura of inevitability. Some have gone further, explicitly observing the successes of Singapore, South Korea, Hong Kong, and Taiwan in upgrading their export production with equipment purchased from trade earnings. Chinese economic reformers describe this as a strategy that could in large part be planned and adopted in China.[36]

On the other hand, many of the same pro-reform economists reject an export-based development model, because it would expose the domestic economy to international market fluctuations, threatening internal economic stability.[37] They note that Japan relied successfully for decades on protectionist restrictions and tariffs as its industries developed stage by stage.[38] Yet they do recognize the positive side of competitive pressure: one of the benefits of more foreign trade, some Chinese have argued, would be a higher degree of competition in society. Published articles have asserted that domestic competition in Japan is a prime reason for that country's economic successes. One such article described Japan as an "athletic field" for companies. The article was entitled "A Society without competition has no way to open completely to the competitive world."[39] Such suggestions directly addressed the realization of economists that many Chinese enterprises "lack motivation" to enter the international sales market.[40]

At the same time, international competition among China's trade partners could work to the country's advantage, Chinese economists have noted. One suggested in 1987 that if more equipment and parts orders were placed with the US and West Germany, this would "strengthen [our] position in trade negotiations" with Japanese companies, by making them realize that the Chinese do not need them.[41] Such an approach depends on treating various trade partners similarly, and hence thrives on a foreign policy of equidistance from the two superpowers, leaning slightly to put pressure on one or the other, while drawing benefits from both of them as well as other partners.

Domestically, Chinese economists now generally recognize that to attain national goals by expanding foreign trade requires decentralized administration. This includes the principle of separating government from enterprise management.[42] The weekly *World Economic Herald*, as usual going as far as possible toward a liberal position as the current Party line allowed, commented in 1985 on "a profound change of attitude in every country and region in Asia" about government interference in economics. Remarking positively on the widespread attitude favoring relaxation of government controls, it quoted with implied approval the Minister of Commerce and Industry in unrecognized South Korea: "'We can't take charge of everything. We must change and adopt an attitude of facing the market.'"[43] The new Chinese policies, in theory, embraced decentralization of control and domestic competition as means to spur the nation to success in the international marketplace. But even in theory, abundant reservations were attached to the opening in foreign trade.

Rather than promoting export substitution or an export production orientation, Chinese officials and analysts of trade policy consistently advocate import substitution: restricting imports of goods China can or could produce, and promoting domestic production to replace imports. "Protectionist policy...does not conflict with an opening up policy" was the concise summary of a Beijing economics journal in mid-1982.[44] A few quotations give ample illustration of what the policy means. *People's Daily*, May 8, 1979:[45]

> We must oppose extravagance and reckless actions, such as importing those items we can make ourselves and acquiring complete sets of equipment, including parts that can be made in China.

Beijing Daily, May 28, 1982:[46]

> Some localities and departments have imported a large quantity of products which can be manufactured at home, thus wasting a large amount of foreign exchange and deterring the development of the country's industry.

Caijing Wenti Yanjiu (Dalian), July, 1982:[47]

> Why...do we not expand production of domestically-produced...machines rather than importing equipment to meet production needs?

Fujian Daily, July 30, 1982:[48] to import consumer goods that can be produced with equal quality in China brings the result that

> "the fertile water flows into other people's fields."

Economist Teng Weizao:

> We should become self-sufficient in all those things that are being produced domestically or can be produced economically once the correct measures are taken.[49]

Economics Daily, January 22, 1983:[50]

> It is completely legitimate for [developing countries] to
> adopt a protective policy in trade.

Teng Weizao (also President of Nankai University in Tianjin)
provided a succinct list of the benefits for China of its import substitution
policy: it protects industries that are training technical personnel; promotes domestic industry and (he believes) diversification; reduces reliance
on imported commodities; saves foreign exchange; and is compatible with
the use of joint ventures to help develop export industries. The drawbacks, Teng admits, are "high costs and low efficiency."[51] A lengthy
1987 article in a leading Chinese economics journal bluntly warned that
without an import substitution policy, Chinese enterprises could be forced
out of production by foreign competition.[52]

Official Chinese speeches and commentaries have supported
import substitution and denounced "blind imports" of both foreign productive equipment and consumer goods.[53] Exactly why China might act
blindly in this regard they did not explain, but both the quality and style of
imported goods attract Chinese consumers. There have been frequent
complaints about expensive purchases of too much foreign equipment. A
National People's Congress delegate in April, 1985 expressed a common
view:

> The state spends a lot of foreign exchange to bring in
> several thousand microcomputers, and what is the result in
> the end? We can't just let whoever has foreign exchange
> spend it blindly on imports. That makes waste, as well as
> influencing the development of the country's electronics
> industry.[54]

Such complaints have often blamed state losses on decisions made by
enterprises using their newly granted autonomy.[55] Thus, the opening up
policy, declared *Caimao Jingji* (Finance and Trade) in 1982, is not

> an unprincipled opening of our doors to allow unrestrained
> infiltration of foreign capital into our country or the flood-
> ing of our market with foreign goods, leaving us at the
> beck and call of foreign businessmen.[56]

Confusingly, demands for tighter central control of both imports
and exports often came together with calls for greater efficiency, expansion of foreign trade, or reform of certain aspects of operation. Far from
being seen as the root of all evil, central control has been the habitual,

preferred Chinese remedy for virtually any unfavorable results. *People's Daily* set this theme at the outset in May, 1979:

> Under the present system [of import regulation] there are too many overlapping control units which have not been properly coordinated...a centralized organ should be set up to coordinate functions, divide responsibility, and increase efficiency.[57]

The instinct to rely on the state to solve problems is understandable when one considers the central government's role in stopping inflation after the civil war of the late 1940s, in achieving sweeping social changes, in restoring order after the Cultural Revolution, and in providing a livelihood for a majority of the Chinese people.

Contrary to the impression of some commentators that China is undertaking a revolutionary decentralization of foreign trade administration, Chinese analysis often stresses (and not only during periods of readjustment) that unified central planning and implementation of foreign trade goals is essential.[58] There are several reasons why. First, to protect China's existing and developing industries from competition and unpredictable market forces. Second, to reduce duplicate purchases of imported equipment by separate, autonomous Chinese enterprises.[59] According to published Chinese analysis, when firms begin to act autonomously there is the benefit of competitive pressure, but also the risk of misjudged capital investment. Third, there is the "corrosive influence of moribund bourgeois ideology"[60] and (worse yet) "there is still the danger of peaceful evolution" to capitalism.[61] Fourth, as authority is partially decentralized, conflicts arise between new and old managers, as well as turf disputes among the new agencies and enterprises.[62] Fifth, adjustment of overall export composition to include a higher proportion of manufactured goods requires administrative intervention by foreign trade departments into production matters otherwise left to enterprises.[63] Numerous localities have called for creation of new local or provincial government organs to coordinate and promote export production. Finally, there is the less often stated, but in the long term crucial, concern about balanced development of China's disparate regions.[64] For these reasons, the perceived need to have higher authorities coordinate trade activity has provided some counterweight to every decentralizing step.

The desire for continuation of strong centralized guidance of foreign trade extends to China's import priority, advanced technology. A 1985 analysis of China's technology imports administration published in the relatively liberal magazine *Weilai Yu Fazhan* (Future and Development) recommended that China should form a specialized central administrative structure to guide technology imports; establish an investigative body to ensure their soundness; and create a "technological imports responsibility system" with enterprise leaders and managers held accountable to a higher reviewing organ for major mistakes.[65] Such suggestions reveal that even many pro-reform theorists do not conceive of a complete separation of government from enterprise administration. Firms will not be left to buy technology in the international marketplace, then have profits or losses determine the degree of success and future investment capacity. Rather, it is central oversight (some theorists suppose) that will guarantee sound purchase decisions. In the period of the Seventh Five Year Plan (1986 through 1990), technology transfer and equipment purchases are to play key roles in upgrading existing Chinese enterprises; the issue of who is responsible for purchase decisions will be of increasing importance.[66]

The Foreign Trade Opening in Practice

Despite reservations and qualifications, a fundamental reform of China's foreign trade operations took place after 1979. It involved both structural reform--a qualified decentralization of authority--and a sharp increase in the levels of trade and export earnings China sought. Some of the levers of control established before 1979 were modified, others kept in place but put to amended use. Because of the continuities of structure as well as guiding ideology, the opening up in foreign trade should be considered a major reform, not a revolution.

A wave of reform of foreign trade operations took shape in the three years after 1978. During this period, the twelve state Foreign Trade Corporations under the aegis of the Ministry of Foreign Trade, which were already handling most import and export arrangements, began to grant greater operational autonomy to their regional branches. As the volume of trade jumped rapidly, officials from China's numerous state industrial production ministries were also itching to participate directly in trade deals. They, after all, had technical expertise relevant to the goods being traded that the Trade Ministry bureaucrats did not. Although they were not granted this right until 1981,[67] the government did expand its plans for foreign trade activity, rapidly heightening the expectations of foreign business.[68]

A wide variety of small signs pointed to a new Chinese attitude. In a gesture of openness, after 1978 Chinese foreign trade negotiators routinely began to distribute individual business cards with their full names and exact positions. Of equal significance, in October 1979, Shanghai People's (official) Radio announced it would henceforth broadcast foreign exchange quotations to provide "a yardstick for our nation's daily progress in foreign economic activities."[69] Also in 1979, demonstrating its increased commitment to export growth, China began to accept production contracts that required the use of foreign trademarks.[70] All of these steps revealed a new willingness to accept, even embrace, international standards in foreign trade work.

Meanwhile, China successfully negotiated new bilateral trade agreements with Western countries in 1979. These included the first US-China mutual trade agreement in thirty years, as well as an extension of the Sino-Japanese agreement to 1990 with a projected value of $60 billion.[71] A textile export agreement, doubling China's annual quota, was signed with the European Economic Community (EEC) later in 1979.

The foreign trade reforms broadened and deepened in the early 1980s. New product-specialized Foreign Trade Corporations were set up, controlled by the state but under the aegis of the central production ministries rather than the Ministry of Foreign Trade. This meant that Chinese traders had specific expertise relevant to export or import products.[72] Furthermore, cities and provinces were granted the rights to form their own foreign trade organizations, to approve some routine import and export contracts, and to retain a portion of hard currency export earnings. For many provincial exports this proportion has been 25 to 30 per cent, but the ethnic minority areas (Xinjiang, Ningxia, Guangxi) have been allowed to retain 50 per cent of their few hard currency earnings, while Tibet and the Special Economic Zones could keep all of theirs.[73] Initially four cities--Shanghai, Canton, Tianjin, and Beijing--were also given autonomous trade prerogatives,[74] and coastal provinces were to handle trade matters on behalf of interior provinces. However, the latter plan raised the potential for quarrels between wealthier coastal provinces and poor interior ones. To alleviate this tension, by 1985 most provinces were also given autonomous trading rights for at least some commodities. Furthermore, in order to foster growth in foreign trade, central and provincial governments supported the establishment of over 180 local export production districts (many very small) with capital, loans, tax preferences, and other special assistance.[75]

Decentralization of trade activity was complemented by continuous issuance of new laws protecting the interests of both Chinese and foreign partners in trade agreements. Especially noteworthy were the Economic Contract Law (adopted December 13, 1981), which makes detailed assignments of responsibility for breach in various kinds of business agreements; and the Patent Law (effective April 1, 1985) which, as one non-Chinese analysis puts it, recognizes "products of mental labor as a form of individual wealth giving rise to proprietary rights and having measurable economic value."[76] This carefully written law was intended to reassure foreigners involved in technology license agreements that industrial designs not yet publicly disclosed would have legal protection. Certain types of items are excluded, notably pharmaceutical and chemical substances. The former (remarks a Chinese commentary) "relate to human life and health," while chemical patents "will put the [chemical] industry under strong foreign influence, which is undesirable."[77]

The administrative structure that emerged was a complex hybrid of decentralization (allowing various agencies to take the initiative and promote trade) and overlapping layers of authority that left central authorities plenty of levers of control to use when necessary. Such complexity was due not only to built-in limitations in the terms of the opening up policies, but also to a fundamental trait of People's Republic politics: it is easier to build new administrative structures than to dismantle old ones. Those already existing have established networks of human relationships, patron-client arrangements, and routine modes of operation. The legacy of institutions and bureaucratic officials from previous phases of policy lives on in these structures long after old policies themselves (such as those of the pro-Soviet period and the Cultural Revolution) have been discredited and rejected. Therefore, the task for China's reformers is to build new structures and add new personnel that surround, outweigh or outmaneuver existing ones.

The new structure of foreign trade administration has been led since March, 1982 by the Ministry of Foreign Economic Relations and Trade (Mofert), which was then created by amalgamating several former ministries and commissions. The Ministry does foreign trade planning (in collaboration with the State Planning Commission), administers foreign trade operations in general, approves import and export licenses, negotiates international trade agreements, and supervises provincial trade bureaus.[78]

Next in the structural hierarchy are the state Foreign Trade Corporations. Their duties are to act as middlemen, negotiate trade contracts under existing binational agreements, and supervise provincial offices to which specific negotiations are often referred. Each corporation is responsible for a category of commodities or services. They are under either Mofert or the state production ministries, or provincial or local governments. To complicate matters further, each province has a foreign trade bureau responsible both to the provincial government and to Mofert. These organs are supposed to plan and oversee trade operations by enterprises in their areas of jurisdiction. Many of the provincial Foreign Trade Corporations (FTCs) and enterprises are in competition with the national FTCs to conclude deals under de facto import quotas.

This mixture of older, newish, and new organizations coexists with other long-established agencies. The Chinese Council for the Promotion of International Trade promotes trade and oversees state arbitration commissions; the Bank of China arranges trade financing; the State Administration for Exchange Control regulates use of foreign exchange; the People's Insurance Company of China has a monopoly on providing necessary insurance. Finally, in part because of overlapping authority among these competing bureaucracies, there has been structural evolution within them as well. Thus, the competing authority of provincial trade bureaus prompted Mofert in 1983 to attempt to improve its own regional administrative efficiency, by decentralizing approval operations to four special trade offices (in Shanghai, Dalian, Tianjin and Canton), each responsible for designated regions of China.

Innovative procedures and structural decentralization under the opening policies do not mean, however, that the ability to regulate trade and restrict imports is lacking. Although on two occasions (1980 and 1984), government controls on hard currency expenditure did seem to melt under the widespread demand for imported goods, order was restored. What were the mechanisms of regulation used by central authorities over the new foreign trade system?

Several levers of state control over Chinese foreign trade activity have remained important since 1978: export and import licensing; restrictions on foreign exchange retention and use; commodity inspection; customs regulation and protective duties; and state pricing of traded goods, especially imports. Every one of these levers existed prior to the opening up reforms, but the uses to which they are put have evolved. To start with, Mofert in Beijing decides which products can be licensed for import by state, provincial or municipal trade bureaus;[79] and which require central approval for any imports at all. The exemptions and product lists can be adjusted by Mofert to restrict consumer good imports, to uphold bilateral trade agreements, to preserve national hard currency reserves, or to promote China's foreign policy aims.

An equally important lever of state trade control is formally in the hands of the Chinese Customs Administration. In February, 1980, this agency was reorganized and put directly under the State Council in an apparently successful effort to maintain its bureaucratic independence from the Foreign Trade Ministry. In addition to inspecting goods and levying duties, the Customs investigates, judges, and exacts penalties in smuggling cases.[80] The Customs Administration's primary job has been to enforce duties first promulgated in 1951, and revised since with the explicit purpose of protecting domestic industry.[81]

Since 1982, Chinese customs tariffs have followed several general principles.[82] The first is that tariffs on imported products that China can or will soon be able to produce are set relatively high, in comparison with prices of equivalent Chinese-made goods. Luxury goods face even higher tariffs. Goods produced in insufficient quantities by China and needed for industrial or agricultural production have lower tariffs. Preference is also given to imports from countries that have bilateral trade agreements with China.

In January, 1982, import duties were comprehensively adjusted. Specific categories subject to reduced rates included raw materials for industry; commodities temporarily in short domestic supply; components and spare parts for machines and instruments[83]--all items essential to industrial development and expansion. But duties on consumer goods, autos, ships, and most types of industrial equipment produced in China were raised. Under this regime, duties ranged from 5-20 per cent for priority imports to 150-250 per cent for most consumer goods. In 1985, the Chinese government published its once again revised list of tariffs, covering every type of good imported into the country.[84] These follow the same principles as the 1982 duties. To name a few examples, imported beer, carpets and autos, all competing with Chinese production, face levies of 100-150 per cent. By contrast, pig iron has a duty of 3-8 per cent; diesel engines for propelling vehicles, 9-14 per cent; drilling machinery, 6-17 per cent. Customs tariffs are clearly being used to implement the import substitution policy.

Through the initial decade of the opening up policies, the central government continued its active use of yet another lever of interference in international trade: control of foreign exchange expenditures. The nonconvertibility of the domestic currency, the renminbi, prevents ordinary Chinese individuals and many enterprises from purchasing imported goods and equipment unless they pay heavy black market premiums. In early 1985 the government enacted new penal provisions for violation of the exchange controls, that are lenient toward one-time offenders who confess, but severe toward repeated acts of illicit money changing.[85]

However, the central government has relaxed restrictions on authorized spending of foreign currency holdings. Each province, locality, and enterprise has been given the right to retain a set portion of its foreign exchange earnings to spend on imports. Provincial and local enterprises can borrow further hard currency from the Bank of China, or form joint ventures to raise foreign capital. These methods do not require central government approval unless a major project is involved.

China's currency exchange rates, and related accounting system, have supplemented and in part replaced foreign exchange controls. The accounting here refers to how the Chinese have reconciled world prices of imports they purchase, with domestic (partially controlled) prices used in transactions between enterprises.

In late 1980, a special exchange rate of US $1 = Rmb 2.8 was established for trading organizations to use in all internal accounting. Since at that time the official exchange rate was still an overvalued $1 = Rmb 1.5, this meant a de facto devaluation of the renminbi for Chinese traders, i.e., an increase of 75 per cent in import prices[86] (though even this did not discourage importing because it did not reflect the renminbi's market value). Since this measure increased profits to be had from selling exports, it was potentially an export-promoting step as well.[87] (Again, however, it would have had to go farther to be effective.)

A more straightforward method of achieving the same ends then followed. The renminbi was devalued in a series of stages, to $1 = Rmb 2.2 in mid-1984 and $1 = Rmb 3.7 in mid-1986. As it passed the 2.8 level in late 1984, the internal rate was no longer needed, and it was abolished at the end of the year. The currency devaluation promotes exports and increases the real price of imports, and can supplement other trade controls.

The final lever of state control over foreign trade is the pricing of imports. Chinese economists maintain that some protection is necessary from international price fluctuations that can disrupt domestic stability and growth. But they also accept, as one Chinese study pointed out, that as foreign trade develops, "the influence of movements in international market prices on our country's domestic prices of imported commodities will be ever greater."[88]

A bit of background provides helpful perspective on how this policy has developed. Until 1979, most imports were priced similarly to comparable (subsidized) domestic goods.[89] Their Chinese sales prices were thus far below international market prices, and often equivalent to Chinese goods of inferior quality. This meant, perversely, that the government despite its "self-reliance" slogans was actually giving price subsidies to purchasers of the limited number of goods that were approved for import. Central economic policymakers, with apparent confidence in their ability to allocate imported goods by fiat, for nearly thirty years overlooked this.

Beginning in 1979, China began to implement an utterly different import pricing system, which would support rather than undercut the nation's evolving long term trade policy. The new pricing system was formalized in a State Council resolution in 1981.[90] Now, state price controls would be used to promote exports and restrict imports. Goods imported under state plans would henceforth be priced according to delivery (market) price plus applicable duties and taxes, rather than according to (lower) domestic good prices. This would also apply to purchases by provincial and local units. Also, the State Council rules specify[91]--and here selective administrative authority enters in--that if international prices of imported goods are too low and threaten domestic goods with competition, they can be readjusted to higher levels when applied to domestic sales. This system keeps import prices in general higher than those of subsidized domestic goods, but permits price relief where it is vital to enterprises that have to import equipment or raw materials.

Provinces active in foreign trade activity, such as Guangdong, have approved their own import commodity price regulations, indicating that they too will not give full play to the invisible hand. "It is necessary strictly to control imported commodities," declared Guangdong's provincial government in 1982:

> ...Prices of imported commodities directly for sale to the masses in the market must be examined and approved by the departments in charge of commodity prices. Business units are not allowed to fix their own prices.[92]

Imports competing with present or possible Chinese production will have relatively high prices. This principle applies regardless of whether the imported good falls into the category of those priced domestically by fixed, guidance, or market methods.

Besides government use of indirect policy levers to influence trade, there have been periodic reminders that reassertion of direct central control remains a preferred Chinese remedy for many forms of economic uncertainty or weakness. For example, in 1981 and 1982 the Chinese despite previous reassurances unilaterally cancelled contracts for iron, steel, petrochemical and other plants involving well over $2 billion.[93] In this case the center had to correct for its own overambitious financial planning, in the face of a cash shortage and need to cut consumption. Another example: effective June 1, 1982, the central government abruptly raised export duties on more than 30 items, mostly raw materials and foodstuffs, including coal, pig iron, tungsten ore, rice and soya beans. Enterprises had discovered that exporting these items was more profitable than selling them to the state.[94]

Government intervention was also required at times when trade policy became a bilateral international issue. For example, in early 1983, in retaliation against newly imposed American textile quotas, China banned imports of cotton, synthetic fibers, and soya beans from the United States.[95] Since imports of these items were already in decline following bumper Chinese harvests, China's move was not a major escalation in the trade conflict. Nonetheless, it revealed a firm hand in asserting what the Chinese consider rightful trade prerogatives.

The United States government has been remarkably compliant in conceding the Chinese position in bilateral trade issues. This held true even during the relatively hardnosed Reagan administration. In 1982, for example, President Reagan had to cast a deciding vote after the US International Trade Commission split 2-2 on a complaint by US producers about allegedly market-disruptive Chinese canned mushroom exports. The Chinese government shrewdly suggested possible retaliation against US grain exports to China--prompting US grain producers to lobby the administration to rule in favor of China and dismiss the complaint. The President did so.[96] In 1986, the US textile industry filed a petition to request countervailing duties against subsidized Chinese textile exports. The Reagan administration applied behind-the-scenes pressure on the industry to have the petition withdrawn. The reason: concern that bringing up the issue would upset the Chinese government. The Commerce Department then promptly dropped its investigation into Chinese export subsidies in this sector.[97]

The Chinese have proved to be forceful opponents of other governments' trade restrictions. In 1987, for example, China strongly protested Japan's temporary restriction of exports by Toshiba Machine Corporation to Communist countries, which delayed shipments of urgently needed equipment.[98] In an unrelated decision the following year, China let it be known that most imports of cars from Japan would be sharply curtailed in order to support domestic production.[99] In Chinese eyes, their own government's interference with trade would be necessary and justified by the shortage of foreign exchange.

* * *

All in all, foreign trade reform was a multifaceted process involving much more than decentralization. While authority over many individual transactions was being devolved to provincial or even local authorities, the state was sharpening its use of indirect tools of control--licenses, tariffs, prices--which served not only as macroeconomic regulators but also as methods of restoring central direction as a corrective when economic results were unsatisfactory. The following chapter assesses the results of these complex reforms in more detail before drawing overall conclusions about their outcome.

Notes

    1.   James Tsao for US International Trade Commission, "China's Economic Development Strategies and their Effects on U.S. Trade," Publication 1645 (Washington, D.C., Feb. 1985), 42.
    2.   Wang Linsheng and Chen Yujie, "Economic Relations with Foreign Countries," in Yu Guangyuan, ed., *China's Socialist Modernization* (Beijing: Foreign Languages Press, 1984), 676.
    3.   Jamie P. Horsely, "The Regulation of China's Foreign Trade," in Michael J. Moser, *Foreign Trade, Investment and the Law in the PRC* (Hong Kong: Oxford University Press, 1984), 23.
    4.   *Ibid.*, 12-13, 18-19.
    5.   Hu Changnuan, ed., *Jiagexue* (Beijing: Renmin Daxue Chubanshe, 1982), 500-505.
    6.   John K. Fairbank and others, *East Asia, Tradition and Transformation* (Boston: Houghton Mifflin, 1973), 913.
    7.   Teng Weizao, "Socialist Modernization and the Pattern of Foreign Trade," in Xu Dixin, ed., *China's Search for Economic Growth* (Beijing: New World Press, 1982), 171.
    8.   Wang and Chen in Yu Guangyuan, ed., *China's Socialist Modernization*, 677.
    9.   Ma Hong and Sun Shangqing, eds., *Zhongguo Jingji Jiegou Wenti Yanjiu* (Beijing: Renmin Chubanshe, 1983), 468.
    10. The World Bank, *China, Long-term Development Issues and Options* (Baltimore: Johns Hopkins University Press, 1985), 103. See also Ungsuh Park in Robert A. Scalapino and others, eds., *Asian Economic Development--Present and Future* (Berkeley: Institute of East Asian Studies, 1985), 94; and Edward K. Y. Chen in *Ibid.*, 134.
    11. Compare *1984 Almanac of China's Foreign Economic Relations and Trade* (Hong Kong: China Resources Trade Consultancy, 1985), 829, which gives manufactured goods as 36.4% of exports by 1957; and Edward K. Y. Chen (see previous note), 134, who gives the following proportions of manufactured exports in 1960:

> South Korea   14%
> Singapore   26%
> Taiwan   32%

It is what happened since 1960 in these states and China that has made all the difference.

12. Teng, "Socialist Modernization," 169-170.

13. James Tsao, "China's Economic Strategies," 43.

14. *Ibid.*, 43, 45.

15. Hu Changnuan, ed., *Jiagexue*, 501-503. Details that follow are from this source.

16. Teng, "Socialist Modernization," 170.

17. James Tsao, "China's Economic Strategies," 46.

18. *Ibid.*, 47-48.

19. *Zhongguo Tongji Nianjian, 1983* (Beijing: Zhongguo Tongji Chubanshe, 1983), 421, 426.

20. *Ibid.*, 679, and Ma Hong, *Jiegou Wenti*, 472.

21. James Tsao, "China's Economic Strategies," 49. See also *Zhongguo Tongji Nianjian, 1983*, 438.

22. James Tsao, "China's Economic Strategies," 50-51.

23. *Ibid.*, 51. For yearly figures see *1984 Almanac of China's Foreign Economic Relations and Trade* (Hong Kong: China Resources Trade Consultancy, 1985), 817ff.

24. James Tsao, "China's Economic Strategies," 52-53.

25. *Ibid.*, 54-55.

26. John C. Hsu, "Hong Kong in China's Foreign Trade: A Changing Role," in A. J. Youngson, ed., *China and Hong Kong, The Economic Nexus* (Hong Kong: Oxford University Press, 1983), 160-166.

27. Teng, "Socialist Modernization," 169-170.

28. James Tsao, "China's Economic Strategies," 55-56.

29. *China Reconstructs*, XXXIII:9 (Sept., 1984), 2.

30. Per Xinhua report, Feb. 25, 1981; trans. FBIS, Feb. 26, 1981, L16-17.

31. Teng Weizao in Xu Dixin et. al., *China's Search for Economic Growth* (Beijing: New World Press, 1982), 168.

32. *Renmin Ribao*, July 8, 1978; trans. FBIS, July 12, 1978, E7-10.

33. *Da Gong Bao* (Hong Kong), Dec. 21, 1978; trans. FBIS, Dec. 21, 1978, N1.

34. *Guoji Maoyi Wenti*, No. 3, 1981; trans. JPRS 79742, Dec. 24, 1981, 109-118. See also *Guoji Maoyi*, Aug. 1982, especially the article by Wang Yaotian; trans. JPRS 82457, Dec. 14, 1982, 47-54.

35. *Renmin Ribao*, May 17, 1985, 3.

36. *Shijie Jingji Daobao*, Sept. 10, 1984, 2.

37. See, e.g., Teng Weizao in *China's Search*, 173-5.

38. *The Economist*, Oct. 3, 1987, 73-76.

39. *Shijie Jingji Daobao*, April 8, 1985, 6.

40. *Renmin Ribao*, May 17, 1985, 3.

41. *Shijie Jingji Daobao,* June 15, 1987, 5.
42. See article by Liu Mingxin, Zhang Chuanfang, and Wang Chengfeng in *Caimao Jingji* No. 6 (June 15, 1982); trans. JPRS 81938, Oct. 6, 1982, 64-71.
43. *Shijie Jingji Daobao,* April 22, 1985, 3.
44. *Guoji Maoyi,* Aug. 1982, article by Wang Yaotian; trans. JPRS 82457, Dec. 14, 1982, 47-54.
45. FBIS, May 15, 1979, L2-4.
46. FBIS, June 4, 1982, R1-2.
47. JPRS 82364, Dec. 2, 1982, 63.
48. JPRS 82018, Oct. 19, 1982, 50-51.
49. Teng Weizao in *China's Search,* 188.
50. JPRS 83018, March 7, 1983, 69.
51. Teng Weizao in *China's Search,* 175.
52. *Jingji Yanjiu,* No. 8, 1987, 35-44. For additional arguments supporting China's import substitution policy, see Wang Zhenxian, "Transnational Corporations and China's Economic Development," in Teng Weizao and N.T. Wang, eds., *Transnational Corporations and China's Open-Door Policy* (Lexington, MA: Lexington Books, 1988), 193; and Zhang Yangui, "The Economic Environment and China's Model for the Utilization of Foreign Capital," in *Ibid.,* 187. The latter sees export substitution as a "supplement" to "the dominant component" of China's foreign economic policy--namely import substitution.
53. *Hongqi* No. 8, April 16, 1982, 2-10, trans. FBIS, May 11, 1982, K4-16. See also *Renmin Ribao,* Oct. 3, 1980, trans. FBIS, Oct. 3, 1980, L16-17; and *Renmin Ribao,* Aug. 10, 1980; trans. SWB FE/6498, Aug. 15, 1980, BII/9-10.
54. *Renmin Ribao,* April 5, 1985, 2.
55. *Ibid*; also *Renmin Ribao,* June 14, 1985, 1.
56. *Caimao Jingji,* Nov. 15, 1982; trans. JPRS 82724, Jan. 25, 1983, 48-52.
57. *Renmin Ribao,* May 8, 1979; FBIS, May 15, 1979, L2-4.
58. See e.g. Beijing domestic service report, Sept. 2-3, 1982; trans. JPRS 81938, Oct. 6, 1982, 59-63.
59. See *Renmin Ribao,* Jan. 4, 1983, 5; trans. FBIS, Jan. 7, 1983, K7.
60. *Ibid.,* K8.
61. Guangdong Provincial report, April 3, 1982; trans. FBIS, April 5, 1982, P1-2.
62. See article cited in note 42.
63. *Renmin Ribao,* Sept. 28, 1979; trans. FBIS, Oct. 9, 1979, L13. See also *Guangzhou Ribao,* July 29, 1982; trans. JPRS 82018, Oct. 19, 1982, 54-6.
64. *Renmin Ribao,* Sept. 23, 1984, 5.
65. *Weilai Yu Fazhan,* Feb. 15, 1985, 17.

66. See Madelyn C. Ross, "China's New Investment Zones," *China Business Review*, Nov.-Dec., 1984, 14-16.

67. Thomas D. Gorman, "China's Changing Foreign Trade System, 1975-85," in Robert Delfs and others, eds., *China* (London: Euromoney Publications, 1986), 86.

68. In 1979, based on official Chinese statements foreign businessmen were expecting $40 billion in import orders over the following five years. *Quarterly Economic Review of China, Hong Kong, North Korea* (London: Economist Intelligence Unit), first quarter 1979, 13.

69. *Jiefang Ribao* (Shanghai), Oct. 29, 1979; trans. JPRS 74921, Jan. 14, 1980, 68.

70. John C. Hsu, "Hong Kong in China's Foreign Trade: A Changing Role," in A. J. Youngson, ed., *China and Hong Kong, The Economic Nexus* (Hong Kong: Oxford University Press, 1983), 174.

71. *Quarterly Economic Review of China, Hong Kong, North Korea*, third quarter 1979, 11-12.

72. Gorman, "China's Changing System," 86.

73. David L. Denny, "Provincial Trade Patterns," *China Business Review*, Sept.-Oct., 1987, 21.

74. On Shanghai, see Xinhua, May 16, 1983; trans. FBIS, May 17, 1983, 03.

75. *Jingji Zongheng*, No. 6, 1987, 36.

76. Ellen R. Eliasoph, "China's Patent System Emerges," *China Business Review*, Jan.-Feb., 1985, 50.

77. Dong Shizhong in *Intertrade Supplement*, Nov. 1985, 6-7.

78. Jamie P. Horsely, "The Regulation of China's Foreign Trade," in Michael Moser, ed., *Foreign Trade, Investment and the Law in the PRC* (Hong Kong: Oxford University Press, 1984), 9-10.

79. For example, in mid-1985, provincial and municipal trade bureaus could license 126 kinds of products. Thirty products required Mofert approval for each contract. Yang Jixiao and Li Yushi of Mofert Foreign Trade Research Institute, interview, Beijing, June 1, 1985.

80. See legal provisions in *The Official Chinese Customs Guide, 1985/86* (London: Longman, 1985), 29-33. A separate agency under the State Council inspects exports. See Horsely, "Regulation of China's Foreign Trade," 19.

81. Horsely, "Regulation of China's Foreign Trade," 23; Hu Changnuan, *Jiagexue*, 498.

82. Hu Changnuan, *Jiagexue*, 498-9.

83. Horsely, "Regulation of China's Foreign Trade," 23-4.

84. See *The Official Chinese Customs Guide, 1985-86*.

85. *China Daily*, April 9, 1985, 2.

86. Hu Changnuan, *Jiagexue*, 497.

87. *Quarterly Economic Review of China, Hong Kong, North Korea*, first quarter 1981, 14.

88. Hu Changnuan, *Jiagexue*, 495.

89. *Ibid.*, 500-503.

90. *Ibid.*, 504-5.

91. *Ibid.* Imports from Communist countries are priced at the agreed international transaction price plus a special surcharge of 30%. If this duty brings the price too high, central authorities can reduce or waive it, taking into consideration the Chinese purchaser involved.

92. Guangdong provincial report, Apr. 15, 1982; trans. FBIS, Apr. 19, 1982, P1.

93. *Quarterly Economic Review of China, Hong Kong, North Korea*, second quarter 1981, 10-11.

94. *Ibid.*, third quarter 1982, 15.

95. *Ibid.*, first quarter 1983, 16.

96. Winston K. Zee, "The Application of United States Foreign Trade Laws to Imports from China," in Michael J. Moser, ed., *Foreign Trade, Investment and the Law in the People's Republic of China*, second edn. (Hong Kong: Oxford University Press, 1987), 505.

97. *Ibid.*, 499-502.

98. *The Economist*, Oct. 3, 1987, 73.

99. *The Economist*, April 16, 1988, 81.

6

The Opening Up in Foreign Trade: Results and New Problems

China's opening up in foreign trade involved a mix of reorganization, decentralization, and some continued use of central levers of control. The policy was able to benefit from new external trade agreements with Japan, the United States, and EEC countries, and increased economic cooperation with Hong Kong. Among the economic results of post-1979 reforms were a rapid increase in trade volume made possible by China's change of mind about the desirability of foreign trade; a gradual shift in trade composition due to greater Chinese flexibility, export orientation, and some success in selling manufactured goods abroad; and a continued tendency to conduct the overwhelming majority of trade with partners from capitalist countries. But the following pages will show that foreign trade reform remained incomplete and self-contradictory.

This chapter begins with an overview of the effects of reform on the volume, structure, and direction of China's foreign trade. It then describes the extent to which bursts of spending on newly available imported goods severely eroded state control. It assesses how, in the reassertions of control that followed, the state failed to reconcile the habit of central interventions with its ostensible goal, stimulation of local initiative. A full decade after reform began, this dilemma remained, because Beijing preferred a strict import substitution policy to the trade liberalization that had been recommended by a major World Bank study of Chinese policy. (Those recommendations are summarized in a concluding section of this chapter.)

Economic Results of Foreign Trade Reform

The most dramatic effect of the new policy was a jump in the volume of China's foreign trade. That volume doubled during the period 1977 through 1979, and continued to rise rapidly thereafter, except during periods of temporary retightening (see Table 6-1). China's exports, benefiting from rapid domestic growth in both industry and agriculture, climbed from US $2,267 billion in 1970, to $13.66 billion in 1979, to $21.8 billion in 1982.[1]

Table 6-1

Chinese Foreign Trade: Total Two-Way Volume

1950	US $1.13 billion
1955	3.14 "
1960	3.81 "
1965	4.25 "
1970	4.59 "
1975	14.75 "
1978	20.64 "
1980	37.82 "
1981	44.02 "
1982	41.60 "
1983	43.62 "
1984	53.55 "
1985	69.60 "
1986	73.85 "
1987	82.65 "

SOURCE: *Zhongguo Tongji Nianjian, 1988*, 721.

A recent World Bank report summarized: "China's trade ratios [of foreign trade relative to GNP] have recently risen to levels well within the 6-15 percent range of other very large countries."[2] (Of course, that measurement neglects to include China's low per capita GNP, and thus gives an exaggerated impression of China's trade levels.)

The opening up policies also accelerated changes in the composition of China's foreign trade. A higher proportion of industrial products among exports indicates progress in industrial development. In China, both the absolute and relative volume of textile and light industrial products grew. And state planning pushed up the relative proportion of heavy industrial products among the total (see Table 6-2). The World Bank reckoned China's proportion of manufactured exports by 1981 to be 53 percent, higher than the average for other low-income countries (30 percent) and comparable to the level of many "upper-middle-income" countries.[3] This is striking when one considers that China's utilization of industrial inputs is inefficient even in comparison with the world's poorest countries. According to the World Bank:

Table 6-2

Composition of Export Products

	Agricultural, Sideline	Light Industrial	Textiles	Heavy Industrial
1955	46.1%	19.5%	11.7%	22.7%
1960	31.0%	17.1%	29.1%	22.8%
1965	33.1%	23.4%	20.1%	23.4%
1970	36.4%	26.2%	21.4%	15.7%
1975	29.6%	23.9%	17.9%	28.6%
1980	18.7%	24.0%	17.9%	39.4%
1985	17.5%	20.0%	19.7%	42.8%

SOURCE: *Almanac of China's Foreign Economic Relations and Trade, 1987*, 398.

Although international comparisons of economic efficiency are particularly difficult, it appears that China's usage of intermediate material inputs--most conspicuously energy, but also other industrial and agricultural products--is unusually high. (Indeed, inefficient use of industrial intermediate inputs appears just as important as the high savings rate in explaining the large share of industry in China's national income).[4]

Such inefficiency has hindered the country from producing a larger absolute volume of manufactured exports. Nonetheless, China now accounts for over 5 per cent of world trade in textiles, and that share is growing.[5] At the same time, the opening up policies led to accelerated growth in the volume of raw materials exports. Since 1973, China had allowed itself to become a net exporter of oil, and during the following years mineral and petroleum exports increased even more quickly than manufactures. From 1978 through 1982, China exported 47 million tons of crude oil to Japan alone. In the early 1980s, gasoline also became a leading export item.[6] By 1980 China was expanding other raw material exports, earning foreign exchange by selling rare and strategic minerals, and showing interest in exploiting its reserves of gold.[7] These would all help pay for needed imports of industrial technology and equipment.

Another aspect of opening up that has supplemented China's hard currency income and thus its import purchasing capacity has been the rapid growth of foreign tourism (see Table 6-3). China reaped substantial benefits from these visitors. Although tourist services account for less than 10% of China's foreign exchange earnings, they give a significant boost. In 1981, a crucial year of turnaround in the national balance of payments, income from tourism was equal to over one-half of the overall trade surplus, as illustrated in Table 6-4.

Table 6-3

Foreign Tourists to China

1980	5.70 million
1981	7.77 m
1982	7.92 m
1983	9.48 m
1984	12.85 m
1985	17.83 m
1986	22.82 m
1987	26.90 m

NOTE: includes overseas Chinese tourists.

SOURCES: *Zhongguo Tongji Nianjian, 1983*, 420, 441; *Ibid., 1984*, 395, 415; *Ibid., 1986*, 586; *Ibid, 1988*, 738.

Table 6-4

	Income from Foreign Tourists	Chinese Trade Surplus (Deficit)
1980	US $ 617 million	($ 1.28 billion)
1981	$ 785 m	0
1982	$ 843 m	($ 3.07 bn)
1983	$ 941 m	$ 0.84 bn
1984	$ 1,131 m	($ 1.27 bn)
1985	$ 1,250 m	($14.89 bn)
1986	$ 1,531 m	($11.97 bn)
1987	$ 1,844 m	($ 3.77 bn)

SOURCES: *Zhongguo Tongji Nianjian, 1986*, 563, 586; *Ibid, 1988*, 721, 738; *1986 Zhongguo Jingji Nianjian*, III-74.

Tourism does not directly add to China's productive infrastructure, but it gives the state cash income with which to purchase imported equipment and technology. Export growth and diversification under the opening up policies were indeed dramatic, but this should not distract from the fact that they were building on a long term trend. As Table 6-5 demonstrates, growth in some key developing exports had long been underway.

Table 6-5

Chinese exports of:

	cotton cloth	manufactured silk
1950	28 million meters	1,546 tons
1960	591 m	2,380 t
1970	696 m	4,283 t
1980	1,086 m	7,731 t
1983	1,325 m	9,330 t
1984	1,733 m	8,557 t
1985	1,673 m	10,893 t

SOURCES: *Zhongguo Tongji Nianjian, 1984*, 401-2; *Ibid., 1986*, 569-70.

What previously hindered Chinese growth was not just a lack of economic capacity, but poor political relations with potential trade partners, central interference in the operations of trade enterprises which diminished their incentives to perform, isolation of enterprises from world markets, and ideological opposition to trade activity of any kind. These factors help explain why, for example, leather shoe exports (the inputs for which China has in abundance) stood at the same level in 1980 as in 1960.[8] Shoe enterprises, isolated from world markets and lacking incentives, failed to learn international standards and styles and suffered no penalty for doing so until the 1980s.

To turn now to import composition, relative proportions of various components have remained fairly steady, but absolute levels have jumped (see Tables 6-6 and 6-7).

Table 6-6

Relative Proportions of Total Annual Imports

	machinery and equipment	industrial raw materials	raw materials for agriculture	food and consumer goods
1955	62.8%	27.8%	3.2%	6.2%
1960	49.7%	41.6%	4.1%	4.6%
1965	17.6%	40.1%	8.8%	33.5%
1970	15.8%	57.4%	9.5%	17.3%
1975	32.1%	45.7%	7.6%	14.6%
1980	27.5%	44.1%	7.3%	21.1%
1981	26.2%	39.4%	7.2%	27.2%
1982	19.4%	43.5%	7.9%	29.2%
1983	17.6%	51.5%	9.6%	21.3%
1984	20.5%	52.3%	8.2%	19.0%
1985	31.9%	46.6%	4.3%	17.2%
1986	37.2%	46.2%	2.7%	13.9%

SOURCE: *Almanac of China's Foreign Economic Relations and Trade, 1987*, 401.

Import composition during the opening up policy continued the government's priority of obtaining capital goods and advanced technology. Chinese imports from 1970 to 1976 had consisted of 81 per cent capital goods and 19 per cent consumer goods.[9] This pattern continued, though somewhat unsteadily. In the last years of the 1970s the government decided to purchase a large number of complete sets of plant equipment. In 1978 alone, new contracts equaled 48 per cent of the number of items signed for in the previous thirty years.[10] After that the government decided to avoid the prospect of huge deficits, and slow down. A sharp cutback in orders and several unilateral contract cancellations followed during the next two years. Consumer good imports were cut drastically, while even some production good purchases were temporarily curtailed. These results were symptomatic of poor initial planning, based on assumptions of rapidly expanding hard currency earnings, which led to overambitious purchasing, deficits, and sudden sharp cutbacks.

Table 6-7

Absolute Levels of Annual Imports (US $100 million)

	machinery and equipment	industrial raw materials	raw materials for agriculture	food and consumer goods
1955	10.88	4.82	0.56	1.07
1960	9.70	8.13	0.80	0.90
1965	3.58	8.08	1.76	6.75
1970	3.69	13.36	2.20	4.01
1975	24.06	34.17	5.70	10.94
1980	53.75	86.20	14.25	41.30
1981	51.05	76.69	14.09	52.99
1982	33.94	75.96	13.82	51.06
1983	32.54	95.37	17.84	39.55
1984	51.96	132.61	20.87	48.12
1985	109.65	159.83	14.91	58.92
1986	122.91	152.74	9.09	46.08

SOURCE: *Almanac of China's Foreign Economic Relations and Trade, 1987*, 401.

The government continued to restrict consumer good imports, and upgrade productive capacity with foreign capital and technology. Even in years when consumer imports were held back, capital imports (except for complete plants) continued to grow. Within the category of capital goods, the proportion of machinery grew at the expense of the share of other industrial materials, underscoring China's priority of expanding productive capacity.[11] The centrally-directed readjustment after 1980 was two-pronged: reduced orders for complete plants, and a sharp cutback in imported consumer goods that the government decided could be produced domestically. Under the renewed protectionism that denounced "blind" imports, imported motorcycles were reduced nearly to zero, imported watches from 2.4 million to 940,000.[12] Only in 1984 did consumer imports again rise sharply, to be cut once again a year later. The central government was unable to balance consumer and protectionist demands.

The distribution of China's trade among its foreign partners revealed the effects of relatively unfettered exchanges. They largely followed international market forces with the result that trade remained overwhelmingly with capitalist countries, which had the capital and technology China wanted to import and markets it could sell to.

In addition to bilateral trade agreements with Japan, the US, and West European countries, by late 1982 China had established trade relations with most countries of all types and ideologies. These included unrecognized states such as South Korea, Taiwan, and possibly Israel. Japan remained China's largest trading partner, with 21.4 per cent of total two-way trade in 1982. Following Japan were the other major capitalist partners: Hong Kong, the United States, and the EEC.[13] The relative importance of these partners varied by region: three-quarters of Canton's exports in 1983 went to Hong Kong.[14]

Japan remained China's leading trade partner during the 1970s and much of the period of opening up. In addition to traditional exports such as soybeans, silk, and minerals, crude oil became China's leading bilateral export item in 1974 and helped pay for subsequent growth of trade. Textile exports to Japan grew in importance in the early 1980s. China's imports were mainly production or capital goods: chemicals, machinery and equipment, steel, chemical fertilizers, etc. Another tendency was established before the opening policy began: a bilateral trade deficit of US \$5.04 billion from 1972 to 1978.[15] In subsequent years up to half of China's large trade deficits would be accounted for by adverse balances of trade with Japan. The main reason was Japanese disinterest in purchasing Chinese finished goods. After its trade deficit with Japan persisted through 1987, China began to protest Japan's tariffs and other trade restrictions, which interfered with Chinese export growth.[16] There was no report of China offering bilateral reductions of such obstacles.

China's growing trade with Hong Kong had several components. China was the colony's main food supplier throughout the 1970s and after. It also used Hong Kong as a principal link for indirect exports as well as (after 1978) sales point for goods processed or assembled in China. Hong Kong's re-exports of Chinese goods in 1980 alone amounted to US \$1.68 billion.[17] The decentralization of foreign trade authority and establishment of Special Economic Zones near Hong Kong encouraged local cross-border trade in all kinds of commodities and consumer goods, some of it illicit.

China's trade with Hong Kong increased exponentially in the early 1980s, spurred on by Hong Kong's function as the major re-export center for finished Chinese goods. These included textiles as well as increasing amounts of light industrial goods. Many Chinese food products were also sold to and through Hong Kong. In exchange, China purchased growing amounts of raw materials and semi-finished goods needed by the thousands of small assembly operations set up by Hong Kong firms in the Guangdong area. As China relaxed its centralized trade controls, consumer goods also began to flow into the country from Hong Kong: televisions, cassette tape recorders, home appliances, and so on, including many produced in Japan, South Korea and Taiwan. By 1985 China began to run a trade deficit with Hong Kong, now approaching Japan as its largest trade partner. This increased the pressure to restore direct central management of trade.

Normalization of Sino-American relations on January 1, 1979 and granting of most-favored-nation status a few months later led to a sharp increase in bilateral trade between these two countries:

Two-way U.S.-China Trade[18]

| 1978 | $.992 billion | 1980 | $4.81 billion |
| 1979 | $2.45 billion | 1981 | $6.85 billion |

In 1982, friction caused by US textile protectionism helped reduce trade back below the 1980 level. China's leading exports to the US were textiles, clothing, and raw and crude materials including petroleum and gasoline. On the import side, before 1979, China mainly imported grain from the US, especially wheat and corn. Starting in 1979, however, imports of machinery and transportation equipment rose rapidly. During the 1980s, the Reagan and Bush administrations steadily relaxed US restrictions on exports of advanced technology to China, including even that with potential military applications. In the early years of the opening up policy, China repeatedly ran a trade deficit with the US, but after 1985 the balance turned favorable to China. This was caused largely by growth in clothing exports, which accounted for one third of American imports from China in 1987. In reaction, the US negotiated a four-year bilateral trade agreement, limiting textile exports from China to annual growth of 3 per cent starting in 1988.[19] US restrictions on textile exports from Hong Kong would also limit growth of trade with China, which uses the colony as a re-export center. Nonetheless, these factors will probably affect the rate of growth in US-China trade, rather than threatening the trade as a whole.

In the mid-1980s, some of the most rapid growth in China's foreign trade was with the Soviet Union. By the time they signed a bilateral technical and economic exchange agreement with Moscow in December, 1984, the Chinese were experienced enough to insist on terms favorable to their long term modernization goals. Beijing received promises of assistance in upgrading several major industrial facilities.[20] The Chinese wanted the Soviets to help develop their electric and chemical industries, and possibly even subway systems for Canton and Shanghai. Both sides hoped to develop joint ventures. In the short term, however, trade was more mundane. China bought Soviet cars, civilian aircraft, electrical generators, railroad cars, industrial raw materials, fertilizer, construction materials, and lumber. In exchange China sold textiles, clothing, daily use consumer goods, meat (unprocessed and processed), fruits, and vegetables. Despite growth in these areas, trade with the Soviet Union lagged far behind that with Hong Kong, Japan, and the US; by 1986 the Soviet trade was roughly at the same level as China's trade with Britain. Continued growth will be hampered by market restrictions on both sides (bilateral trade slowed markedly in 1987), and by the unavoidable red tape involved in dealing with two nonconvertible currencies. Measuring the trade in Swiss francs, as Beijing and Moscow have decided to do, hardly diminishes this problem. Nor is there much sign of a dramatic increase in Soviet tourism to China, despite Chinese hopes.[21]

Under the opening up policy, the overwhelming share of foreign trade continued to be with non-Communist partners--a proportion which remained well over 80 per cent. To put the evolution of China's trade partners into historical perspective reveals the tendency caused by China's desire for advanced equipment and technology from capitalist countries (see Table 6-8).

In summary, the opening up reforms had significant effects on the volume, structure, and direction of China's foreign trade. Accepting a wide range of competitive trade partners, China succeeded in promoting its exports (including manufactures) sufficiently to raise the levels of productive capital it was bringing in. But this success created a new dilemma:

Table 6-8

Total Value of Trade with: (US $100,000)

	Japan	W.Germany	USSR	USA	Hong Kong
1950	472	194	3,384	2,381	1,512
1955	833	192	17,898	0	1,894
1960	2	1,137	16,639	0	2,083
1965	4,543	1,266	4,074	0	4,636
1970	8,065	2,750	472	0	5,925
1975	37,955	8,155	2,972	4,707	16,835
1980	92,011	20,433	4,924	48,113	49,231
1985	164,344	30,720	18,814	70,250	108,941
1986	138,640	37,544	26,377	59,935	115,184

SOURCES: *Almanac of China's Foreign Economic Relations and Trade, 1984*; and *Ibid., 1987*, 404-8.

how could central authorities impose their production-oriented import priorities while simultaneously decentralizing authority over the growing level of trade activity?

Losses of Control During the Opening Policy

Foreign trade, under restored relations with capitalist countries and with decentralized initiative, grew quickly but not smoothly. Wild swings in import purchasing created a persistent threat of payments deficits, especially with key capitalist trading partners. Not only the volume and balance of trade, but even the recording of statistics went out of control, prompting central authorities to reassert their authority.

The most noteworthy feature of China's trade deficits and other imbalances is that they appear to have stemmed from an inability to use indirect levers of control to regulate transnational trade patterns to China's advantage. Poor planning (the first time) and decentralized import purchasing (the second) resulted in spurts of orders that shot past China's newly enlarged foreign exchange reserves, leading in turn to reactions that restored tighter regulation.

The trouble centered around 1979 and 1984, two years of wildly excessive importing: excessive, especially from the point of view of avoiding trade deficits and using state protectionism to limit outside competitive pressure on domestic enterprises. On the first occasion, concern developed in 1979 over potential Chinese inability to finance rapidly expanding orders for Japanese goods and equipment with oil sales. China had already signed US $5 billion in contracts and was considering $15 billion more, while crude oil sales to Japan stood at $6-800 million per year. By late 1979 foreign businessmen realized that China would be financing many imports through deferred payments or loans, which had been ideologically unthinkable until 1978. The overall real deficit was $1.6 billion in the first ten months of 1979 alone. Nonetheless, despite retrenchment on some of Hua Guofeng's more grandiose projects (such as a $14 billion integrated steel plant at Jidong, Hebei Province), others such as the $1.9 billion Baoshan steel plant near Shanghai were going ahead--for one more year. Then, as the deficit continued into the first half of 1981, the Chinese retracted on portions of the signed contracts, and only after protracted negotiations agreed to pay the Mitsubishi group some $40 million compensation.[22]

After a severe readjustment, China's trade with leading partners came back into surplus in late 1981. Both consumer goods and major machinery imports had had to be cut back, the latter by 50 per cent in one year. Meanwhile, China was successfully promoting its exports, particularly textiles, to Japan. Trade deficits with Hong Kong and the US diminished. Only US wheat sales to China increased; China raised exports to the US in almost all categories. Although China's imports from Taiwan and South Korea, which had grown exponentially in 1981, suffered a setback, China's exports to both nearly doubled in 1982.[23]

By mid-1982 China had, by a combination of export promotion, import order reductions and new trade barriers including higher customs duties, built a trade surplus of $1 billion in six months. While making a

15 per cent increase in oil exports, China also attempted to diversify its exports to include a larger proportion of manufactured goods, although many of these (including 85% of machinery exports) went to developing rather than developed country markets.[24] The following year (1983), imports began to rise again. China earned a trade surplus of $500 million in the first half of the year, in spite of placing import orders for increased quantities of steel, non-ferrous metals, and equipment as well as chemical fertilizers, sugar, and grain. By October of that year China's foreign exchange reserves stood at $14.6 billion.[25]

One year after 1983 recovery, China's foreign trade swung into hyperactivity again. For the whole year of 1984, imports surged 37.8 per cent to $25.5 billion while exports rose only 10.1 per cent to $24.4 billion--leaving a deficit of $1.1 billion. This time it was not primarily plant and equipment orders, but consumer imports such as television sets and tape recorders, that were out of control.

By the time of the 1984 import boom, foreign trade authority had been extensively decentralized. This as much as poor planning accounted for a burst of spending by importing enterprises on consumer goods that went beyond China's proclaimed financial cautiousness and forced another radical tightening a year later. In 1984, to take only one aspect of the boom, Japanese exports to China were 47 per cent higher than the previous year and China became the number one purchaser of Japan's color televisions--with imports 15 times the 1983 level--and number two purchaser of its refrigerators.[26] Purchases of foreign autos, motorcycles, cassette recorders and other consumer goods that had so recently been cut back all jumped, only to be cut again just over a year later.

Market forces could not rectify imbalances that developed with the rapid growth of foreign trade, because enterprises were not following free market signals in making decisions. True, in the early 1980s many Chinese state enterprises began to follow the profit incentive as they were now allowed to retain a portion of hard currency earnings from exports. However, until at least 1987, many of their domestic purchases of production inputs and of finished goods for export sale were subsidized by the central government, to compensate for price increases brought on by domestic reforms. Many Chinese enterprises thus made a perfectly rational decision to purchase inputs and goods domestically, and sell whatever goods they had or made at a 10 to 15 per cent discount abroad. The central government reimbursed all their costs, while they retained a good share of the hard currency income.[27]

The other aspect of loss of central control during the 1984 import boom was a burst of smuggling activity. Wherever there was contact between a still rigid planned economy with state-set prices on nearly all types of goods, and market forces offering incentives to those who could obtain access to closed markets or subsidized goods, opportunities abounded. The $1.5 billion Hainan Island smuggling scam, in which local officials took advantage of decentralized trading rights to profit from importing tens of thousands of autos, motorcycles, televisions, and video recorders and reselling them to the more tightly controlled interior,[28] was only the largest episode of many, noticed or not. These too were symptoms of a structure of control which was not adapting smoothly to decentralization.

Even the numbers were beyond management. In early 1985 Chinese bureaucrats differed by up to $7 billion over the sum of the trade deficit for the first three quarters of 1984. Mofert (the relevant ministry) put the deficit at $4.1 billion; the more disinterested Customs Bureau, $10.07 billion for the same period. This difference was equal to more than half of China's total foreign exchange reserves. Since Mofert's administrative effectiveness might be called into question by the figures, it used various creative accounting methods to make them appear more favorable: counting retail transactions in domestic "friendship stores" as exports; leaving out imports of materials by processing and assembly projects; omitting imports of equipment and materials by Chinese-foreign joint ventures; and using "import substitutes" produced domestically to subtract from overseas expenditures.[29] Statistics in China rarely have independent verification. But in this case a separate agency with parallel figures exposed the extent to which bureaucratic interests use their ingenuity to fiddle with the bottom line.

In the summer of 1985 began the next import crackdown. New import licensing rules were issued and customs duties were once again raised. Some imports such as cars were banned altogether. The renminbi was further devalued. Inspections were tightened. Yet even after these measures were taken, imports continued to grow faster than exports. Only after a de facto freeze in national import spending did the huge deficit begin to shrink.[30] By that time China's foreign exchange reserves of over $15 billion had shrunk by nearly a third.[31]

The rollercoaster ride of results from the opening up in foreign trade amply explains why the government limited its decentralization activity. From Beijing's perspective, devolution of authority was one cause of these problems and to carry it further would only aggravate them. The benefits of the opening up were manifest, and it would not be scrapped; but the problems encountered led the government to add complex layers of reservations and to extend its interventions to uphold national policy goals.

Cycles of Central Control and Opening Up

The record of Chinese foreign trade activity after 1979 reveals the symptoms of groping for a balance between often contradictory policy goals. These included trade surplus; expansion of trade volume; upgrading the composition of both imports and exports to give China a more diversified role in the international division of labor; maintenance of a centrally guided economy; and stimulation of local initiative.

The tensions between these goals account for the shifts back and forth between opening up and retightening restrictions. Loosening up led each time to a deficit-producing flood of import purchases which in turn prompted the central government to intervene and use its levers of influence to restore stricter control. Each crisis led to an ad hoc set of solutions. The aim remained as described in a 1980 government statement: "changing the centralized management and rigid[ity of] regulations while remaining under a unified policy and plan..."[32]

Thus, administrative changes sometimes contradicted one another. On one hand, central oversight of hard currency spending was consolidated in the hands of the new Ministry of Foreign Economic Relations and Trade (Mofert) in March, 1982. On the other, immediate authority over most trade activity was shifted to Foreign Trade Corporations under other ministries, to provinces, and even to some localities. Mofert continued to handle major staple commodities, complete sets of equipment, and intergovernmental trade arrangements.[33] Otherwise, Mofert's role became one of overall planning, guidance, deciding approval procedures, and active regulation using import and export licenses.

In any case, the tightening of import expenditures after the booms of 1979 and 1984 showed that the central government still had levers of control to use when necessary. The first set of interventions occurred during a general tightening of capital construction expenditure in 1981, in response to the previous year's ballooning balance of payments deficit. In 1981, import duties on more than 100 items were adjusted to allow in needed production goods while protecting domestic consumer goods industries. More control was slapped on in October, 1982 with Mofert-approved import licenses required for vehicles; electronic, household, and consumer goods; and chemical fabrics.[34]

Central interference with foreign trade activity extended to the export side of the ledger as well. On June 1, 1982, China attached export duties of up to 60 per cent on more than 30 items. The primary purpose of this unexpected measure was also protectionist: to prevent a drain of goods still in scarce domestic supply including coal, pig iron, rice, soya beans, sugar, fresh fish and several others.[35] A second purpose was to regain some control over provincial trading organizations that found a way to make a higher cash income through exporting than from selling to state enterprises. A third concern was competition among export producers that drove down sale or barter prices. Most of the categories of products involved had already been subject to special export licensing since February, 1982, but apparently that measure had not been enough to slow down the drain caused by local managers trying to duck the state-controlled price system. In April, 1983, the list of goods requiring export licenses was lengthened further.[36] Even while promoting exports through incentives to localities from partial retention of earnings, the central government implemented new levers of control "effectively [to] forestall the confusion in China's exports, check the impact made on the market [prices] by parallel [export] goods and protect the interests of the state and overseas retail businessmen," in the words of a Chinese economist.[37] These measures led to recovery of trade surplus, and were in turn followed by a general loosening up in 1984--and another trade deficit.

The second major wave of central government interventions was necessitated by an impending trade deficit of up to $18 billion for 1985. If not brought under control, this deficit threatened to exceed China's total foreign exchange reserves. In response, Mofert again added to the export and import licensing lists, and signaled that all imports would be brought under direct central control if necessary to reduce the deficit.[38] Mofert also issued new requirements that it approve all trading operations of provincial and local organizations.

In addition, customs tariffs were again adjusted in early 1985. Although public announcements emphasized reduced duties on some items, they also stated that duties on a range of other goods were raised "to protect domestic production."[39] In fact, only raw materials, machinery and equipment needed for production purposes, and which China could not produce, had duties reduced.

In July, 1985 a further "import regulatory tax" announced by the State Council took effect, raising effective duties on imports of consumer goods to all parts of China to levels as high as 200 per cent.[40] This despite a recent decentralization of authority over imports that had relinquished the requirement for central approval of many purchases. Local authorities could still approve some trade contracts, but how many Chinese enterprises or consumers could pay the money required by the new 1985 tariffs? Finally, in July, 1986 the renminbi was devalued a further 15.8 per cent against the US dollar, primarily in order further to encourage exports and limit imports.[41] The effect of all these measures was to restore central guidance of an economy swayed by local Chinese enterprises seeking to purchase imported goods of all kinds.

The government interventions of 1985 and 1986 again succeeded in rapidly reducing China's trade deficit, which in turn encouraged another phase of relaxed control and decentralization. The national trade deficit fell from $12.8 billion in 1986 to $3.7 billion in 1987, thanks to a 24 per cent increase in exports while imports were successfully held down.[42]

The Late 1980s: Deepening Dilemmas in Foreign Trade

As the decade approached its close, the central government continued to try to manage the consequences of relaxed control through direct interventions--an impossible task which simply aggravated existing problems. A telling remark developed within the central government: "As soon as you loosen up, there's a mess; as soon as there's a mess you take charge; as soon as you take charge, it becomes deadening; as soon as it becomes deadening, you loosen up."[43] One Chinese analyst complained in 1987:

> Because the policy and interests of every department and locality are not coordinated, and because [policy] decisions lack a basic foundation, the validity of policies is diminished....For example, sometimes foreign exchange earnings quotas are followed [by enterprises] even if they have to take a capital loss, while sometimes large losses are controlled by strictly prohibiting exports of products that experience large losses....Recently, in the heatwave of propaganda about the 'new technological revolution', [the state] emphasized bringing in advanced technology and fervently wished to improve the industrial structure within one morning. The result was a very large foreign trade deficit and spending of hard currency went out of control....But now, [the state] emphasizes bringing in [imported] materials for processing, and developing labor intensive production in order to attain the goal of earning more foreign currency. This situation of shifting from one extreme to another and of policies swinging upwards and downwards fully demonstrates that we lack not only the goal of complete and long-term reform, but also the goal of complete and long-term development of foreign trade.[44]

This conclusion might seem surprising in light of administrative changes China had recently undertaken in foreign trade work. In 1988 the State Council issued internal regulations stating that henceforth the center (presumably Mofert) would merely issue three-year export assignments to each of the provincial governments, and it would be up to them to determine how to carry these out. This encouraged a tendency latent in Deng Xiaoping's economic reforms from the beginning, one that has always been a problem in China: a widening divergence among local policies as they respond more and more to the interests of local powerholders rather than the dictates of the central government. Every province and locality immediately began announcing its own "responsibility system" to promote exports, each system with its own unique characteristics and its own poetic-sounding slogans.[45] In order to promote exports, provinces and localities grant tax rebate and profit retention incentives to manufacturers and Foreign Trade Corporations that normally operate profitably but now find themselves sandwiched in the market between inflationary domestic purchase prices and low international product prices.[46] (Plans to implement a policy of *zi fu ying kui*, letting enterprises be responsible for their own profits and losses, have still not been realized.) Some provinces subsidize raw materials purchases by export producers, which encourages them to ignore their production costs.[47]

This new set of reforms sought to penalize units and enterprises that incurred foreign exchange losses. In March, 1988, the central government issued regulations informing all state Foreign Trade Corporations and production enterprises that they could make their own import and export plans, but the government would no longer compensate their foreign exchange losses.[48] But as usual, the apparently sweeping new rights were heavily qualified: enforcement of the export license system was also to be reemphasized with an additional 26 items added to the list of affected goods.

(Export licensing, though diminishing in importance, had never been phased out completely.[49] State and provincial Foreign Trade Corporations had been granted authority to export independently in their areas of expertise without obtaining licenses. However, Mofert always reserved the right to revoke that authority for economic or foreign policy reasons.[50] Similarly, export taxes, which had supposedly been abolished in February, 1980,[51] reappeared after several years. Import licensing was also renewed in October, 1982.[52])

By 1988 enterprises were given rights to set their own export prices according to market conditions, and to determine the other terms of their trade contracts, tasks previously performed by the Foreign Trade Corporations. The latter, now including provincial and local corporations which had proliferated to well over 1,000,[53] were supposed to begin using their international contacts to work as "agents" for Chinese enterprises, on a commission basis rather than issuing directives.[54] More enterprises would be allowed to do without them altogether--a return to the direction undertaken in the previous reform phase, four years earlier. Authority within the Foreign Trade Corporations themselves was further decentralized, with provinces taking control of their branch offices. Furthermore, the newly created province of Hainan Island would also assume full responsibility for all its foreign trade profits and losses.[55] This established a model for possible application to other provinces in the future. And as a national export promotion incentive, the proportion of foreign exchange earnings from exports that most enterprises could retain was raised to around 50 per cent (even higher in priority industries such as electronics).[56]

Once again, however, a possible limitation emerged. To prevent severe price competition among Chinese exporters, the government began in 1988 to encourage export price regulation by cartels of domestic producers.[57] This could counteract their newly granted rights to pursue export sales and profits autonomously. It was again the "two hands" approach: one opening up, the other adding a restriction.

Despite the relaxation of controls, provincial and local trade enterprises continue to chafe at obstacles to efficient operation created by the central government. Many complain that, apparently because of an internal regulation, their second-ranking managers must be appointed by higher level government authorities. There are also internal regulations issued by the central government on their hiring of workers, especially trained ones--restrictions which led one trading company to hire retirees that already have pensions and social welfare benefits to fill one half of its staff requirements (a total of 800 out of 1,600).[58] State Foreign Trade Corporations still interfere with the work of provincial ones by handing down export plans and quotas, regulating expenditures, and limiting profits and losses. The degree of state control varies sharply from place to place. In some localities such as Hangzhou (the city with the eighth largest industrial production in China in 1987) export manufacturers remain under the control of state Foreign Trade Corporations with regard to all production- and foreign trade-related decisions, including the expenditure of any foreign exchange.[59] Yet state control is sometimes welcomed by provincial trade officials in order to prevent price gouging and speculation by private businessmen. Export enterprises have often been victimized by Chinese speculators: there have been numerous cases of private distributors of export goods stuffing packages with false substitutes before selling them to provincial trade companies.[60]

The central government's major concern was that the "independent kingdoms" of provincial and local officials were increasingly subverting its intentions. It became apparent by 1988 that many of Beijing's policy pronouncements were being honored in the provinces with a show of superficial obedience that masked the real basis of implementation, namely local advantage.[61] To a certain extent, this was caused by local ignorance of the policy changes constantly being issued in Beijing; more often, local officials developed their own laws, regulations, and administrative practices in competition with their neighbors. With the relaxation of many state prices, newly autonomous provincial and local trading enterprises have begun bidding furiously against each other for export goods which they can sell for foreign exchange--thus pushing up (in some cases doubling or even tripling) prices of key commodities and products and making them less competitive (and less profitable to the state) when sold on the international market.[62] This activity did little to increase the efficiency of China's export producers, which remained protected by the state from much of the risk of market competition.

The same local and provincial officials who help policy take on different coloration in various parts of the country also participate in profiteering commerce known in Chinese as *guan dao* (from *guan*, "official").[63] Cadres have formed thousands of "trade" or "technology" companies loosely affiliated with local or provincial governments and ostensibly operating with their approval, whose sole activity is short term speculation. In some cases they buy up supplies of particular commodities until prices rise, then dump their supplies on the market. One county in Hebei Province managed with official connivance to obtain a near-monopoly of the national supply of certain medicinal herbs, an operation costing hundreds of millions of yuan.[64] Such activities have caused wild price swings and disrupted supplies of various production and export goods. This is the main reason why in early 1989 foreign purchasers of silk from the state trading companies under Mofert were suddenly asked to pay 30 to 50 per cent more than their contracts specified. The price of silk inside China had risen due to free trading and speculation, and the central government wanted to protect itself from possible resulting losses.[65]

Another emerging problem has been mutual price gouging between China's relatively underdeveloped interior and the richer and more experienced coastal provinces.[66] As state price controls are relaxed, export factories on the coast find the prices of their inputs from other regions of China increasing sharply and supplies shrinking, which raises production costs and hampers their ability to remain price competitive.[67] On the other hand, enterprises in the interior that want to export their products often find, despite their newly granted autonomy, that they have to go through traders on the coast, with which they must share most of their foreign exchange earnings.

Competition among the provinces in the rapidly growing textile and clothing export industry is especially fierce, and has costly results for China. Mofert's system of export licenses is supposed to keep overall national textile exports within the limits specified in bilateral agreements with the Western industrialized countries. But provincial and local trade companies, pursuing their own interests, often exceed the quotas issued to them by overseeing trade officials who get their overall ceilings from Mofert. There is tremendous competition among China's exporters to fill each developed country textile and clothing import quota at the beginning of each year, with some enterprises using false labelling (of less restricted categories like children's clothing) or ignoring the quotas issued by Mofert altogether in their eagerness.[68] Provincial and local trade officials who are ostensibly in charge of issuing export licenses often turn a blind eye to these abuses. The result is that national export quotas to the developed countires are frequently exceeded, and more and more Chinese shipments are stopped at incoming ports. In 1986, Canadian customs blocked the entry of 3,800,000 pieces of clothing from China that exceeded bilaterally agreed quotas. In the same year, West Germany, France and Britain blocked 2,200,000 pieces of clothing and the US blocked 44 categories of textiles from China, for the same reason.[69]

A conflict also arises between Chinese enterprises involved in together producing the same export good. There is no standard method for allocating export-earned hard currency among them. To let each retain an equal share hardly solves the problem, since they have incurred unequal production costs. Many factories have found a solution: those making raw cloth, for example, instead of selling their state-subsidized output to Chinese clothing factories, prefer to export the cloth themselves. That way, they earn foreign exchange directly rather than waiting to see what the clothing factories will share with them.[70] Unfortunately for China, this sort of competition between enterprises does little to raise overall hard currency earnings.

Another area of growing tension under decentralized administration is between the hundreds of government Foreign Trade Corporations (FTCs) and production enterprises, as they compete for authority over foreign trade work. According to a Chinese report in 1987,[71] relations between the two types of entities prior to the latest reforms had not been fruitful. Most producing enterprises were required to export through FTCs. The producers concealed their true production costs from the FTCs, which in turn concealed from their comrades at the factories the international market value of the products the FTCs were to sell for them. Under the 1987 reform, reducing the FTCs to "agents" of the production enterprises was supposed to make them start working harmoniously, with the FTCs happy to share useful market information because they now receive a share of all export earnings. In a less ideal outcome, the FTCs are more likely to try to grab back their lost authority during the current phase of retightening central controls. That will be resisted by production enterprises that are most successful at exporting, and don't need "agents." In fact, 130 production enterprises have been excused from relying on "agents" at all in their export activities.[72]

Oddly, the newly granted right of Chinese enterprises to retain some of their hard currency earnings is sometimes still not a sufficient incentive to pursue export activities vigorously. The reason is that many domestic manufacturers find it is much more profitable and easier to sell in the domestic market, because it is protected by the state from international competition and thus maintains ever more inflated prices for consumer goods, than to sell to trade companies or export in competition with cut-price Asian producers. Furthermore, the quality standards, sizing specifications, and delivery and packaging requirements of the domestic market are well known by Chinese manufacturers to be far lower than those of potential foreign purchasers. In one steel factory, the profit rate in 1986 for domestic sales was 10.8 per cent while the profit rate from export sales was 2.6 per cent.[73] For these reasons, some domestic producers have avoided exporting and sought domestic sales instead. According to a 1987 report by the Economics Research Center of the Shanghai Social Sciences Academy, a majority of the export manufacturers in both Shanghai Municipality and neighboring Jiangsu Province were "unwilling" to continue export production.[74] There is no evidence, however, that their preferences were accepted by supervising authorities.

All of the above problems diminished China's capacity to earn hard currency through exports, and (in official minds) once again justified central government interventions to hold China's 1988 trade deficit in check. This subsequently tightened into a major austerity program with domestic as well as foreign economic dimensions. However, the government did not rely on extra export promotion measures to restore a trade balance. Instead, it acted against Chinese enterprises that were making state-subsidized purchases of goods on the domestic market, and then selling them abroad at cut-rate prices to earn foreign currency some of which they could then retain. This was profitable for them but drained capital from the state. To discourage such practices, the central government in late 1988 recentralized control over certain key exports such as silk under the state Foreign Trade Corporations, reimposed export license requirements on 165 major items (such as cotton cloth, silk and rubber), and raised export duties on some materials needed by domestic manufacturers.[75] In January, 1989 the central government further banned or restricted several export items that were in short domestic supply.[76] This may have diminished speculative trading by provincial and local companies, but at a cost of aggravating China's overall trade deficit problem, improvement of which depended on promoting all kinds of exports. Of course, import restrictions have also been renewed. The central government in 1988 doubled import duties on many electrical consumer goods to keep domestic demand for them in check,[77] but Beijing had great difficulty restraining purchases of imported production equipment by provincial enterprises engaged in overheated expansion.[78] New restrictions created new economic distortions. For example, a new central restriction on importing refrigerator compressors led to speculation in import licenses for this sought-after good. The licenses were soon trading for more than the market price of compressors themselves.[79]

Government intervention failed to solve China's economic and foreign trade problems. The central government began tightening credit and imposing extra domestic price controls in the fall of 1988. Its purpose was to slow down economic growth driven by booming and largely uncontrolled provincial investment, growth which had fueled price inflation of over 30 per cent per annum. These measures proved inadequate to their intended purpose, and had the inadvertent effect of curbing needed infrastructure developments.[80] In March, 1989, Premier Li Peng announced an even tougher economic austerity program intended to last a few years. But inflation and rampant corruption had already eroded popular tolerance of the government and fueled support for the student movement that would erupt in April and May. Then, the central government's bloody response led to conditions of much greater austerity for the country, as many foreign loans and investments were either postponed or cancelled altogether.[81]

Other Developments in the Late 1980s

In the last years of the 1980s, the trend toward gradual diversification of China's trading partners continued. Hong Kong, Japan and the United States remained the most important partners, purchasing oil and coal (Japan) and low-value products such as clothing, shoes and toys (the

US) while supplying technology and capital equipment. America continued to export large amounts of grain to China to cover the domestic production deficit as many Chinese farmers shifted to producing cash crops. But labor intensive Chinese exports began to generate a substantial bilateral trade surplus with US, which may well become a thorny issue between the two in the future. Some of the most rapid growth, however, occurred in the two-way trade between China and its former ideological enemies, Taiwan and South Korea. As the Japanese yen appreciated and the cost of Japanese production goods and equipment rose, the economic advantages of purchasing from substitute suppliers of such goods became increasingly obvious. Trade between China and Taiwan was facilitated by Beijing's "united front" tactic of encouraging as much contact as possible between the two sides, which left the Taiwan government appearing to be the more stubborn of the two. China-South Korea trade benefited from the political changes underway in the latter country, which encouraged a more flexible and pragmatic stance toward Communist states; from informal contacts developed at the 1988 Seoul Olympics and other international meetings; and from the partial decentralization of trade authority in China which allowed coastal provinces such as Shandong to go full speed in developing their South Korean economic relations without much central interference.

While relaxation of government attitudes in China and South Korea facilitated the development of bilateral trade to a level exceeding US $2 billion per year, it has above all been driven by the complementarity of the two economies. Many types of industrial machinery and mid-range industrial products for which there is tremendous demand within China could be imported from South Korea at prices far less than those of their Japanese competitors. The proportion of Korean exports to China accounted for by machinery grew from one tenth to nearly one third by 1987, while the total volume of trade was also increasing.[82] South Korea also supplies artificial fibers for synthetic textiles, yarn, paper products and steel. In the other direction, China sells coal, natural fibers used in textiles and some semimanufactured products to South Korea.[83] Put in more general terms, the complementarity of the two economies becomes even more obvious:

> ...whereas primary products comprise a relatively high proportion of China's exports at 36.4 per cent and industrial goods comprise a significant portion of its imports at 86.8 per cent, industrial goods make up 91.7 per cent of South Korea's exports (1986) while primary products account for 34.6 per cent of its imports.[84]

This makes apparent the long term possibility that South Korea could play an increasingly important role in stimulating Chinese development by providing some of the means to develop new export industries. (Most

Chinese economic planners continue to maintain, however, that their country's economy cannot be as export-oriented as that of South Korea because China is so much larger.)

The role of South Korea in China's foreign trade is supplemented by that of Taiwan, whose trade with the mainland reached US$ 2.5 billion in 1988. Taiwan's rapidly growing trade with the mainland also stems from a complementary relationship between two economies. But rather than industrial equipment, Taiwan supplies China with synthetic textile raw materials, consumer products (such as color televisions, bicycles, motorcycles, and watches) while China exports primary materials such as fish and traditional medicinal ingredients to Taiwan. Because of the limited types of its exports that are in demand in Taiwan, China tends to run very large deficits in this trade, most of which goes through Hong Kong as an intermediate port (in part because of the Taiwan government's traditional ban on contact or negotiations of any kind, which is only gradually being relaxed).[85]

China's trade with the Soviet Union also continues to develop, but more slowly and much of it in the form of bilateral barter agreements with a total value of less than US $3 billion per year. The most active trade has been in a number of border cities. The Chinese are supporting this with some infrastructure developments, notably a planned extension of the Lanzhou-Urumqi railroad through Xinjiang Province in western China to the Soviet Union, which could eventually become an artery for Asian goods being shipped to Western Europe as well.[86] The slow growth of Sino-Soviet trade is surprising when contrasted with the two countries' defreezing of political relations, accelerated at the end of the decade by the Soviet withdrawal from Afghanistan and the reduction of bilateral border tensions. Part of the problem is the awkwardness of dealing in two nonconvertible currencies. Beyond that, the complementarity of the two economies is limited. The Soviet Union exports raw materials, steel, electrical equipment and fertilizers to China in exchange for textiles, agricultural products and light industrial products. But the Soviet Union, hampered by its own severe systemic weaknesses, can supply only a limited portion of the capital and industrial technology that China urgently seeks to further its state-led modernization drive. While bilateral border trade will no doubt continue its gradual expansion, there is no possibility that the Soviet Union or East European countries could replace the capitalist nations of Europe, America and Asia as China's primary trade partners.

China's overall trade deficit began to widen again in 1988, and it was only partly offset by rapidly increasing income from tourism. The latter grew at annual rates of over on quarter to reach more than US $2 billion in 1988,[87] while the trade deficit that year exceeded $5 billion. The deficit was this time caused primarily not by purchases of imported consumer goods, which the central government used various methods to keep under control, but rather by imports of agricultural goods in short supply and by purchases of production goods used to fuel regional profit-oriented expansion.[88] Much of the purchasing was by cash-rich provincial enterprises.

China's Application to Rejoin GATT

The Chinese government has found an important new avenue in which to advance its international trade interests. Although it has a limited commitment to free trade as far as its own policies are concerned, it is pressing ahead with its application to rejoin the multinational General Agreement on Tariffs and Trade (GATT). It could thereby obtain permanent most-favored nation status and assured long term entry for its products into Western markets. The threat of American political demands for a "level playing field" and the possibility of human rights concerns influencing China's market access would then recede. Beijing hopes that the existence of its opening up policies will be sufficient qualification for admission to GATT, and that China will only face a requirement to make its foreign trade rules "transparent" (i.e. state them explicitly). That diverts attention from the real issue: What *are* China's trade rules? How many Chinese enterprises will be authorized to engage in foreign trade without central government interference? Will China's comprehensive system of protectionist import duties, licenses and nontariff barriers remain in place? How will China's foreign trade partners measure the national and provincial subsidization of export production by Chinese enterprises?

China was a member of GATT from its founding in 1947, but after the Communist victory in the civil war, the Republic of China (ROC) on Taiwan resigned the seat in 1950. The Beijing government is now preparing to argue that the ROC's resignation did not represent the will of the PRC, which is internationally recognized as the legitimate government of China. To explain why the PRC failed to apply for readmission during the 35-year interim, China will argue that during that period it was giving priority to gaining admission to the United Nations, and that it did repeatedly serve notice to the international community that the PRC regime was the legal representative of China, thus implicitly rejecting the ROC's withdrawal as legally invalid.[89]

China has already taken several steps towards readmission. In 1982, the Beijing government was granted observer status in GATT, and began sending delegations to its meetings. In 1984, China was granted special observer status, giving its representatives the right to attend meetings of the GATT Council.[90]

The PRC would gain several benefits from being admitted to GATT. It would obtain the right to file formal grievances where access to developed country markets was not granted. For example, if China as a full GATT member were not given most-favored nation (MFN) status by the United States, it could claim a violation of GATT rules.[91] Membership in GATT would provide China not only with most-favored nation status from all GATT members (it has been granted this by the US since 1980), but also (subject to the approval of the President) with tariff-free importing rights for some goods under the Generalized System of Preferences for Third World exporters. By obtaining market access through GATT, China would diminish its dependence on negotiated bilateral trade agreements.[92] China would also have a voice in bargaining the rules of the world trading system. Finally, China would realize a public relations benefit: it could, to its overseas trade partners and Hong Kong, cite its admission as yet another sign of its good intentions in economic reform and opening up.

In support of its application, Beijing will point to the movement China has made in the direction of market-oriented reform: its decentralization of foreign trade authority; the expanded administrative and financial autonomy given Chinese foreign trade enterprises; the supposed reduction of controls over imports; as well as other domestic economic reforms (especially in agriculture and in partial lifting of price controls). Those Western commentators inclined to give China the benefit of the doubt will argue that admitting the country to GATT would, by letting China benefit more fully from opening up, help forestall possible domestic opposition to continued economic reform.[93] As for its remaining restrictions on foreign trade, China's supporters argue that these represent "inhibitions [that] can only be overcome in time."[94]

There are precedents for admitting nonmarket economies to GATT. In fact, five Eastern European countries as well as Cuba belong. The terms of admission for Poland, Romania and Hungary included provisions allowing their Western trading partners to continue restricting their volume of imports from these countries.[95] However, the potential for rapid expansion of China's exports is widely regarded with more apprehension among potential competitors in the West than the capabilities of any of these other (until recently) socialist members.[96] Western governments may therefore seek more specific "safeguards" before agreeing to China's readmission.

Concerning the possible terms of China's readmission to GATT, several options exist besides immediate full membership. Special provisions could include limited membership subject to a set of obligations for China.[97] Limited membership, however, might water down the intended purpose of GATT, namely promotion of free trade. And there are serious problems with many of the possible requirements that might be applied to China in exchange for immediate readmission. To require Chinese tariff reductions would still not ensure market access for China's trade partners, given the variety of other restrictions by which China's import substitution policy is realized.[98] To try to limit China's price markups on imports would be horrendously complicated, could be undercut by exchange rate manipulations, and would require state price controls--exactly contrary to the kinds of reforms China is promising to carry out in order to gain admission to GATT in the first place.[99] To specify "import commitments" could well turn out to be as ineffective as it was in the cases of Poland and Romania, due to difficulties in specifying, agreeing on, and realizing import targets.[100] Another possibility would be to assign China some sector-specific or GNP-linked import commitments. But such rigid schemes would probably be rejected as an infringement of Chinese sovereignty.

A more practical approach proposed by a former US trade official would be for China to be allowed to enter GATT in a series of specified stages, with benefits of fuller membership being granted in exchange for realizing certain market opening "milestones" (including price decontrol measures).[101] This approach recognizes the persistent limitations on China's opening up: it still relies on considerable mandatory state economic planning, it maintains export subsidies, remains unwilling to open some closed sectors of its economy such as banking and insurance services to foreign competition, and maintains nontariff barriers including a nonconvertible currency. To admit China in stages, with market access assurances broadened as economic reforms continue, would provide incentives to both China and its partners to continue fostering its integration into the world economy.

Prior to the 1989 turmoil, there seemed to be a consensus among diplomats from Western countries that China's GATT application should be approved.[102] It remains to be seen whether their governments have the political will to raise the above issues in negotiations before China receives the automatic trade preferences associated with GATT membership. The US Government position alludes to China's nontariff barriers to trade, but does not specify which ones and how many must be removed before the US will support China's application. The US position makes no reference to China's comprehensive published system of protective customs duties. [103] Yet the Chinese appear to be anticipating criticism in that area as well. Some Chinese researchers in Mofert are suggesting that the government plan a shift to nontariff barriers in substitution for protectionist tariffs, to achieve the same purpose: "that way, our country can avoid international criticism and at the same time we won't lose the necessary protection for some domestic industries."[104] In any case, Chinese researchers have an argument ready when China is accused of protectionism. In their eyes, China is already relatively open:

> Currently, the trade protectionism practiced by the Western industrialized countries led by the United States is more and more serious and intense. But our country's economic and trade systems are more and more open. The environment for foreign investment [here] is continually improving; we have ample reason to demand that America exert itself in the same direction.[105]

Partial Decentralization Does Not Mean Liberalism

Even before the June, 1989 massacres and policy retrenchment, China's national trade deficit was growing steadily as imports of most products grew at some four times the rate of exports, suggesting that austerity and recentralization would have to be severe if Beijing was to restore full control and a trade surplus. Conditions do seem severe: inflation has recently exceeded 20 per cent per annum; the state continues to pour billions of dollars of subsidies into loss-making state enterprises; and in the fall of 1989 national light industrial output fell for the first time in a decade.[106] The financial crisis that has ensued after crushing the "counterrevolutionary rebellion" will paradoxically benefit ultracapitalist South Korea and Taiwan, which can deliver high quality industrial and consumer goods to China at the best prices.

The trading partner which will feel the effects of Chinese political upheavals most directly is Hong Kong. But even for the British colony with its uncertain future the consequences may well be tolerable. Some sectors in Hong Kong such as banking have limited exposure to China, while others such as the property market will probably experience a slump that was due anyway.[107] It is true that Hong Kong is the major port for a great deal of the trade between China and the Western world, and to that extent it will feel the effects of China's political instability. It is also true that as confidence in the Chinese government erodes, long term investment in Hong Kong (notably in the manufacturing sector) will suffer. But as a regional trade center and a highly sophisticated financial headquarters for the region, Hong Kong has other roles not entirely dependent on China--and no obvious replacement candidate is available. In the immediate aftermath of the Beijing massacre, some American buyers of Asian merchandise urged their Hong Kong agents to shift their bases of supply from Guangdong Province in China to southeast Asia. But in the longer run, the fact that Guangdong was largely uninvolved in the political turmoil will allow it to continue offering itself as an attractive, convenient, and profitable base of cheap-labor assembly and processing operations for Hong Kong entrepreneurs. This will help neighboring Hong Kong maintain its position as a production center. And finally, the Chinese government itself has potent incentives to keep Hong Kong flourishing: not only because of its literally immeasurable investments in all sectors of the colony, but also because of the political cost to Beijing's already wounded prestige among overseas Chinese if Hong Kong's prosperity should be destroyed.

Nonetheless, despite wild swings in the volume and balance of trade activity, China's opening up policy has generally continued to follow principles first outlined in May, 1979 by *People's Daily*. China, it then argued, needs imported technology to raise production, but the financial constraints of a backward economy require the central government to uphold purchasing priorities. The key idea is not to allow China to become interdependent with other nations, but rather that

> Importing technology and acquiring the latest advances in technological development for our own purposes aim at strengthening our ability to do things in a self-reliant way.[108]

Therefore, the government must "strictly control and rationally organize imports, so that only essential technology, key items of equipment and raw materials in short supply are imported in a planned order of priority."[109]

On the other hand, China has sought both to expand export sales and to upgrade the composition of export structure. Chinese policymakers advocate increasing exports of light industrial and textile goods. But what will bring about these changes? "An export production system will be set up," runs a typical official Mofert statement of 1986.[110] During the seventh Five Year Plan, concentrated export production zones "will be set up." The composition of export production "will be arranged and developed..." Rather than letting market forces determine production priorities, "we will do research" on market demand. These phrases are all found in an article firmly supporting managerial decentralization. As they reveal, reform is not intended to displace a central guiding hand: "Decentralization and control are two sides of one coin."[111]

Chinese officials believe central guidance is necessary to realize the import priorities of the Seventh Five Year Plan. These are energy (including several nuclear power plants), transportation, advanced technology, and communications equipment. The emphasis at present is on production technology which (authorities believe) can increase the quality and output of existing operations without requiring expensive purchases of complete plants or duplicate buying of major pieces of equipment by independent enterprises.[112]

Similarly, on the export side, an emphasis on central guidance and control remains in official explanations, independent of phases of decentralization and readjustment. Prominent economist Xue Muqiao wrote in early 1986 about exporting, for example, that "Multiple lines of management authority have proved to be defective and should not be allowed to continue."[113] Foreign trade companies that have no clear justification (he went on) should be closed, to prevent profiteering, tax evasion, speculation, and unnecessary competition. Further, according to a Beijing foreign trade official in 1986, export licensing should prevent such "abnormal phenomena" as "parallel [Chinese] goods....flooding overseas markets [and] upsetting traditional [domestic] distribution channels."[114] At the provincial level, too, officials see a need for trading monopolies. For example, a Beijing analyst urged that Fujian Province, in response to complaints from Japanese buyers about the quality of some oolong tea, should grant its provincial tea trading company exclusive rights to handle exports and impose product standards.[115] The Chinese are still far from rejecting the Soviet view that the key to administrative effectiveness lies in improving central or higher-level control.

A look at delegates' speeches at the third plenum of the sixth National People's Congress (NPC) in April, 1985 dispels any idea that this emphasis on higher-level guidance is only a figment of power grasping by the center itself. On the contrary, at the grassroots level, the first instinct is to turn to higher authority to rectify real or perceived ills that arise in the course of opening up to foreign trade. A few typical comments by delegates published in *People's Daily* during the session are illustrative. Zhao Jinsheng of Tianjin demanded stricter control of technology imports to prevent duplicate or premature purchases. Chen Jiexin of Shanxi denounced imports of inferior quality foreign goods. Cong Shen of Heilongjiang complained that the biggest smugglers were still flourishing while "little fish" were penalized for trade abuses. Ma Dashi of Liaoning called for protection of the domestic construction industry from foreign competition. Song Ping, the State Planning Minister, called for tighter management of foreign exchange to prevent excessive imports: "It's not easy to obtain foreign exchange, it definitely must be controlled well, and used well."[116] Other delegates made speeches along similar lines. The conviction with which these views were expressed seems to reflect a broad-based desire to strengthen, and (in Soviet style) make more effective, central regulation of foreign trade and purchasing activity.

Central government involvement in trade matters may take new forms. In 1986 trade officials in at least two provinces suggested[117] that the increasing number of industrial factories run by Chinese army units would be a useful strength in developing the country's export programs. This suggestion, if enacted, could complicate China's admission to GATT. But it indicates that in the midst of decentralization, the "center" is still looked to as the fountainhead of new initiatives.

Chinese at all levels are understandably confused about how to reconcile central guidance with decentralization. Under the Deng Xiaoping reforms, the state owns major resources and plans the use of all elements of production, while allowing local initiative to provide a market stimulus. It is easier to talk about using indirect economic levers than to decide which to use, when. One example: Xue Muqiao is ambivalent about giving enterprises a tax reduction to encourage their export sales. To do so would add a performance incentive to enterprises, but lower tax rates would also diminish revenues collected by local authorities (at least in the short term; supply-side economics has not made it to China yet). Local authorities thus tend to oppose such incentive tax reductions--and have helped stall their implementation.[118] Should incentives to enterprises be enlarged despite such local opposition? To this and many similar dilemmas, China has no clear answer.

One cause of confusion over how to use economic levers is that Chinese analysts are fundamentally uncertain about the cause and effect mechanisms their opening up policies are bringing into play. It is common for Chinese commentators to bring emotional feelings of national "honor" or "shame" into discussions of foreign trade achievements.[119] And their analysis of problems often begs questions. Why, for example, is there a constant threat of "blind" importing? How can market forces be both included and limited? Will a centrally planned change in the structure of exports make them more welcome in the international market, as a Mofert spokesman suggests,[120] or will market forces themselves produce a new structure of production? Chinese foreign trade officials lack guiding concepts, as their policies move beyond the past experiences of state socialism.

The analytical confusion is understandable, given that Chinese trade policymakers face problems beyond the scope of nearly any theory. The most profound of these is that the consequences of foreign economic policy touch only indirectly on large rural, interior areas of the country that are still largely disconnected even from major domestic markets. According to the World Bank, in the early 1980s the ratio of export procurement to net material production was three times as high in the coastal provinces (12% on average) than in the interior (4% on average)--and nearly eight times higher in Shanghai.[121] The World Bank could have added that if differences in regional net output among the provinces were weighed into the comparisons, the relative differences in foreign trade activity among provinces would appear much greater. Regional concentration of trade activity can bring problems: the four small Special Economic Zones plus Hainan Island accounted for more than a fifth of the entire country's trade payments deficit in the first half of 1985.[122] But while the government pays lip service to balanced development of China's regions[123] and the need to help the poor and backward interior, it recognizes that existing infrastructure only allows rapid development near the coast. The many imponderables involved in regional distribution add further confusion to Chinese policies that aim to attain specific economic goals through opening up.

Chinese government officials, because of their inexperience with the kinds of problems caused by the opening up policy, are hardly in a position to make clear and decisive resolutions of their political dilemmas. Rather, they will continue to waver between bold reform intentions and the realities of a sluggish economic structure and widespread political reluctance to change.

To consider the policy aims, dilemmas, and confusions of the Chinese government shows why the well-intentioned recommendations of a report sponsored by the World Bank on foreign trade policy will be, at best, deferred for a prolonged period. The Bank's authors, in a series of reform proposals partially disguised as an empirical analysis of China's international trade situation, sided with the most radical of China's economic reformers and provided them with some well-written debating ammunition.[124] Among the viewpoints advocated by the Bank are the following:

1. China would probably increase the efficiency of its overall production by greater specialization in its areas of foreign trade strength, even if this meant becoming a net importer of agricultural products with which it is not well endowed. The Bank concedes that such specialization could expose the domestic economy to foreign competition, price fluctuations, and increased regional inequalities (pp. 98-9, 103).

2. China should expose its enterprises to foreign competition to encourage them to introduce better products. True decentralization would disconnect enterprises from central control and lead them to act on foreign market signals of values and costs (pp. 99-100).

3. China's present restrictions on foreign investment and sale of foreign products in the domestic market inhibit the growth of its exports, by limiting competitive pressure on producers. Chinese export enterprises (not just joint ventures as at present) should be allowed freely to import equipment and components made abroad if superior in quality to Chinese equivalents. This would help upgrade quality and salability of export output (pp. 104-5).

4. China's import substitution policy, which prevents the entry of many potential foreign suppliers, harms national capacity to achieve technology transfer. Domestic firms must be able to contact and choose from a much wider range of Chinese and presently excluded foreign suppliers of goods and services, in order to absorb new productive technologies (p. 106).

5. China's domestic pricing system discourages export production. It sets price levels for manufactured goods at such a high level that Chinese producers of these goods lack strong incentives to export. To compensate by further subsidizing exports could bring "dumping" charges from developed countries (p. 106).

6. About high technology that Chinese constantly discuss their need of: "productivity and product quality in Chinese industry could often be dramatically improved without new technology, whose introduction may indeed divert attention from more elementary problems." Such problems include proper use of existing equipment; adjusting work habits and management to make use of new technologies effective; selectivity in purchasing; allowing market incentives to encourage technological innovation within enterprises themselves; and creating incentives for diffusion of existing technology among industries (pp. 110-120).

The World Bank's viewpoint coincides with the direction taken by economic reformers in China, but goes beyond what most of them advocate. It rejects the protectionism, central interference, and import substitution that are integral parts of the opening up policy. But the Bank overlooks the interrelated forces of past habit and politics. Central authorities are reluctant to relinquish control, not just from selfishness but from fear of the unknown. Lower ranking officials often share this instinct. Since the Party controls the state and thus manages the economy, these attitudes prevent the unqualified decentralization that the Bank advocates. The potential results--higher efficiency, incentives to innovate, diffusion of technology--do not come about. Instead, a pattern of behavior cited by the Bank predominates:

> Some officials of the Tianjin [elevator] company believe that. . . problems would be solved by replacing electromechanical controls with sophisticated microprocessors. The immediate problem, however, lies more in work practices and the quality of material supplies. Workers now hold metal pieces for drilling rather than using clamps, measure pieces manually rather than mechanically, and move partially assembled pieces by dragging them rather than using a conveyor. The result is that holes do not line up and parts are damaged or do not fit together. Moreover, castings supplied by other companies are of low quality, thus causing waste and excessive wear on tools. Solving these basic problems would probably contribute more than the proposed introduction of sophisticated controls to achieving the joint venture's export targets.[125]

Why were these habits preserved despite China's apparently unanimous wish to develop? Part of the reason lay in protection from competitive pressure to improve performance. *People's Daily* on September 20, 1984 reviewed the state of China's foreign trade system after five years of reform and opening up:

> Administration and management are not separated; duties, rights and benefits are not unified; management is deadening, restrictions are too many, industry and trade have become disjointed; profits and losses must altogether be borne by the state, and eating from the "iron rice bowl" reduces economic benefits.[126]

Neither the reformist intentions of the government, nor the stimulating effects of the opening up policies, had yet altered the prevailing pattern of state bureaucratic control, administrative inertia, and inability to apply performance incentives and penalties to individual workers. These factors still combine with the objective limitations of the country's already over-loaded transportation system to hinder the potential for rapid growth of China's labor-intensive exports.

Conclusions

As the Chinese commentators cited in Chapter Two advocate, their government's opening up in foreign trade maintains the role of the state as an intervening participant in import and export activity. The state acts as a trusted guarantor of efficiency; as planner and manager; as habitual source of authoritative direction; as provider of necessary or comfortable protection for infant industries--and therefore sometimes as an unintentional upholder of existing work practices. China has renounced the political class struggles essential to Marxism, but neither in ideals nor in practice is it moving toward free-trade liberalism. It is rather developing state guided foreign trade, letting potential partners compete with each other so that China can obtain the best possible terms for the means to develop its own industries.

This aspect of the opening up policy accords more closely with China's declared political aims of using state activism to promote national strategic autonomy and strength than does the free trade decentralization promoted by the World Bank. First, state protectionism, despite the effect on growth levels of preserving some inefficient enterprises, can ensure that development includes a broad base of key industries as a guarantee of autonomy from external market conditions. For the Chinese this is as much a national strategic priority as is growth through specialized export production. Second, a neomercantilist, state-centered approach to trade is easier to reconcile with politically necessary lip service to Marxism than would be profit-oriented, competitive enterprise capitalism. In practice, neomercantilism shares with many states that have professed Marxism a pervasive streak of nationalism, and a reliance on state intervention and control. Many of the policies and habits of a Marxist system need not change under neomercantilism; whereas liberal capitalism would require an inconceivable relinquishing of central authority. Third, there is in China an incoherent but broad protectionist constituency consisting of workers, managers, officials, and enterprises that would lose wealth or comfort as a result of introducing foreign competition into the domestic economy. The institutional remains of Marxism-Leninism include countless inefficient state industries with just such constituents, and a professed ideology that gives prime attention to their complaints. These factors explain why there is a neomercantilist policy today and why, World Bank notwithstanding, it is likely to remain. In the minds of those who make policy there, China's perceived national interest does not coincide with international interdependence.

Nor is there any sign of China returning to Marxist-inspired egalitarianism in its trade and development strategies. As Chinese planners are aware, the interventions of their government in foreign trade activity are intended to foster national productive capacity, not to diminish the wide regional inequalities of wealth in China that the opening up policies aggravate. A survey of 1985 statistics reveals that imports per capita in some coastal provinces are twenty or more times as high as in interior provinces.[127] (Although the same source reports that foreign trade growth figures for the interior have been higher than for the more developed coastal provinces, this was largely caused by changes in reporting procedures as the interior provinces began to manage and account for their own exports.) The fact that sensitive outlying minority provinces such as Xinjiang and Tibet have been allowed to keep a larger proportion of their small export earnings will not compensate for the differentials in export sales that leave them relatively far behind.

Rather than free trade or domestic egalitarianism, China's statist foreign trade policy emphasizes expansion of trade and rapid industrial development. The manufactured proportion of exports has grown during the 1980s to the point of surpassing the 60 per cent level. In the area of textiles and garments, export growth has been especially rapid, despite US restrictions limiting annual growth of such imports--measures which encourage China to develop other markets. The Chinese economy already contains sectors with a stake in trade that know the profitability of growth. Managers, workers, and enterprises in that sector have an interest in giving political support to further opening up. And rapid growth of the economy depends on equipment and technology imports obtained through trade. These are political and economic factors likely to oppose protectionism. However, they remain subordinate to the prevalent Chinese desire, reflected in policy, to balance growth with other priorities: developing broadly based national industries and maintaining sovereign control, exercised through the state, over the factors of production.

Independent of further growth in foreign trade and its tangible benefits, state involvement and interference will remain. The structure and system of foreign trade will in that sense continue to have "Chinese characteristics," even as the opening up process continues.

Notes

1. *1984 Almanac of China's Foreign Economic Relations and Trade* (Hong Kong: China Resources Trade Consultancy, 1985), 817.
2. The World Bank, *China, Long-term Development Issues and Options*, (Baltimore: Johns Hopkins University Press, 1985), 101.
3. The World Bank, *China, Economic Structure in International Perspective* (Washington, DC: 1985), 15-19.
4. *Ibid.*, 2.

5. The World Bank, *Development Issues*, 104.

6. James Tsao for US International Trade Commission, "China's Economic Development Strategies and Their Effects on U.S. Trade" (Washington, DC, 1985), 58-60.

7. *Quarterly Economic Review of China, Hong Kong, North Korea*, third quarter 1981, 13.

8. *Zhongguo Tongji Nianjian, 1984* (Beijing: Zhongguo Tongji Chubanshe, 1984), 405-6.

9. Wang Linsheng and Chen Yujie, "Economic Relations with Foreign Countries," in Yu Guangyuan, ed., *China's Socialist Modernization* (Beijing: Foreign Languages Press, 1984), 679.

10. Ma Hong and Sun Shangqing, eds., *Zhongguo Jingji Jiegou Wenti Yanjiu* (Beijing: Renmin Chubanshe, 1983), 474-5.

11. Harry Harding, *China's Second Revolution* (Washington, DC: Brookings, 1987), 141.

12. *1983 Zhongguo Jingji Nianjian* (Beijing: Jingji Guanli Chubanshe, 1983), 440.

13. *1983 Zhongguo Baike Nianjian* (Beijing: Zhongguo Da Baike Quanshu Chubanshe, 1983), 439.

14. *Guangzhou Jingji Nianjian, 1984* (Canton, 1984), 333.

15. James Tsao, "China's Economic Development Strategies," 55.

16. *Jingji Yu Guanli Yanjiu*, No. 3, 1987, 62-64.

17. John C. Hsu, "Hong Kong in China's Foreign Trade: A Changing Role," in A. J. Youngson, ed., *China and Hong Kong, The Economic Nexus* (Hong Kong: Oxford University Press, 1983), 175.

18. James Tsao, "China's Economic Development Strategies," 57.

19. *Wall Street Journal*, Feb. 1, 1988.

20. This and following, see discussions by Soviet officials in *Shijie Jingji Daobao*, Dec. 7, 1987, 16, and *Guoji Maoyi*, No. 10, 1987, 43-44. See also Nicholas R. Lardy, *China's Entry into the World Economy* (Lanham, MD: University Press of America, 1987), 14-15.

21. *Shijie Jingji Daobao*, Sept. 7, 1987, 15.

22. *Quarterly Economic Review of China, Hong Kong, North Korea*, second quarter 1979, 12-13; third quarter 1979, 11; first quarter 1980, 12; fourth quarter 1981, 14.

23. *Quarterly Economic Review of China, North Korea*, second quarter 1982, 12; third quarter 1982, 14.

24. The World Bank, *China, Development Issues*, 104-5.

25. *Quarterly Economic Review of China, North Korea*, fourth quarter 1982, 13-14; second quarter 1983, 12-13; fourth quarter 1983, 14; first quarter 1984, 16-17.

26. *FEER*, Jan. 31, 1985, 67-8; June 27, 1985, 110.

27. *Caimao Jingji*, No. 6, 1987, 41.

28. *FEER*, Aug. 22, 1985, 100.

29. *Quarterly Economic Review of China, North Korea*, third quarter 1984, 6; first quarter 1985, 6, 27; fourth quarter 1985, 31-3. On statistics, see *Intertrade Supplement*, May 1986, 20.

30. *Quarterly Economic Review of China, North Korea*, fourth quarter 1985, 31-3; first quarter 1986, 29-31.

31. *The Economist*, Jan. 4, 1986, 53-4.

32. Xinhua, Dec. 30, 1980; trans. FBIS, Dec. 31, 1980, L41-2.

33. Teng Weizao, "Socialist Modernization and the Pattern of Foreign Trade," in Xu Dixin, ed., *China's Search for Economic Growth* (Beijing: New World Press, 1982), 190-2.

34. Jamie P. Horsely, "The Regulation of China's Foreign Trade," in Michael J. Moser, ed., *Foreign Trade, Investment and the Law in the PRC* (Hong Kong: Oxford University Press, 1984), 17.

35. *Quarterly Economic Review of China, North Korea*, third quarter 1982, 15.

36. Horsely, "Regulation of China's Foreign Trade," 15; Fei Shunlian, "Streamlining Foreign Trade," in *Intertrade Supplement, Guidelines for Investment in China* (Hong Kong: May, 1986), 6.

37. Fei Shunlian, "Streamlining Foreign Trade," 6.

38. *Quarterly Economic Review of China, North Korea*, first quarter 1986, 31; David L. Denny, "Provincial Trade Patterns," *China Business Review*, Sept.-Oct., 1987, 21.

39. *Renmin Ribao*, March 7, 1985, 4.

40. *Quarterly Economic Review of China, North Korea*, third quarter 1985, 26-7.

41. *Guoji Shangbao*, March 5, 1987, 2.

42. *FEER*, March 24, 1988, 72.

43. Yi Boshui, "Waimao Fazhan Yu Waimao Tizhi Gaige," *Gaige yu Zhanlue*, Jan., 1988, 43. A Chinese source provides an interesting example of plans changing in Beijing: in 1982 and 1983, the central government strongly encouraged exports of certain types of electrical machinery and instruments in order to upgrade the mix of the country's overall exports and raise foreign exchange income. They did begin to grow, but only because of their very low prices on the world market rather than any other reason. After two years central government officials were dissatisfied with the income this produced; in 1984 they changed the policy and limited exports of products that have high costs of production. Exports of machinery and instruments promptly fell from 12.7 per cent of total exports in 1984 to 8.5 per cent in 1985, which was the same proportion as in 1981. Huang Zihua, "Dui Kuoda wo guo Chukou Maoyi de Tantao," *Shijie Jingji Yanjiu*, No. 5, 1987, 49-50.

44. Lu Jinhao, "Shilun woguo Waimao Hongguan Guanli Jigou de Gaige," *Caijing Yanjiu*, Oct., 1987, 44.

45. Xu Yu and Zhu Mingxia, "Liang Quan Fenli yu Duiwai Maoyi Chengbao Jingying Zeren Zhi," *Guoji Maoyi Wenti*, Dec., 1988, 22-25.

46. Li Lanqing, "Zhongguo de Waimao Tizhi Gaige," *Zhongguo Duiwai Maoyi*, Jan., 1988, 6-7.

47. Li Jianfeng, "Dangqian Waimao qie kuair Chengbao de Xiaoying Fenxi," *Guoji Maoyi Wenti*, Dec., 1988, 22-25.

48. *Wall Street Journal*, June 17, 1988, 10.

49. Horsely, "Regulation of Foreign Trade," 14ff.

50. *Ibid.*, 15.

51. Hu Changnuan, *Jiagexue* (Beijing: Renmin Daxue Chubanshe, 1982), 497.

52. Horsely, "Regulation of Foreign Trade," 16.

53. *Guoji Shangbao*, Jan. 10, 1987, 3.

54. Madelyn C. Ross, "Changing the Foreign Trade System," *China Business Review*, May-June, 1988, 34-36.

55. *Beijing Review*, May 2, 1988, 21.

56. Ross, "Changing the Foreign Trade System," 35-36; *FEER*, March 24, 1988, 74.

57. *Ibid.*

58. Zhou Shude, "Lungao Huo Waimao Qiye," *Guangdong Duiwai Jingmao*, March, 1987, 10.

59. Wei Zhangyao, "Hangzhou Fazhan Waixiangxing Jingji Wenti de Jianxi," *Tansuo*, No. 2, 1988, 23-25.

60. Zhou Shude, "Lungao Waimao Qiye," 9-13.

61. See *FEER*, Sept. 29, 1988, 110.

62. Zhou Shude, "Lungao Waimao Qiye," 9-13.

63. *FEER*, March 2, 1989, 54.

64. *FEER*, Oct. 13, 1988 96-97.

65. *FEER*, March 2, 1989, 54.

66. See Denny, "Provincial Trade Patterns," 19-22; *Wall Street Journal*, June 17, 1988, 10; Ross, "Changing the Foreign Trade System," 36.

67. *Caijing Yanjiu*, No. 6, 1987, 35-38.

68. Sun Nanshen, "Woguo Fangzhipin Chukou de Falu Zhangai Yu Xiangying Cuoshi," *Guoji Maoyi Wenti*, July, 1988, 42-45.

69. *Ibid.*, 43.

70. *Shijie Jingji Daobao*, May 25, 1987, 14.

71. *Shijie Jingji Daobao*, Nov. 23, 1987, 5.

72. *FEER*, March 24, 1988, 73.

73. Han Jingtang, "Zong he Yun Yong Jingji Ganggar Guli Chukou Tigao Jingji Xiaoyi," *Duiwai Jingji Maoyi*, Feb., 1987, 18-20; and Zhang Jianshan and Zhang Renli, "Jianping 'Waixiao buru Neixiao'," *Guoji Maoyi Wenti*, Aug., 1988, 25-28.

74. Huang Jianping, "Duiwai Maoyi, Liyong Waizi yu Guomin Jingji Fazhan," *Guoji Maoyi Wenti*, June, 1988, 45-47.

75. *FEER*, Nov. 17, 1988, 90; and March 2, 1989, 54.

76. *Beijing Review*, Jan. 2, 1989, 30.

77. *FEER*, Nov. 17, 1988, 91.

78. *Guoji Maoyi Wenti*, No. 4, 1987, 9; and *FEER*, March 24, 1988, 72-3.

79. *Wall Street Journal*, June 17, 1988, 10.

80. *Business Week*, April 3, 1989, 54.

81. *Wall Street Journal*, June 22, 1989, A10.

82. *JETRO China Newsletter* No. 76 (Sept., 1988), 16.

83. *Ibid.*

84. *Ibid.*, 18.

85. Wang Jianmin, "Taiwan Yu Dalu Jianjie Maoyi Xianzhuang Fenxi," *Yatai Jingji*, No. 5, 1987, 47-49.

86. Lardy, *China's Entry into the World Economy*, 16-17.

87. *FEER*, Nov. 17, 1988, 89. Note: Chinese statistics on income from tourism apparently include all hotel receipts, which means that much of the rent and other living expenses paid by resident foreign businessmen are included.

88. See *Beijing Review*, March 6, 1989, 16-17.

89. Robert E. Herzstein, "China and the GATT: Legal and Policy Issues Raised by China's Participation in the General Agreement on Tariffs and Trade," *Law and Policy in International Business* XVIII:2 (1986), 403-404.

90. J.E.D. McDonnell, "China's Move to Rejoin the GATT System: an Epic Transition," *The World Economy* X:3 (Sept., 1987), 331-2.

91. Herzstein, 382-3.

92. *Ibid.*, 372.

93. McDonnell, 332ff.

94. *Ibid.*, 341.

95. *Ibid.*, 342.

96. Herzstein, 406.

97. McDonnell, 345ff.

98. Herzstein, 375.

99. *Ibid.*, 390-392.

100. *Ibid.*,386-388.

101. Herzstein, 408ff.

102. For the US position, see *FEER*, May 11, 1989, 57-58.

103. *China Business Review*, May, 1988, 33-34.

104. Yi Boshui, "Waimao Fazhan yu Waimao Tizhi Gaige," 43.

105. He Jianxiong and Zhou Shijian, "Meiguo Yuanwai Huodong dui Jingmao Lifa de Yingxiang ji wo Ying Caiqu de Duice," *Guoji Maoyi Wenti*, June, 1988, 55.

106. *The Economist*, Sept. 16, 1989, 33; and *Wall Street Journal*, Oct. 21, 1989, A9.

107. *FEER*, June 29, 1989, 52-54.

108. *Renmin Ribao*, May 8, 1979; trans. FBIS, May 15, 1979, L2-4.

109. Teng Weizao, "Socialist Modernization," 181-2.

110. Huang Wenjun, "Exports are the Key," *Intertrade*, June, 1986, 30-1.

111. *Ibid.*

112. Yang Jixiao and Li Yushi, Mofert Foreign Trade Research Institute, interview, Beijing, June 1, 1985.

113. Xue Muqiao, "Readjustments in Prices and Exchange Rates Deemed Essential," *Intertrade*, March, 1986, 19-20.

114. Yang Jixiao, "Import Growth Hinges on Export Expansion," *Intertrade*, March 1986, 24.

115. Fei Bian, "Southern Fujian Wants a Piece of the Action," *Intertrade*, May, 1986, 58-9.

116. *Renmin Ribao*, March 5, 1985, 2; April 7, 1985, 2; April 13, 1985, 2; see also April 5, 1985, 2.

117. Liu Gang in *Jiangxi Caijing Xueyuan Xuebao*, No. 5, 1986, 67; Dai Yunzheng (Shanxi) in *Jishu Jingji yu Guanli Yanjiu*, No. 2, 1987, 5.

118. Xue Muqiao, "Readjustments in Prices," 20.

119. See e.g. *Red Flag*, April 16, 1982; trans.in *1984 Almanac of China's Foreign Economic Relations and Trade*, 382; cf. Chapter 3 on the affront to "national dignity" from popular preference for Hong Kong dollars over renminbi.

120. Huang Wenjun, "Exports are the Key."

121. The World Bank, *China, Long-term Development Issues*, 109.

122. *FEER*, August 22, 1985, 100.

123. E.g. *Renmin Ribao*, Sept. 23, 1984, 5.

124. This and the following discussion are based on The World Bank, *China, Long-term Development Issues and Options*, Chapters 6 and 7, 97-122.

125. *Ibid.*, 111.

126. *Renmin Ribao*, Sept. 20, 1984, 1.

127. Denny, "Provincial Trade Patterns," 19.

7

China's New Foreign Investment Policies

> In cooperating with China, one must not only weigh immediate advantages and disadvantages, benefits and losses of each individual case, but, more importantly, have farsightedness and courage in opening up new areas of cooperation. Some projects might not be very profitable in a short period of time, but in the long run, they may prove to be really profitable and wise undertakings.
>
> --Communist Party General Secretary
> Hu Yaobang (forced to resign
> January 18, 1987) as quoted in
> *China Daily*, April 18, 1985

By the time China's Party leader issued this invitation, thousands of contracts between Chinese state enterprises and foreign capitalist partners had already been signed. The purposes of the foreigners were as diverse as the projects they helped develop: some wanted a bridge to the domestic Chinese market; some desired to establish good relations with China, hoping that its market would in future become more accessible; others sought a short-term direct payoff for technology transfer or introduction of equipment; still others were willing to cooperate in producing goods for possible export. Chinese motivations could be put more simply: by allowing regulated foreign participation in the economy, to obtain productive technology and equipment which could raise the state's hard currency export earnings.

The Chinese government after 1979 permitted profit-oriented foreign joint ventures which could take a variety of forms. Government protection, labor, and tax policies were intended to encourage these ventures, provided they served Chinese interests. For this latter purpose, China's economic nationalism again established a preeminent regulatory role for the state. The arrangements in joint ventures usually included provisions for transfer of all assets to the Chinese side after a limited number of years. They also put many restrictions on the means by which a foreign investor could earn profits--and what he could do with them--during the life of a venture contract.

This and the following two chapters present a study of some important aspects of Chinese foreign investment policy. This chapter begins with a discussion of the broad aims of the policy as enunciated in officially approved Chinese statements. It then surveys what the "opening up" to foreign investment has actually meant in practical policy terms. A third section examines how certain convenient ambiguities in China's foreign investment laws leave room for flexibility to strengthen the bargaining position of state enterprises in negotiating high-priority projects with foreign partners.

The Context: Aggressively Seeking Out Foreign Capital

For the Chinese government, foreign investment policy was part of a larger strategy which began in the Deng era of seeking out financial support from a variety of foreign sources on the best available terms.

From shortly after the outset of its opening up policy, China found ways to enhance its resources by participating in two key international economic institutions, the World Bank and the International Monetary Fund. The major functions of the World Bank are economic development-related financing, technical assistance, and research in poor countries around the world. Most World Bank project assistance takes the form of loans to Third World governments when private financing is unavailable. Most of the funds for these loans come from contributions by developed countries, based on assessments of their national economic resources, and from bonds issued in major capitalist world markets.

The International Monetary Fund (IMF) was founded in 1944 with the purposes of promoting international monetary cooperation and stabilizing currency exchange rates. It has also become a major research center on international monetary issues. The IMF has developed means to assist national members that experience temporary imbalances in their trade payments.

The Chinese government's switch from deriding to accepting large grants from these international institutions was conducted with amazing rapidity. Beijing discontinued its disparaging political attacks on the World Bank only in 1978. In February, 1980 Deng Xiaoping declared: "to accelerate China's modernization we must not only make use of other countries' experience. We must also avail ourselves of foreign funding."[1] In April, China entered the IMF. The following month China was welcomed as a member of the World Bank Group (including the International Bank for Reconstruction and Development [IBRD] and the International

Development Association [IDA]). By December, the Chinese government had drawn US $278 million in reserve funding through the IMF, and with additional below market-rate loans the following year, it received nearly $1.5 billion within its first year of IMF membership.[2]

As though not to be outdone, the World Bank promptly undertook for China an exhaustive study of its economy (the most detailed ever attempted), involving a 30-member study team which produced a nine-volume report with detailed sectoral analyses. Even before that report was complete, China in July, 1980 produced a list of 19 major projects for which it wanted support. The Chinese angered other Third World governments by understating Chinese per capita GNP in order to qualify for the most preferential loan treatment.[3] And in the project negotiations, the Chinese government managed to raise the proportion of loans to be granted at extremely low interest rates (through the IDA) from one quarter to one half of the package. By 1988, the Chinese government had received $5.6 billion in 52 project loans (many interest-free, but all at favorable rates) as well as a $300 million "structural adjustment" loan from the World Bank. These included major railroad development, airport, factory, coal mining, and agricultural research projects.[4] As for China's behavior as a member of the World Bank, despite rhetorical support for Third World interests (as a scholarly observer noted), "China has operated...as a Group of One within the World Bank Group to maximize its own [economic] advantages", rather than joining a political campaign for collective transformation of the rules.[5] This disinterest was reciprocated: there was no evidence of Third World governments coming to China's defense when the World Bank suspended new aid projects after the June, 1989 turmoil in Beijing.[6]

By 1986, China had also received at least $75 million from the United Nations Development Program, $500 million from the World Food Program, and benefited from the establishment by the UN of several first aid and medical centers around the country[7]--not to mention the payoff from dozens of scientific and technical "exchange" (in fact, aid) programs negotiated with the United States and American universities.[8] China also benefited from its admission to more than 110 world and regional scientific organizations, which give it access to scientific and technical information in many fields while at the same time conferring further international recognition on the Beijing regime.[9]

During the 1980s, Japan contributed official development aid and low-interest loans to the Chinese government approaching $1 billion per year (some of which, by modernizing branches of the railroad system linking Chinese coast and interior, will help assure long-term availability of Chinese coal exports to resource-poor Japan[10]). Japan has remained China's largest aid donor.[11] Its contributions have been supplemented by assistance from other developed countries; total economic aid actually used by China during the Sixth Five Year Plan (1981-1986) came to $3-5 billion.[12]

Another source of soft loans for China is the Asian Development Bank (ADB), a UN-associated organization with a large headquarters staff in Manila. The ADB administers multilateral economic development loans to Asian countries, with most of the funds coming from developed countries both in and outside the region. China's entry into the ADB was delayed by US support for the continued membership of Taiwan, which had been a founding member of the organization in 1966. China was finally admitted in 1986, with Taiwan kept in under the designation "Taibei, China" (a label the Taiwan representatives protested first by boycotts and then verbally, to no avail). After China began to attend ADB meetings in April, 1986, then-Premier Zhao Ziyang announced that China would seek a seat on the governing board of the ADB: "China is boosting its economic development by introducing foreign funds and technology. Our participation in the ADB has opened a new channel for achieving our objectives."[13] China obtained loans worth $283 million from the ADB in 1987 and hosted its annual meeting in Beijing in May, 1989. The organization was contemplating a substantial increase in lending to China in the early 1990s.[14] After the June massacre in Beijing, the ADB temporarily suspended new loans to China, but lending is planned to resume soon.[15]

Finally, the Chinese government has also issued bonds in foreign capital markets to supplement the capital obtained from other international sources. From 1982 until April, 1986, China issued 14 bonds overseas (11 in Japan, two in West Germany, and one in Hong Kong) with a total value of about US$ 1.5 billion.[16] Chinese bond issues have generally (at least until 1989) received high safety ratings and a huge number of underwriters, most of which are using their participation as a means to demonstrate "goodwill" to the Chinese government.[17] The issuing of bonds in London and New York, however, has been delayed by the slowness in settling the claims of holders of pre-1949 Chinese railroad bonds.

By 1989, China was successfully sustaining not only a continuing inflow of foreign capital, but also a foreign debt which reached US$ 33.1 billion, much of the latter consisting of "soft" long-term loans at concessionary rates.[18] The most dramatic means of utilizing foreign capital, however, has been the invitation to outside investors themselves to develop factories and other profitable facilities inside China, and actively participate in their management.

The Aims of Foreign Investment Policy

The general legal principles of China's policy were embodied in the Joint Venture Law of July, 1979.[19] Except where law or policy stated otherwise, all foreign investments have been given the same treatment as joint ventures. The Joint Venture Law gave foreigners the right to form equity joint ventures to which they and their Chinese partners make capital contributions. The Law contains vague declarations which allow leeway in implementation. Products "may" be distributed in China; profits may be remitted abroad "in accordance with foreign exchange regulations"; "legitimate" personal income of foreigners may be remitted abroad; the "lawful rights and interests" of foreign investors are fully protected; and so forth. Besides vague, general statements of foreign investors' rights, the Joint Venture Law identifies important demands: technology contributed by the foreign partner "must be advanced...and ...actually suit our country's needs." Joint ventures are "encouraged" to market their products outside China. In subsequent years, these general provisions would be supplemented by more specific demands from the Chinese government.

Much of Chinese foreign investment law is more a signal of policy intentions than a guide to the rights and duties of each side. Nonetheless, in allowing profit-oriented capitalist investment by foreigners on Chinese soil, the Communist Party three years after the death of Mao took a step it had previously considered anathema. Why?

Chinese authors on the subject have repeated what appears to be a standard list of the advantages to China of allowing foreign investment.[20] One crucial goal is to develop China's export production. By one Chinese account, fully 80 per cent of all the country's industrial equipment needed technological transformation as late as 1984.[21] China needs steady growth in its export earnings in order to be able to buy new equipment for its state enterprises. Yet in the early 1980s it was still depending largely on exports of petroleum, agricultural and mineral products, all of which it produces at low efficiency by international standards and which are highly susceptible to fluctuations in world demand.

The second prime goal of foreign investment policy has been to introduce foreign technology, equipment and managerial methods for exposure to the Chinese workforce and transfer to Chinese-run operations. According to some Chinese analysts, through joint ventures, even technologies held secret by large capitalist companies can be obtained: "The mutual benefit from joint ventures [which gives each side a stake in their profitability] makes the foreign investor willing to bring out some secret technologies that he is not willing to make available in ordinary commodity trade."[22] Related advantages the Chinese perceive from foreign investment, besides training of the workforce at every level, include creation of employment, stimulation of regional agriculture, increasing Chinese skills in related areas of international trade, and "enlivening" the domestic economy.[23] The goals of earning foreign exchange and obtaining technology, however, are paramount and mutually reinforcing. In theory, each adds to the capacity of state enterprises to produce export quality goods. In practice, to obtain, adapt to, and utilize technology from the outside have all been highly problematic for China.

Chinese government spokesmen have been equally explicit about how the general goals of foreign investment policy translate into project objectives. Official statements became clearer as the Chinese learned through experience what sectors most needed technical upgrading. By late 1985 an official statement[24] defined the "right" investment focus as emphasizing:

1. Projects that import advanced technology, or produce import substitutes or productive equipment.

2. Projects involving very large capital expenditure, especially in the areas of natural resource development or technological upgrading of key state enterprises.

3. Development of new export industries or facilities.

     An official in the Ministry of Foreign Economic Relations and Trade (Mofert) spelled out in more detail the priorities for state-planned utilization of foreign investment during the Seventh Five Year Plan (1986-90):[25] energy development (especially coal and petroleum resources); electronics (especially computers and electronic components); equipment manufacturing; construction industries and infrastructure development; and modernizing the productive equipment and goods output of existing enterprises. To obtain advanced technology (which is usually treated as a uniform category in Chinese writings, without any reference to the capacity of particular sectors of the economy to absorb it), China has approved contracts in a variety of forms. These include direct purchase of technology licenses, co-production with foreign firms by contract, and hiring technical consultants. In each case part of the objective is to "help raise the quality of Chinese technical personnel."[26] Joint ventures have the advantage, in Chinese eyes, of making technologies available for eventual transfer to Chinese ownership while earning profits in the meantime; a tempting bargain.

     The Chinese government realizes that foreign capitalists must receive compensation for investment in China, but its spokesmen are vague on the subject. "Legitimate" profits, explains Chu Baotai of Mofert, are defined to mean legally permitted ones. There is no maximum permissible profit, but there is an official conception of "reasonable" profit:

> To bring in more foreign funds, technology, and managerial experience, China pursues a policy under which the foreign investor can, by his independent operation, earn a profit that is higher than the interest on bank deposits. And this is exactly what we mean by reasonable profit.[27]

Chinese writings on the subject often assert that a capitalist's motivation is to seek a steady return higher than bank deposits (the time and place of which are unspecified). This assertion ignores an investor's desire to obtain higher returns in compensation for greater risks. In the official Chinese view, profits more than double the bank rate of interest are "excess" and may in future be subject to supplementary taxation.[28] While some foreign investors are satisfied with these conceptions and the results they allow, their ideas of reasonable profits differ from the government's in many cases.

Chinese cautions about the motives of foreign capitalist investors go beyond the possibility of their extracting excess profits, however defined. The suspicions are not surprising given the historical abuse of Chinese under imperialism, and in light of Chinese officials having absorbed and disseminated anti-capitalist propaganda for thirty years. Their ideological past does not determine policy, but leaves a reluctance to make more concessions than necessary. Concessions to whom? Given the fervently nationalist character of Chinese Marxism, it is never clear whether the objection is more to foreign, or to capitalist interests. In remarking on perceived dangers of foreign investment, Chinese analysts usually make the two indistinguishable.

A Chinese handbook on all aspects of joint venture activity, published for domestic consumption, gives a list of the potential drawbacks and dangers of foreign investment that largely coincides with the perceptions outlined in Chapter Two. First, capitalist investors seek higher rates of profit in developing countries than in developed ones. The book then repeats the potentially contradictory claim that "the goal of foreign investors is to receive a higher profit rate than the bank rate of interest."[29] Second, foreign investors want to obtain influence over some of the 51 per cent equity stake that is normally under Chinese state control. Third, continues the list, foreign investors often "extort" huge sums for technological licenses. Fourth, foreign investors will try to go through joint ventures "to monopolize and control our domestic market." Indeed, many foreign investors in China are hoping to penetrate the domestic market; to do so would threaten with competition the existing market control by state monopolies. Fifth, developed country firms export their heavily polluting industries to developing countries. Capitalists in general, according to such Chinese descriptions, behave more ruthlessly and destructively in developing countries, and this requires state measures to protect national interest. A more recently published article also expresses concern that joint venture products might compete overseas with other Chinese-made exports; and that joint ventures, by borrowing from foreign banks, could add to China's national debt burden.[30]

These reservations about any dealings with foreign capitalists are reflected in limitations in China's foreign investment policy. A spokesman for the State Council's Foreign Economic Research Group has listed types of projects that are officially prohibited:[31] those which threaten China's sovereignty; are illegal; pollute the environment; or projects which do not conform with the requirements of China's national economy--for example those which merely introduce assembly lines, import spare parts to assemble machines for sales on the domestic market and profit from price differences between domestic and world markets.

The point about assembly projects is an area of confusion in China's foreign investment policy. It describes what many foreign investors have tried, and in Shenzhen Special Economic Zone succeeded in doing for a time. Yet the Shenzhen experiment had substantial local benefits. The mixed results explain Chinese ambivalence, reflected in a contradictory statement by a Mofert spokesman in the same year (1986) as the statement cited above:

> The Chinese Government encourages processing and assemblage [sic] business, and exempts from customs duties goods imported or exported for the purpose.[32]

The government could never quite bring itself to ban low-tech foreign investment, which did create jobs and enhance local incomes.

What other compromises has China made since 1979 in its attempt to obtain productive capital and technology?

The Terms of Foreign Investment Policy in General

China's foreign investment laws and policy after 1979 were flexible, in two senses. They offered the foreign capitalist partner a variety of forms and means by which to conduct his profit-oriented operations. At the same time, numerous provisions gave the government ways to reinterpret and readjust policy to resolve emerging problems.

Coinciding with or even prior to the Joint Venture Law of July, 1979, China began to accept a variety of forms of cooperation with foreign capitalism. Most of these are designed to give the foreign side an inherent interest in seeing that any technology or equipment it supplies is properly and profitably used, in contrast to technology license agreements which can leave the purchaser short of necessary practical expertise. Technology licensing, while also undertaken by the Chinese, has been overshadowed by other investment arrangements.

The simplest type of foreign investment contract is compensation trade (*buchang maoyi*), which as Michael Moser has pointed out "in its pure form is essentially a loan transaction."[33] The foreigner brings in productive equipment and is repaid within a set time period with products made using the same equipment. A similar arrangement is processing for fee using foreign-supplied equipment. Although few specific laws or regulations have been issued governing this form of investment, there are provisions of foreign exchange, tax, and customs rules that apply; as well as standard procedures for registration similar to those specified for joint ventures. Compensation trade agreements are typically of three to five years' duration and small (less than US $1 million).[34] Their relative simplicity appealed to foreign investors: during several years, three times as much foreign investment went into them as into equity joint ventures.[35] The Chinese have been ambivalent about them because they bring in capital equipment, but not advanced technology. Nevertheless, the equipment is often an improvement on what it replaces.

A special form of joint Chinese-foreign investment called joint development (*hezuo kaicai*) was created for exploring natural resources that involve major capital expenditure, such as offshore oil and gas. A Chinese source summarizes:[36]

> In the competitive field of petroleum exploration, the Regulations of the PRC on the Exploitation of Offshore Oil Resources in Cooperation with Foreign Enterprises provide that during the exploratory stage, the foreign partner is to cover investment for the entire exploration operation and bear all risks alone. The two cooperating partners will invest together at share levels specified in the contract after the discovery of oil with the foreign partner taking full management responsibility. Profits will be allocated according to contract while taxes will be paid separately by both individual partners. When the contract expires, all assets...pass to the Chinese partner.

Under the general authority of the Ministry of Petroleum Industry, the China National Offshore Oil Corporation obtains bidders and project partners under a standard contract designed for such ventures. No independent new legal entity is set up. Twenty-six contracts of this type for exploration and development of offshore oil were signed by 1985.[37] These were typically very large items: in 1983, 18 joint exploration contracts together involved over U.S. $1 billion in foreign investment (versus 107 joint venture contracts worth only $188 million total in the same year).[38]

Under such cooperative development agreements, China again gains productive capital, which over time the state takes full possession of. The foreign side is paid off with a negotiated share of hard currency income. China can thus attempt to satisfy foreign oil companies for their risks and costs with a stream of income, while itself gaining resources and taking all further income after a set period. In the meantime, parts of the labor force get paid training and experience working with advanced resource exploitation equipment that the state eventually owns.

The third major type of foreign investment project China has accepted is the cooperative joint venture (*hezuo jingying*). Until 1988, these followed the general terms of the equity Joint Venture Law, with the difference that cooperative joint ventures set up a much simpler profit-seeking entity that may not even need its own Board of Directors. In such ventures, each party to the contract has its own profits, liabilities, and taxes. Capital contributions take the variety of forms outlined in the original Joint Venture Law: essentially any factor of production including labor.[39] Since there are no fixed equity shares in such ventures, there is no set formula for profit distribution and it can be decided flexibly by the parties to each contract. Tax rates for the foreign partner are higher at 30-50 per cent (under the Foreign Enterprise Income Tax Law), than the 33 per cent or below for equity joint ventures--except in the Special Economic Zones where cooperative ventures have a preferential rate of 15 per cent. Foreign exchange restrictions are the same as those faced by equity joint ventures.

Examples of cooperative ventures are "cooperative construction" and "cooperative production." In the first, the Chinese side contributes land and the foreign side contributes capital to build hotels or housing; each derives a contractually-set profit from the sale or rental of finished units.[40] In the second, the foreign side supplies production technology and jointly engages in production (with Chinese-made parts rising to 100 per cent of composition) for profit to both sides over a set period--necessarily giving the Chinese some practical instruction in the use of the technology.[41] Because of their relative simplicity, contractual joint ventures have appealed to foreign investors considerably more than equity joint ventures, and have outnumbered the latter.[42]

The National People's Congress published a Cooperative Joint Venture Law in April, 1988. The fact that several thousand such ventures had already been approved before the issuance of this law gives an idea of the ability of the Chinese government and its foreign partners to operate without legal guidance. Like most Chinese foreign investment laws, this one simply makes explicit certain principles developed over years of practice without the benefit of law. The new law is flexible on such points as the distribution of earnings among investors, the assignment of Chinese and foreign members to the Board of Directors, and sources of financing (Cooperative Joint Ventures are not required to borrow from the Bank of China).[43] The law also reveals considerable sophistication on the Chinese side in using incentives to get favorable results: Cooperative Joint Ventures will not be granted the benefits that go with limited liability status unless there are substantial cash (as opposed to merely in-kind) contributions from the foreign partner.[44]

Equity joint ventures (*hezi jingying*) are more well-known, because they were the subject of the 1979 law that symbolized China's rejection of Maoist self-reliance. However, as already noted, that law is short and vague. Only numerous subsequent regulations and policy statements would make clear what the policies were and how they could change over the years. In brief, each equity joint venture creates a new legal entity, a registered limited liability company, with equity shares and corresponding profit distribution split between the Chinese and foreign sides as specified in the original contract. Equity joint ventures are given preferential tax rates, and are reassured that they can obtain production supplies, land, and necessary labor locally in much the same manner as Chinese state enterprises. In practice, most labor and supply arrangements that are not part of the initial capital contributions of each side under the contract are undertaken by the Chinese partner through its own connections, sometimes through a formal contract with the joint venture. And the state, as will be seen shortly, keeps its hand between the venture and the domestic economy in ways that prevent free interaction.[45]

Most equity joint ventures have 51:49 Chinese and foreign share holdings respectively, with seats on the binational Board of Directors as well as any profits or losses distributed in the same proportion. The minimum requirement is that the foreign partner contribute 25 per cent of original registered capital. Each side can, according to the law, make capital contributions in a variety of forms. However, in practice the contracts usually specify that the foreign side contributes machinery, equipment, technology rights, or hard cash; while the Chinese side contributes labor (often employees of the Chinese partner's other production activities) and land use rights:

> If the land use fee is contributed as investment [says a
> Mofert source], the total amount due over the entire period
> of the joint venture's operation is counted as a lump sum
> for the purpose. However, the profit accruing from this
> part of the investment must be turned over to the state as its
> financial revenue if the Chinese joint venturer is a state
> enterprise. If the land use fee is not used as investment, the
> joint venture can obtain the right to the use of land by
> paying such a fee to the state.[46]

Either way, the state gets a profit from making land available. More important than that is the knowledge that the foreign partner has an inherent stake in the success of the venture and its ongoing productivity--and thus has an incentive to make sure that any technology supplied is being effectively utilized.

The foreign side is required to supply equipment "indispensable" to production, that China cannot produce sufficiently at reasonable cost, at standard international prices.[47] Any technology contributed must facilitate production of "urgently needed" or export goods; raise productivity or quality of existing products; or diminish the energy and raw materials consumption of existing production. In reality, things did not work out this way, since most foreign investment went into commercial and property development-related sectors, and light assembly. Nonetheless, the developing legal structure put bargaining chips in the hands of negotiators, who could insist on a substantial capital contribution from the foreign side.

In this bargaining process, China has made much of its respect for intellectual property.[48] The Patent Law that became effective April 1, 1985 protects proprietary technology for five to fifteen years, when it is part of the foreign side's capital contributions to joint ventures. "The state protects ownership of the technology transferred to joint ventures by foreign investors, ownership of proprietary technology introduced into China under licensing agreements, and the property rights of inventors."[49] According to this official source, Chinese courts will enforce patent protection provisions if necessary against Chinese state enterprises. But the government has stated several conditions that are necessary before proprietary technology will be accepted as a capital contribution:[50]

1. The technology must be "advanced and...suitable for use in China" (Chinese statements rarely acknowledge the possibility that these two characteristics might be contradictory).

2. Its price must be "fair and reasonable."

3. There are no product sales restrictions or exclusive distribution agreements.

4. The technology should facilitate new and "urgently needed" or export products.

5. It should increase productivity.

6. It should cut raw materials or energy consumption.

7. Proprietary technology should not exceed 15 per cent of total investment--although Mofert (which approves major joint ventures) admits that "it is rather complicated to ascertain the price of any intangible property because of its exclusive possession."[51]

Chinese law preserves ambiguity about the definition of "advanced technology," which it demands of foreign investors as a condition for preferential treatment. On October 24, 1986, the Mayor of Shanghai certified 26 foreign investment ventures as "technologically advanced."[52] Three months later, the city's rules on making such decisions were made public. The "Rules for Confirming and Examining Export and Technologically Advanced Enterprises with Foreign Investment" (January 27, 1987) provide in Article 4 the following criteria of decision:

> Enterprises that meet the following requirements can be confirmed as "technologically advanced enterprises:" The technology, production techniques, and key facilities of the

enterprises with foreign investment should pertain to the projects proclaimed by the state as appropriate and advanced; they should be in short supply on the domestic market; and the products should be newly developed or capable of expanding exports or substituting for imported products or upgrading similar domestic products.[53]

That is the entire article. It is copied from Ministry of Foreign Economic Relations and Trade guidelines issued for national use.[54] Clearly something other than precise legal definitions would determine whether a venture could receive special treatment by being certified as "high tech:" namely, the current supply of and demand for foreign investment projects of the type under negotiation.

After learning the market value of the foreign side's capital contribution, Chinese negotiators typically assign equal cash value to the land and buildings they allow to be used for the project.[55] This practice led to complaints from foreign businessmen, and after foreign investment dropped markedly in early 1986, the Chinese government made assurances that it would standardize land use fees.[56]

Joint ventures are encouraged by law and policy to obtain all possible supplies in China, and to rely on Chinese financial institutions. They must open foreign exchange and renminbi accounts with the Bank of China, if any profits are to be remitted abroad.[57] Chinese partners prefer that any loans should be taken from that same state bank. Insurance on assets must be purchased from the state insurance company.[58] And, of course, many expatriate executives live in state-run or joint venture hotels and spend part of their incomes in state stores. The state takes every opportunity (and there are many) to earn sideline profits from joint venture activity.

One area of government indecisiveness was to what extent to allow wholly foreign-owned enterprises (*waizi qiye*) to operate in China. The US firm Minnesota Mining and Manufacturing, after three years of negotiations, set up a wholly-owned factory in Shanghai in 1983 for producing electric tapes and resins.[59] Even more surprising, the venture has no fixed duration and could go on indefinitely. State control is exerted through supply contracts with state enterprises, local labor bureaus' involvement in recruitment, and renting of facilities. For a foreign enterprise without pre-existing local connections to obtain facilities and supplies is a formidable undertaking, with success far from assured. Still, one might wonder, why did China sacrifice its usual share of equity control in this case? Probably as an experiment to see what kind of hard currency tax revenues would be possible. Chinese experts claim wholly foreign-owned ventures are welcomed,[60] but the number approved has apparently been under a central restriction of at most one per foreign firm.[61] Some thirty wholly foreign-owned ventures worth U.S. $200 million had been approved by 1983,[62] most of these in the Special Economic Zones. By

1986, this experimental type of venture had still not spread widely in China (only 18 were approved that year[63]).

How do capitalist-run joint ventures, many of them with foreign managers, interact with the domestic Chinese economy? The answer is complicated. On one hand, they are in principle treated much the same as state enterprises for many contractual supply arrangements (typically made by the Chinese partner using pre-existing connections). On the other hand, and perhaps not in contradiction, the state puts restrictions on all aspects of foreign investment operations.

The process begins with negotiated capital contributions from each side. The factor of production most commonly supplied by the Chinese side in joint ventures is use rights to land and facilities. Only in 1986 were standard fees set in response to complaints by foreigners of gouging. Previously, the use fees were not even announced until after joint venture approval. Since there were no domestic land sale prices to use as a standard of comparison, Chinese authorities could still claim that local land fee rate schemes were "fair and reasonable."[64] Although the foreign partner is discouraged from making technology more than 20 per cent of its capital contribution, the Chinese partner can without restriction use its existing occupied sites as investment contributions to match foreign capital. The preferred foreign investment ventures (e.g., those that bring in so-called high technology) get land use fee reductions, independent of the quality or location of the land in question.[65] The land use fees thus remain a bargaining chip that helps the Chinese insist on desired capital contributions from the other side.

The second most common "capital" contribution of the Chinese side in joint ventures has been labor. Most frequently the Chinese partner simply shifts some of its own workers from previous operations or production lines to the new ones. In fact, one of the stated qualifications for a Chinese enterprise to enter into a joint venture is that "it must have the skilled workers and managerial personnel required for the joint venture, or at least the ability to provide them."[66] At American Motor Corporation's (AMC's) Beijing Jeep joint venture, for example, all but a few hundred of the 4,000 employees came from the Chinese partner's previous production lines. In the first three years of operation, the few workers whose behavior led to their being "fired" were in reality transferred back to the Chinese partner's regular operations.[67]

Joint ventures are free to hire on the local labor market--insofar as they can draw qualified workers away from their prior work units (which have to consent to their moving). Some joint ventures have hired graduating high school and (in much smaller numbers) college students. But university graduates are subject to quota-based state job assignments.

The government has fixed wage guidelines for workers in joint ventures at 120-150 per cent of the income of state enterprise workers in the same locality (e.g., the Chinese partner's existing workers). Thus, joint venture workers get more than their compatriots in state industries but not so much that the higher wages give "rise to a contradiction between these two sections of people," as a Chinese source puts it.[68] Moreover, the Chinese worker does not and cannot receive "his" full wage. The state takes a portion (perhaps a third) of the wage payment as reimbursement for food and medical subsidies that benefit all Chinese workers. Joint ventures in this way pay a per capita labor tax to the state to help underwrite nationalized social services.[69]

Joint ventures secure their other production inputs in much the same manner as Chinese state enterprises--that is, with the same difficulty. They are required to give preference to Chinese-produced supplies where available. Only if domestic supplies are inadequate may joint ventures import them, and in that case they must use foreign exchange, submit an import plan, and obtain semi-annual import licenses.[70] Thus joint ventures are not relieved of pressure to use Chinese inputs or parts even when these are of inferior quality. Yet joint ventures, unlike many state enterprises, face strong demands to export the output they produce with such parts. No matter where the products are sold, there are bureaucratic obstacles. Goods sold in the domestic market are subject to state resale and price controls and cannot engage in price competition with other domestically sold items. Goods that a joint venture exports must have their prices "coordinated" with the relevant state trade enterprises.[71]

Admittedly, these rules are not always observed. One government policy states: "Chinese enterprises in the Special Economic Zones can only sell their products within the Zones [not inside China]."[72] As Chapter Three has shown, that is far from the case. Laws or policies which proclaim what kind of technology a joint venturer should bring in, or where he should sell his products, contain principles that are enforced with more or less severity according to the perceived importance of the project. There were special political reasons, having to do with Hong Kong's confidence, why enforcement of domestic sales restrictions was lax at Shenzhen.

Beyond purchase and sales restrictions lie issues of allowable earnings and repatriation. What kind of profits can a large capitalist company earn in the new China and what can it do with them? Here, the most important restriction is the nonconvertibility of the domestic currency, renminbi, into foreign exchange. This means that joint ventures have to use hard currency export earnings to pay for necessary imported parts and equipment. On this point they are as hampered as state enterprises. Export earnings are often insufficient to cover hard currency expenditures. Although legislation passed in stages after 1983 attempted to ease this burden on joint ventures (see below), these changes only juggled the burden and did not relieve it.

The basic problem of earnings for joint ventures remained: using Chinese labor and Chinese inputs where available, they had to sell goods in internationally competitive markets if they were to earn profits that could be repatriated. If it meant hotels and commercial service centers for hard currency-spending foreigners in China, this was feasible. If it meant producing manufactured exports, joint ventures had difficulty succeeding where state enterprises had failed. Imported production technology and management were not magic cures for shortcomings in other essential factors of production and in Chinese infrastructure. The inability of foreign investors to convert or repatriate renminbi earnings reduces the benefits of tax concessions that have been made to joint ventures.

China's policy of making concessions to foreign capital went beyond allowing the several kinds of ventures, subject to the constraints briefly outlined above. Equally significant for the People's Republic whose greatest achievement was to unify a torn and complex country, the central government decided to allow provinces and localities considerable autonomy in arranging and approving foreign investment contracts. The gradual implementation of this policy reflected the government's awareness of a fragile balance between local initiative and growth in China's more advanced coastal regions, against dangers of regional inequality and loss of central control.

All foreign investment projects are required to accord with state plans. In practice this means that during the initial negotiating period, letters of intent are submitted by the Chinese partner to its superior authorities for review.[73] Formally, the contract must be approved by the state (i.e., national) or provincial planning commission. However, in 1983 new Joint Venture Implementing Regulations allowed the state Foreign Investment Bureau (itself under the authority of Mofert) to relinquish approval powers for some projects to lower level authorities.

In general, most projects with value under US $3 million could after 1983 be approved by the responsible ministry or provincial government alone.[74] Projects above this value must be approved by Mofert. Several key cities were given higher approval ceilings. After 1983, as it emerged from occasional government announcements, these local approval rights were raised even further. Table 7-1 makes plain the extent of decentralization in approvals as well as the priority given coastal cities which are already the most highly developed in China. Implicit in this policy was a decision to let the coastal region, which could more easily attract foreign capital, develop more quickly than the interior: growth at a cost of inequality. In this respect, state policy became more and more relaxed. Domestic or regional inequality was of far less concern under China's economic nationalist policy than the possibility of foreign capital getting direct influence in the domestic economy.

Chinese policy not only ensures that the state takes a stream of income from profitable foreign joint ventures, but also requires transfer of most capital assets to the Chinese side after the contract period. Thus, even in the case of low-tech items such as hotels and commercial centers, the state gains previously nonexistent facilities or equipment. Admittedly, ten to twenty years (the typical contract life) may seem long enough that

Table 7-1

Ceilings for Autonomous Approval of Foreign Investment Projects

	Late 1983	1985
Provinces and Ministries	US $ 3 million	US $ 5 million
Liaoning Province	$ 5 million	$ 10 million
Dalian City	------	$ 10 million
Beijing Municipality	$ 5 million	$ 10 million
Guangdong and Fujian Provinces	$ 10 million (reportedly)	$ 10 million
Tianjin Municipality	not available	$ 30 million
Shanghai Municipality	$ 10 million	$ 30 million

NOTE: Prior to 1983, provinces and localities had no powers of independent approval.

SOURCES: Michael J. Moser, "Foreign Investment in China: the Legal Framework," 108; Chu Baotai, *Foreign Investment in China, Questions and Answers* , 97.

the assets transferred will be of little value after the contract runs out. But in many cases the items in question have a much longer profitable life: witness the intensive 1980s use of many Chinese hotels built in the 1950s. Equipment may be aging by the time of transfer, but it may well still be productive in the hands of workers by that time experienced in using it.

The issue here is what happens when joint ventures go through a normal termination process. (Premature dissolution and liquidation are rare.) On this key point, a Shanghai law professor stated in 1985:[75]

When a joint venture terminates, its assets can be transferred to either of the partners who wishes to continue
operations. The evaluation of assets shall proceed according to the provisions laid down in the contract and articles
of association.

In other words, each contract can freely determine the final distribution of
assets. Another Chinese publication distributed to potential foreign investors in 1986 contains similar implications.[76]

Such statements are misleading. In practice, after dissolution,
ownership of joint venture assets is transferred to the Chinese side. It is
doubtful whether the Chinese would approve most joint ventures otherwise, whether they are the cooperative or equity type--just as China re-
fuses to sign technology transfer contracts that prohibit "the continued use
of the technology by the transferee on the expiration of the contract."[77]
The government insists that the productive capacity inherent in each
technology transfer or joint venture contract must pass in the end to
Chinese control. Speaking of Sichuan Province's joint ventures, Deputy
Governor He Haoju remarked:

As for projects such as hotels, contracts stipulate that when
the contract expires, all assets will go to the Chinese partner and these contracts are not renewable.[78]

He did not mention any exceptions to this practice. A typical example of
such a transfer is the contract of the Beijing Air Catering Company, a joint
venture between a Hong Kong firm and China's state airline (CAAC) to
supply meals for CAAC passengers. A Chinese summary states:

The two partners have agreed to repay the capital and
compensate for the depreciation of fixed assets in the first
four years of operation. From the fifth year the Hong
Kong partner will transfer part of its shares to the Chinese
partner, who will own all the company's capital and assets
on the expiry of the [8-year] cooperation period.[79]

In this case, both partners had made nearly equal capital contributions of
2.9 million yuan. (The two sides later negotiated an extension of the
contact to 15 years.)

As if to put icing on the Chinese cake, the Chinese policy specifies
that if any assets or property are distributed to the foreign partner on
dissolution, "the excess is regarded as profit and subject to income tax
according to law."[80] There is a preferred alternative: Chinese negotiators
routinely demand valuation of any liquidated venture assets by Chinese
state assessors, which facilitates undervaluation and resale to other Chinese entities.[81]

How long is the contract period before that transfer of assets occurs? This issue, too, has been obscured. The Joint Venture Implementing Regulations of 1983 contain an ambiguous provision that "Joint venture terms for average projects in principle are from ten to thirty years,"[82] and allow over thirty years for "large" projects or those which involve prolonged construction or low rates of return.

In practice, however, most joint ventures have a contract life of less than twenty years before transfer of assets to the Chinese side. In a comprehensive list of US-Chinese joint ventures throughout the country prepared by the United States Embassy in Beijing in January, 1986, only seven out of 134 had terms exceeding twenty years.[83] Listings of Hong Kong joint ventures also show a duration nearly always under twenty years.[84]

The restriction on the number of profitable years was a major deterrent to foreign investors, particularly long term-minded Japanese. Mitsui executives in a published interview, for example, made it plain that duration and capital transfer restrictions were a prime reason why joint ventures in China were not a "viable proposition."[85] The low level of Japanese investment was a source of bilateral friction during the early 1980s.

In response to such complaints, the Chinese announced a change in foreign investment law on January 15, 1986. The provision in the Joint Venture Implementing Regulations was then amended to read:

> ...the term of a joint venture engaged in an ordinary project may be ten to thirty years. That of those projects requiring large amounts of investment, long construction periods and operating on low profit margins, *or having foreign partners who provide advanced or key technology to produce sophisticated and internationally competitive products, may be extended to fifty years. And that of such projects with the special approval of the State Council may be extended to more than fifty years.*[86]

The portions I have emphasized were added in 1986. They seemed to promise a much longer term of profitable operation to foreign investors.

This apparent concession was intended to make an impression on potential investors. In fact, *prior* to the amendment, a Chinese spokesman stated:

> There is no prescribed stipulation in Chinese law limiting the duration of joint venture projects involving large investment figures, long construction periods and low interest rates on funds. It rests with the discretion of the cooperating partners.[87]

The length of term allowed by the new amendment had already been permitted. In addition, joint ventures already had the right to extend their contract terms, subject to prior application and approval by the supervising government department.[88] The issue before 1986 was not that longer term joint ventures were prohibited (they were not), but rather that as a matter of policy they were generally not approved. The 1986 amendment to the law did not affect this policy.

Law and public relations should not distract, then, from what Chinese policy has been, although the interactions of the three are interesting. The policy has offered foreign investors wide latitude in their choice of a form of operation. It has decentralized approval authority. The policy has been designed, however, not only to ensure the state an income from selling various services to the venture, but also to transfer all capital to the Chinese side within a limited period. Although recent provisions have seemed to change this principle, the policy remains much as before. The 1986 regulations are part of an ongoing process of give and take with foreign investors--bargaining facilitated on the Chinese side by loopholes in even detailed legislation.

The Development of Foreign Investment Law as a Bargaining Tool

Chinese foreign investment law from its beginning in 1979 left plenty of room for administrative discretion in granting extra concessions to projects especially desired by state authorities. At first, this was an inevitable result of ambiguities in undeveloped law. Negotiation was always prolonged and contracts had to contain numerous ad hoc features. A 1980 Swiss-Chinese venture to manufacture elevators included in its contract a detailed description of the venture's liability for eight different taxes.[89] Investment proceeded nonetheless. At the same time, a whole category of projects, compensation trade, was flourishing with many contracts signed despite a lack of relevant legislation.[90] In the first few years after 1979, legal gaps left the government negotiating room to make or withdraw concessions in particular cases. And as Table 7-2 shows, great flexibility remained possible on almost every aspect of a contract. This provides attractive points to advertise to foreign businessmen, as well as bargaining chips.

The flexibility was gradually extended to approvals of borrowing by joint ventures. In Tianjin Municipality, for example, after 1983 the local government could allow joint ventures to borrow up to US $50 million abroad, and in 1985 that limit was raised to $150 million.[91]

Table 7-2

Discretionary Concessions Allowed by Chinese Foreign Investment Law

Preferential Item	Ostensible Criteria for Preference	Extent of Potential Flexibility	Agency that Decides
(1) project approval	high-tech, large export-oriented, or project in preferred sectors	rejection or slow to rapid approval	state, provincial or local foreign investment agency
(2) acceptance of equipment or technology as joint venture contribution	indispensability; import substitution; valuation does not exceed int'l. price	acceptance or rejection of proposed capital contribution	"
(3) recruitment of labor outside locality	unsuitability of local candidates	no outside hiring, to open hiring subject to state employment rules	local labor management department
(4) contract term extension (joint ventures and technology transfer)	large, high-tech, low profit margin, or high quality exportable product output	extension of contract to 30, 50 years or even more	state, provincial or local foreign investment agency;State Council (over 50 years)
(5) access to domestic market	advanced technology or equipment; or import substitute products	from zero access to unspecified proportion and period of domestic sales	Mofert

Preferential Item	Ostensible Criteria for Preference	Extent of Potential Flexibility	Agency that Decides
(6) special currency conversion rights	hard currency earnings insufficient to cover expenditures; must be large, high-tech project and export unspecified portion of goods--exceptional cases only	from strict RMB nonconvertibility to state hard currency subsidies	Mofert and State Planning Commission
(7) tax reduction	advanced technology projects	up to two profitable year tax exemption; 50% reduction in 3 subsequent years; 10-30% in reduction up to 10 years after that	supervising foreign investment agency and Ministry of Finance
(8) relief from provisions of subsequently enacted laws	"excessive burden or excessive losses"	possible permission for contract to supercede newly enacted laws	supervising foreign investment agency

NOTE: partial list

SOURCES: (1) Chu Baotai, *Questions and Answers*, 60-61, 99-102. (2) *Ibid.*, 133, 138-9. (3) *Intertrade Supplement*, Nov. 1985, 13. (4) *Ibid.*, May, 1986, 15. (5) *Intertrade*, Sept., 1985, 57; *China Daily*, Jan.21, 1986,1; *Intertrade Supplement*, May, 1986, 15; Chu Baotai, *Qestions and Answers*, 88, 143. (6) *Intertrade Supplement*, Nov., 1985, 11; *Ibid.*, May, 1986, 15; *Intertrade*, Sept., 1985, 57-58; *Ibid.*, Jan., 1986, 14. (7) *Intertrade Supplement*, Nov., 1985, 9, 28; *China's Foreign Economic Legislation, Vol. 1*, 65-66. (8) Chu Baotai, *Questions and Answers*, 106.

On May 15, 1984, local autonomy was broadened when the State Council declared fourteen cities as well as tropical Hainan Island to be "open" areas. For over a year the "fourteen coastal cities" became a catchword and the subject of constant discussion in the Chinese press. The "fourteen coastal cities" policy was an extension to relatively developed municipalities of the right to approve foreign investment projects under specified ceilings, and to give such projects preferential tax and customs treatment.[92] It was soon announced that a limited "opening" (decentralization of administrative discretion regarding foreign investment) would be extended to areas near the fourteen cities;[93] and in even more limited form to as many as 24 inland cities.[94] At first, the most preferential treatment of foreign capital in the "fourteen coastal cities" themselves was restricted to specified development zones there.[95] By early 1988, however, most of these cities adopted some of the preferential policies pioneered in Shenzhen Special Economic Zone; and the government, apparently at the initiative of Party leader Zhao Ziyang, decided to make all of Hainan Island a newly separate province and China's fifth Special Economic Zone.[96]

This was a dramatic gesture to speed up China's coastal development by trying to lure foreign investment that could build the region's export and hard currency-earning potential. Hainan (as government publications pointedly noted) is China's "second largest island"[97] with an area of 34,000 square kilometers. As such it could begin to compete with slightly larger (but far more developed) Taiwan. In order to develop tropical Hainan's potential in cash crops, tourism, and perhaps industry, foreign investors have been promised the right to manage state enterprises on contract, and joint ventures will get tax breaks spread over the first several profit-making years. As in Shenzhen, foreigners will be able to enter and spend money with a minimum of border formalities. However, as throughout China, they can only repatriate profits earned from exporting.

Around the same time, the government announced that the whole 50,000 square kilometer Shandong Peninsula would become an "open zone." This meant that it would emphasize attracting foreign investment on terms similar to other relatively advanced coastal areas such as Fujian and Liaoning.[98] In addition to selective tax preferences, cities in Shandong will be able to approve foreign investment projects valued up to US $30 million. The "opening" of Hainan and coastal "open zones" means in essence extension to additional cities and provinces (including ones with relatively developed infrastructure) of the right to bargain with foreign investors, using points of flexibility built into national law.

However, none of this has deterred central authorities from intervening in projects in which they have some interest. Take the case of a Japanese company negotiating in 1987 to build a factory that would produce edible oils in the coastal "open" city of Dalian. This city had already been granted autonomous approval rights for several years.

Presumably the Chinese enterprise could negotiate for itself. But because central government planners regarded developing China's productive capacity in this item as an important priority, State Council representatives became directly involved in negotiations with the Japanese firm. Their intervention, and that of provincial officials, greatly expedited negotiation--but left the Japanese wondering whether solving operational problems later on would again require high-level bureaucratic intervention.[99]

Nor do the foreign investment policy reforms mean that Chinese-foreign project negotiations are greatly simplified. The many policy decisions that have to be made on the Chinese side about each project are if anything complicated by the extent of flexibility now permitted. Thus, after top executives in the American Express Company's Shearson Lehman unit took an interest in building a large, expensive office and apartment complex in Beijing, letters of intent with a Beijing partner were quickly signed in 1985. The negotiations then took two years, cost American Express $1 million, and required two dozen Chinese approvals.[100] To help bring the negotiations to completion, American Express obtained direct appeals to the Chinese government by the US Ambassador, the Secretary of State, the Mayor of New York, and others. This successful tactic greatly irritated the Chinese negotiators because it involved going over their heads to the Mayor of Beijing and even higher levels. It is a tactic which draws on the importance of *guanxi* (connections) in China--and which recognizes the continuing authority of the state over decisions that are ostensibly to be made by localities and enterprises.

In sum, the substance of China's foreign investment laws has lagged behind their quantity. There is certainly no shortage: the Joint Venture Law was followed by several sets of implementing regulations; then, in 1986, the "22 Provisions for the Encouragement of Foreign Investment," and 16 forthcoming sets of implementing regulations for the Provisions, not to mention provincial and local laws, and others which affect foreign investors. However, this rapidly growing body of law was largely a statement of what *might* be offered foreign investors, rather than a clear delineation of their rights. The law's loopholes and areas of flexibility became more specific, too. Chinese negotiators could therefore make detailed offers of special treatment to ventures their government preferred. After 1983, some of the authority to take advantage of this flexibility was passed downward to provinces and localities. Since this partial decentralization allowed investors to compare different provinces in order to obtain the best treatment, it meant more to them than many of their widely proclaimed but not always realized privileges.

Notes

1. Quoted in William Feeney, "Chinese Policy in Multilateral Financial Institutions," in Samuel S. Kim, ed., *China and the World* (Boulder and London: Westview, 1984), 266-292.
2. *Ibid.*, 274.
3. *Ibid.*, 284.
4. *The China Business Review*, May, 1988, 32-33. See also David Denny, "The Impact of Foreign Aid," *China Business Review* XIII:1 (Jan.-Feb., 1986), 22-24.
5. *Ibid.*, 289.
6. *Far Eastern Economic Review*, October 12, 1989, 62.
7. Denny, "The Impact of Foreign Aid," 23.
8. Some 40,000 Chinese advanced students are in the United States in 1989, concentrated in scientific and technical fields; while there have been, at most times during the past decade, several hundred visiting American students in China, mostly short term.
9. Denis Fred Simon, "The Role of Science and Technology in China's Foreign Relations," in Samuel S. Kim, ed., *China and the World*, 298-300.
10. Nicholas R. Lardy, *China's Entry into the World Economy* (Lanham, MD: University Press of America, 1987), 10-13.
11. *The Economist*, May 6, 1989, 77.
12. Denny, "The Impact of Foreign Aid," 23.
13. *Beijing Review*, May 26, 1986, 8.
14. *Far Eastern Economic Review*, Feb. 23, 1989, 66.
15. Quoted in *Wall Street Journal*, October 31, 1989, A16.
16. Liu Rongcang, "Woguo Waizi Shiyong Xiaoyi de Huigu he Duice," *Shehui Kexue Jikan*, No. 1, 1988, 42.
17. Elizabeth Morrison, "Borrowing on World Bond Markets," *China Business Review* Jan.-Feb., 1986, 18-21.
18. *Beijing Review*, March 6, 1989, 22.
19. Foreign Languages Press, ed., *China's Foreign Economic Legislation, Vol. 1* (Beijing: 1982), 1-12.
20. See Wang Yihe and others, *Zhongwai Hezi Jingying Qiye* (Shanghai: Social Sciences Academy Press, 1984), 88-91; and Chu Baotai and Dong Weiyuan, *Zenyang Juban Zhongwai Hezi Jingying Qiye* (Beijing: Zhishi Chubanshe, 1986), 37-47.
21. Chu Baotai, *Zenyang Juban*, 40.
22. *Ibid.*, 41.
23. *Ibid.*, 42-46.
24. Wu Chao, State Council Foreign Economic Research Group, in *Intertrade Supplement*, May, 1986, 10-11.
25. Chu Baotai, *Foreign Investment in China, Questions and Answers* (Beijing: Foreign Languages Press, 1986), 62.

26. Dong Shizhong of Fudan University in *Intertrade Supplement*, Nov. 1985, 17-18.
27. Chu Baotai, *Foreign Investment in China*, 36-7.
28. *Ibid.*
29. Wang Yihe, *Zhongwai Hezi Qiye*, 88-93.
30. Wang Yibing in *Guoji Maoyi*, No. 3, 1987, 9-11.
31. Wu Chao in *Guoji Maoyi*, Beijing; trans. *Intertrade Supplement*, May, 1986, 11.
32. Chu Baotai, *Questions and Answers*, 28.
33. Michael J. Moser, "Foreign Investment in China: The Legal Framework," in Moser, ed., *Foreign Trade, Investment and the Law in the PRC* (Hong Kong: Oxford University Press, 1984), 109. In the following pages I rely primarily on *Ibid.*, 109-136.
34. *Ibid.*, 110.
35. Xue Muqiao, ed., *Almanac of China's Economy, 1984* (Hong Kong: Modern Cultural Company, 1985), 1095.
36. Dong Shizhong in *Intertrade Supplement*, Nov. 1985, 5.
37. Chu Baotai, *Questions and Answers*, 22-24.
38. *Almanac of China's Economy, 1984*, 1096.
39. Moser, "The Legal Framework," 112-113ff.
40. Chu Baotai, *Questions and Answers*, 24-5.
41. *Ibid.*, 25-6.
42. *Guoji Jingjifa Yanjiu*, No. 4, 1987, 20. See also *Zhongguo Faxue*, No. 4, 1987, 23-28.
43. See the analysis by Jerome Alan Cohen in *China Business Review*, July 1988, 14-18.
44. *Ibid.*
45. Chinese private enterprises were strongly discouraged from forming joint ventures with foreigners until June, 1988, when this was abruptly legalized. See Chu Baotai, *Questions and Answers*, 41-2; and *Beijing Review*, July 18-24, 1988, 10.
46. Chu Baotai, *Questions and Answers*, 43.
47. Moser, "The Legal Framework," 121.
48. Chu Baotai, *Questions and Answers*, 57-8.
49. *Ibid.*
50. *Ibid.*
51. *Ibid.*, 56-57.
52. *China Business Review*, Jan-Feb., 1987, 16.
53. *Business China*, March 9, 1987, 37.
54. *Guoji Jingjifa Yanjiu*, No. 4, 1987, 20-23.
55. Moser, "The Legal Framework," 121-22.
56. *China Daily*, Oct. 14, 1986, 2.
57. *Intertrade Supplement*, Nov., 1985, 11.
58. Moser, "The Legal Framework," 129.
59. *Quarterly Economic Review of China, North Korea*, No. 1, 1984, 19.

60. Feng Datong, Dean of Law, Beijing University of International Business and Economics, interview, June 10, 1985.

61. Robert Taylor, Consul, Economics Section, US Consulate, Hong Kong; interview, April 3, 1987.

62. Moser, "The Legal Framework," 136.

63. *Guoji Maoyi*, No. 10, 1987, 11.

64. Chu Baotai, *Questions and Answers*, 44.

65. Dong Shizhong in *Intertrade Supplement*, Nov. 1985, 14.

66. Chu Baotai, *Questions and Answers*, 39.

67. Robert Steinseifer, Director of Industrial Engineering, Beijing Jeep; interview, Jan. 21, 1987.

68. Chu Baotai, *Questions and Answers*, 91.

69. See *Ibid.*, 90-91.

70. *Ibid.*, 85-6.

71. *Ibid.*, 88-9.

72. Dong Shizhong, *Intertrade Supplement*, Nov., 1985, 10.

73. Moser, "The Legal Framework," 107.

74. *Ibid.*, 108.

75. Dong Shizhong in *Intertrade Supplement*, Nov. 1985, 4.

76. Chu Baotai, *Questions and Answers*, 110-111.

77. *Intertrade Supplement*, Nov. 1985, 40-41. See also p. 5.

78. *Intertrade*, July, 1985, 61.

79. China International Economic Consultants, *The China Investment Guide* (London: Longman, 1984), 342.

80. Chu Baotai, *Questions and Answers*, 111.

81. Moser, "The Legal Framework," 135.

82. *The China Investment Guide*, 394.

83. "U.S.-P.R.C. Joint Ventures in China," Beijing, January, 1986 (xeroxed list prepared by US Embassy).

84. See, e.g., *The Almanac of China's Economy, 1984*, 1152- 1177.

85. *Intertrade*, Feb., 1986, 25.

86. *Intertrade Supplement*, May, 1986, 14-15.

87. Dong Shizhong in *Guoji Maoyi*; trans. *Intertrade Supplement*, Nov. 1985, 3.

88. Chu Baotai, *Questions and Answers*, 107-8.

89. *Quarterly Economic Review of China, Hong Kong, North Korea*, third quarter, 1980, 13.

90. *Ibid.*, fourth quarter, 1980, 13-14.

91. *Intertrade*, Jan., 1986, 13.

92. See *Shijie Jingji Daobao*, Dec. 31, 1984, 5; *FEER*, Dec. 20, 1984, 102-4.

93. *Renmin Ribao*, Jan. 18, 1985, 2.

94. *China Business Review*, Nov.-Dec., 1984, 14.

95. *Ibid.*, 16.

96. *The Economist*, March 12, 1988, 61-62; and *New York Times*, April 22, 1988, 4.

97. *Beijing Review*, May 2, 1988, 18ff.
98. *Beijing Review*, May 30, 1988, 42-43.
99. *Shijie Jingji Daobao*, June 1, 1987, 4.
100. *Wall Street Journal*, May 5, 1988, 20.

8

Foreign Investment Policies and Laws: Some Key Issues

How can poor, socialist China allow ostensibly autonomous, profit-oriented enterprises to operate with foreign participation, and yet hope to maintain centralized economic guidance of national resources? How can it obtain the productive training, equipment, and technology it needs from abroad, without compromising other economic aims that the state considers vital?

To try to shed some light on these questions, this chapter analyzes how the Chinese state maintained its interests with regard to two of the most sensitive issues involving foreign investment: the hiring of Chinese labor, and the repatriation abroad of profits earned in China. Once again the analysis is based largely on Chinese sources.

Policy and Law: Distinctly Separate

Besides serving as a flexible bargaining tool to use in negotiations as described in the previous chapter, the emerging body of foreign investment laws had additional functions. Law used for public relations offered conspicuous concessions to investors, some of them misleading. It also served as a signal of potential future concessions, of policy direction. Policy and law did not proceed simultaneously; sometimes experiments were made with one of the two alone. Throughout the period of the opening up policy, however, the laws were intended to convey sensitivity to foreigners' interests and an impression of underlying permanence of policy.

Law was first of all a means for the government to make conspicuous concessions to foreign investors. The Joint Venture Law of 1979, despite its ambiguities, was a bold announcement of the right of foreign businessmen to hire Chinese labor and extract profits. Subsequent laws such as the 1983 Joint Venture Implementing Regulations and the 1985

Patent Law, usually issued with a fanfare in the Chinese state press, listed numerous specific concessions to foreign interests.

Some of the fanfare was misleading. For example, the October, 1986 "Provisions for the Encouragement of Foreign Investment" declared in Article 3 that export and high-tech joint ventures were exempt from paying the state for workers' subsidies other than labor insurance, welfare, and housing support.[1] In fact, these exceptions happened to include the costliest subsidies. Another example: the State Council's regulation of January, 1986 (see Chapter Seven) stating that certain joint venture projects "may" be extended beyond 30 or 50 years. In fact, existing law had already allowed this; policy, on the other hand, strongly discouraged such contracts both before and after the State Council issued its new regulation. In such cases, law was in part public relations for foreigners, and could be used to distract from potentially awkward issues.

Law, when approved prior to actual policy changes, has been used as a signal of government intentions. In some cases laws have offered specific new concessions that might be granted investors bringing the types of capital investment China seeks at a given time. Foreign investment tax laws have served this function. Legislation approved in 1980 allowed a possible one-year tax exemption and subsequent two-year tax reduction of 50 per cent for joint ventures scheduled to operate ten years or more. Less than three years later, the length of exemption and tax reductions were extended to two and three years respectively, and the scope of *potentially* eligible firms broadened.[2] Most of these reductions are at the discretion of supervising authorities, but hint at generous treatment. A similar signal of possible generosity is the 1986 regulation that allows 30 to 50 year joint venture contracts. Although government policy continues to discourage such terms, the new law indicates willingness to compromise when necessary, even on such sensitive points as when assets must be transferred to the Chinese side.

Finally, the state has on occasion issued several provisions simultaneously to demonstrate its professed sensitivity to foreign investors' concerns. A perfect example is the "Provisions of the State Council...for the Encouragement of Foreign Investment" of October, 1986.[3] This was a melange: new concessions (tax reductions for export-oriented enterprises); promises of preference (assured water and electricity supplies); restriction of abusive land fees (specific statements of charges now written into the law); misleading concessions (exempting some joint ventures from subsidies, all except for the costliest ones); and statements of good intentions (foreign businessmen do not have to pay "unreasonable" charges). The Provisions, a mixed basket of real fruits, promises, and vague statements, served the broader purpose of indicating China's willingness to accommodate foreign investors' needs on an ostensibly point by point basis.

Just as law could anticipate or hint at future policy direction or potential flexibility, policy could itself precede legal changes. I have already given examples of policy changes that occurred under supposedly unchanging law. In some cases policy changes were followed by legal change some years later after being evaluated as successful experiments. This was the case with wholly foreign-owned ventures. The most notable of them, 3M in Shanghai, was approved in 1983, as others were being developed in Shenzhen. But the law allowing them and defining their legal rights was not passed until three years later,[4] by which time perhaps 60 of them were already in operation. The earlier policy change hinted at broader legal concessions to follow. Similarly, national policy allowing contractual joint ventures developed for nearly a decade and several thousand were actually in operation before the law governing them was finally issued in April, 1988.

Law sometimes lagged behind the direction of policy initiatives. In 1985 a private businessman in Dalian received State Council permission to form a joint venture with a Hong Kong company. Despite the economic success of this policy experiment, the government continued to discourage such arrangements.[5] They were not legalized until mid-1988, and were still strongly discouraged thereafter. In some other cases, policy was only slowly enacted into law for a different reason: the touchiness of the issue. For example, joint ventures were under government pressure to export their products from at least 1983, and this became a major sticking point with potential Japanese investors. But this policy was not embodied in legal requirements and incentives until early 1986.[6] The separateness of law and policy allows policy experiments without legal change, as well as avoidance of making controversial policies explicit in the law.

Finally, law can create an impression of firmness or permanence of policy, also useful. "Are the rights and interests of foreign investors protected by Chinese law?" asks a Chinese publication in English.[7] "Yes, of course." They are protected by Article 18 of the 1982 Constitution. "Since the Constitution is the fundamental law of the country, a constitutional guarantee for the investor's lawful rights and interests is a most effective one." Even before the flagrant violations of the Chinese Constitution by the government in suppressing peaceful demonstrations in June, 1989, that claim could have been met with skepticism. Nonetheless, this sort of reassurance is constantly issued and perhaps gives an impression of dependability and longlastingness. The broad strokes of the early joint venture legislation contained rights--such as to "remit [net profits] abroad through the Bank of China in accordance with the foreign exchange regulations..."[8]--which were never amended, but had subtle qualifications attached. Despite the consequences that would later result to foreign investments from the fine print, to have stated rights in the law made them appear fundamental and durable.

To understand either law or policy regarding foreign investment, one must study both, recognizing that they are distinct. The laws have a built-in flexibility that leaves room for policy adjustments and experiments. Also, the conspicuousness and seeming clarity of law give it great public relations value that can distract from important qualifications. In the following two sections which examine labor and profit repatriation policies, therefore, law is treated as only a part of policy and politics.

Foreign Investors and Chinese Labor: Law and Policy

How free shall foreign investors be to hire, manage, pay, and in some cases dismiss Chinese workers? The emerging policy reveals three sets of interests involved: the enterprise formed with foreign capital; its Chinese employees; and the state. The state has put limits, in the form of restrictions on hiring, discipline, and wage payments, on the foreigner's capacity to manage labor independently.

The government tries to satisfy foreign investors' labor needs, but does not allow a free labor market. It restricts the mobility of Chinese workers and keeps a lid on the wage differences among various enterprises. The cost of such policies is to deter some foreign investors from bringing more capital to China instead of its more flexible Asian competitors. The restrictions do, however, prevent the development of a home-grown elite of highly paid Chinese employees of foreign companies. The restrictions also maintain the state's prerogative to be the final arbiter in labor management decisions.

The many laws, regulations, and policy statements issued by Beijing since 1980 in general terms endorsed the principle that Chinese-for-eign joint ventures could recruit their own labor. Under the labor regulations for joint ventures issued July 26, 1980, ventures may employ workers recommended by the local government labor department or, with the consent of the same labor bureau, may recruit on their own.[9] However, on January 19, 1984, new implementing regulations on labor management made a change of emphasis in the rules about recruitment. Henceforth joint ventures must satisfy their labor needs locally, and only if that proves impossible could they recruit workers from elsewhere.[10] The new rules required each joint venture to produce a labor plan regarding recruitment, for approval by local authorities.

Subsequent regulation narrowed further the scope of foreign intrusion into the domestic labor market. The State Council issued new provisions on foreign investment in response to complaints of businessmen on October 11, 1986.[11] These only promised that joint ventures "may recruit and employ technical personnel, managerial personnel and workers in their locality." This time, no mention was made of going outside the locality to recruit skilled workers. The emphasis on local labor sources reveals concern that skilled workers and managers could begin to move around China seeking work with foreign investment ventures, upsetting the state's household registration system which maintains some regional population stability. From the state's viewpoint, orderly direction of the labor force is a higher priority than flexibility in meeting employment needs of joint ventures, which are concentrated in a few locations.

Nevertheless, China's official policy explanations fudged the issue to leave the state some flexibility in bargaining. Legal commentaries published by the Ministry of Foreign Economic Relations and Trade (Mofert) reiterated in November, 1985 that joint ventures have "full authority" to design their own labor programs--and may recruit publicly outside their localities "with the consent of state and collective enterprises."[12] But this fine print means that other work units must agree to let workers go, an unlikely decision if they are the skilled, dedicated types sought by joint ventures. Some Chinese work units have only agreed to let employees go after accepting payoffs of up to RMB 10,000.[13] Many others will not let their more skilled workers go at all. Furthermore, workers themselves may well hesitate before leaving the security and welfare guarantees inherent in a state enterprise job, for a limited-term joint venture with far more work pressure and a wage only slightly higher. As for hiring fresh university graduates, joint ventures are encouraged instead to train their own employees whenever possible, according to the same source quoted above.

Chinese foreign investment law therefore leaves unclear how free joint ventures will be to extend their employment offerings into domestic labor markets. It fails to clarify the role of ubiquitous local labor agencies in controlling access to local and non-local labor supplies. It does not spell out under what circumstances direct, wide recruitment of skilled employees by joint ventures is possible. These ambiguities leave Chinese officials the option of relative flexibility on hiring rights in what they judge to be individually deserving cases, but in practice usually make the foreign investor dependent on his Chinese partner for most recruitment.

The hindrances to direct recruitment and pressure to hire locally aggravate two problems facing investors in China. In joint ventures, the Chinese partners frequently want to provide far more employees than the venture can use.[14] The Chinese often overlook that if the advanced technology they demand is actually supplied, and successfully utilized, even more workers in those factories will eventually be made redundant. The other problem is that emphasizing local recruitment sometimes makes it difficult to avoid taking on friends and relatives of the Chinese partner's staff. This extends the venture's internal structure of *guanxi* or interrelationships, complicating labor management with issues of "face" involved in promotion or discipline.

Most joint venture investors must also negotiate the role and salaries of Chinese managers. Here problems have arisen when the Chinese partner has candidates in mind, who from the foreigner's standpoint may well not be qualified.[15] The Chinese side may see this as a training opportunity, yet still demand salaries equivalent to those of expatriate executives: And the quality of Chinese managers is crucial. After negotiation and start-up, some joint venturers have found that foreign managers are so heavily outnumbered that they only play an overall guiding role. AMC-Beijing Jeep, for example, in 1987 had eight foreigners working in a venture employing over 4,000 local workers. None of the foreigners could speak Chinese. This would make it difficult to fulfill the confident prediction of an AMC executive when the project started up that "Basically, we will run the plant."[16]

Yet Chinese managers often cannot make a full commitment to a joint venture. The reason was pointed out in a Chinese report in late 1987.[17] A joint venture's Chinese managers are often transferred in by the Chinese partner or some other unit with which it has connections. The manager's original work unit often remains his formal employer, and it retains control over his rank, wages, promotion, and housing. Managers in such cases are afraid of "attack from the rear" if they make decisions at the joint venture that are unpopular with their true employers in the original unit. On occasion they have been abruptly transferred back out of joint ventures against the wishes of the Chinese-foreign Board of Directors, an action since prohibited. The 1987 report just cited called for further legal guarantees that would assure a joint venture Board's right to hire its own managers. Even that might not solve the problem, since many Chinese Board members are themselves employees of other work units, and do not necessarily perceive a strong connection between the joint venture and their personal welfare.

Specific hiring and dismissal actions involve more than a simple reading of the law would lead one to suppose. One of the innovations of foreign investment law from normal Chinese practice is that all workers are hired under contract, with at least the implication of direct accountability for their performance:

> The contract is required to contain provisions regarding employment terms, dismissal and resignation, wages, working hours, labor insurance, discipline and other matters, and must be approved by the labor management department of the local people's government where the joint venture is established. In general, the labor contract is to be signed between the joint venture and the labor unit organization established by the staff and workers of the joint venture. In small-scale joint ventures, however, the contract may be signed between the venture and workers and staff members individually.[18]

For these regulations, Chinese sources describe "small" ventures as having fewer than four hundred workers; the union provision applies to ventures larger than this.[19] However, outside the Special Economic zones, a union-signed contract has been the normal case. Intrusion of Party-controlled unions into labor bargaining with joint ventures gives the state another way to influence labor management.

Foreign investment legislation from the beginning carried a clear implication that joint ventures and other projects would have full rights to enforce standards of performance and behavior on workers. The second article of the original Joint Venture Labor Management Regulations states:

> The employment, dismissal, and resignation of the staff and workers of joint ventures, and their production and work tasks, wages and awards and punishments, work schedules and holidays and paid leaves of absence..., labor discipline and other matters shall be prescribed through the signing of labor contracts.[20]

Workers have the right to resign under unspecified "special circumstances," a right they have otherwise generally lacked in China. They can also be fired for disciplinary reasons, but to do so is not simple. The Chinese venture partner (which normally has majority control of equity) must agree, a problem if, for example, the worker has relatives in its management positions. Also, the labor union can protest to the enterprise's Board of Directors; the decision must be reported to the local government labor bureau, and can be appealed to the corresponding provincial bureau, and beyond that into Chinese court.[21] These last steps are rarely necessary.

The laws therefore leave considerable potential limitation on foreign investors' rights of hire and dismissal, through the interference of various levels of government. "As a result of these provisions," concluded Michael Moser, "foreign investors have found that the dismissal of a joint venture employee is extremely difficult to enforce without the agreement of the Chinese partner."[22] This applies to both disciplinary dismissals and technology-caused redundancy layoffs: the case of Fujian Hitachi, which dismissed over one hundred workers who became redundant in 1983, being widely reported precisely because it was unusual.[23]

The scope of foreign investors' rights to hire and fire was not altered by the 1982 Regulations on Rewards and Punishments for Enterprise Staff and Workers. These provisions specified honorific rewards for aiding production, such as citations for merit or "great merit." Such rewards, and special monetary bonuses, must be recommended by the labor union.[24] The regulations also list a series of specific punishments for misbehavior, from warnings to dismissal with one month's notice. The regulations reiterate that if technological changes render workers superfluous, dismissal is allowed, provided that severance pay or other contractually specified compensation is forthcoming.[25] The legal treatment of hiring and dismissal (including the appeal process) in the Special Economic Zones follows nearly identical provisions, except that the contractual role of labor unions is entirely omitted.[26]

In principle, then, foreign investors have considerable freedom in labor management. Nor do the unions play a directly obstructive role in practice. However, the red tape involved in carrying out dismissals is one reason serious disciplinary sanctions are rare. AMC-Beijing Jeep fired only two workers out of 4,000 in three years of operation (though there were more numerous demotions and self-criticisms).[27] The limitations on discipline may save workers from exploitive labor practices; but managers are hampered in dealing with a labor force used to the tolerant treatment implied by the "iron rice bowl."

Nearly always, there is a physical proximity between an industrial joint venture and its Chinese partner's original operations, which can lead to particular problems. Typically, the less productive workers--including the old, infirm, and handicapped--are left behind at the original factory, and their dissatisfaction can become a "factor causing instability" in the neighboring joint venture (as a Chinese report put it[28]). There are plenty of opportunities for friction to arise between the two sets of workers. For example, supportive services for the joint venture (cafeterias, kindergartens, health clinics) are often provided by the original factory and its workers. With constant contact between the two units, any sense that joint venture workers are getting better working conditions leads to resentment (according to the same Chinese source). Managers of such a joint venture have to consider these reactions in making all recruitment and promotion decisions.

The complications concerning labor recruitment and management are repeated and magnified with regard to payment of wages and benefits by foreign investors and joint ventures. The issue is to what extent wages paid to Chinese workers can approach the higher levels and wider disparities that would arise in a freer labor market--rather than being filtered through state agencies so that the real payments received by workers are nearly as low as their domestic counterparts. Behind this issue are three conflicting interests. Workers hired by joint ventures want to get as high a cash payment as possible. The government wants to hold wages low, both to appeal to foreign investors and to avoid exacerbating domestic inequalities among categories of workers. The government also wants to play middleman in distributing wage payments. The foreign investor wants to pay a wage lower than he would pay elsewhere, but slightly higher than Chinese domestic wages (to attract diligent and trained workers)--and he (like the worker) wants it to be paid directly. These conflicting interests concern both the wage level, and the form of payment.

On the wage level issue, the key question is how payments will be set in relation to other East Asian (higher) and domestic (low) wages. There is much less potential dispute about wage disparities within foreign investment ventures among various levels of workers. The Chinese government is willing to accept wide inequalities of wage payments and perks *within* enterprises--witness the widespread use of Mercedes-Benz autos by cadres in Beijing, whose workers are typically paid the equivalent of $25 per month. The acceptability of internal wage disparities is enshrined in Article 93 of the Joint Venture Implementing Regulations (promulgated September 20, 1983): "The wage and incentive systems of joint ventures must comply with the principles of each according to his work and more pay for more work."[29] But concerning the wage level in comparison to foreign and domestic Chinese enterprises, the government maintains a ceiling for joint venture workers only 50 per cent higher than the equivalent wage in state enterprises.[30] (This ceiling does not apply to payment for piecework in some Guangdong Province ventures.)

The apparently simple ceiling raises an issue between the Chinese and foreign management sides: what is the "equivalent" real wage? According to a Chinese interpretation frequently advanced for purposes of negotiation,[31] it includes not only what state enterprise workers receive in cash, but also such indirect subsidies as labor insurance, medical expenses, housing costs, and so forth. If these are included in figuring the basis for workers' wages, then joint ventures pay 350 yuan per month for workers who take home typically 170 yuan. The balance goes into state- or union-run insurance and group welfare funds to provide workers with further subsidies. A similar de facto labor tax exists in the Special Economic Zones. There, the 25 per cent "labor service charge" paid by foreign investment ventures for each worker hired goes to the state to reallocate as various kinds of subsidies. Elsewhere, the foreign investor must contribute a wage to the worker, additional subsidies of sometimes twice that amount to state-run welfare funds, and in some cases annual increases of 10-15 per cent in both figures.[32]

A similar and sharper disparity of interests arises over wages to be paid Chinese managers in foreign investment ventures. In hiring them, the venture is often expected to pay wages comparable to those paid to foreign executives, although the law allows the venture's Board of Directors to decide. The better part of these exceptionally high (by Chinese standards) wages is retained by the Chinese government. In order to dodge such demands, which are of slight direct benefit to the Chinese manager himself, some foreign investors have resorted to paying foreign managers a low wage in China (the basis for equivalency), and a separate salary outside the country.[33]

Besides the basic wage paid for workers and managers, which includes a subsidy reimbursement to the state, foreign investment ventures may need to pay bonuses and other subsidies.[34] Bonuses consist of extra reward pay, usually to groups of workers. Subsidies can include housing charges, transportation allowances, labor insurance and group welfare payments (for recreational, rest and educational facilities, day care centers, etc.), and routine medical care. The foreign investor is thus contributing both to the state, in support of its welfare subsidies to ordinary Chinese workers; and to welfare funds for his own workers.

Another aspect of state involvement in labor management in relatively large foreign investment ventures is through unions which ostensibly protect workers' interests. Under the Joint Venture Implementing Regulations of September 20, 1983,[35] they sign collective labor contracts with joint ventures, can appeal disciplinary decisions, and must be given ten days' notice of firings. Their other responsibilities include promoting education of workers in both skills and discipline. Union representatives attend joint venture Board of Directors' meetings, and the same law requires the Board to "heed the opinions of the trade union" and obtain its cooperation. The union also conducts welfare, cultural, and athletic activities, in facilities provided by the joint venture through a 2 per cent surcharge on all wages paid. (These union roles are omitted in the labor provisions for ventures in the Special Economic Zones.[36])

Although the enterprise unions on paper have great significance, they are politically subordinate to the Party and government. Chinese workers under the 1982 Constitution lack the right to strike.[37] All unions are under the leadership of the national trade union federation, which is controlled by the Communist Party at both the provincial and the national level. This helps explain why in practice, many of the unions' activities consist of resolving personnel problems and encouraging smooth labor management in projects the government supports. How the Party conducts ideological supervision over both Chinese managers and union workers is known only in general. The unions themselves are in the ambiguous position of responding to workers' grievances, instructing them to follow Party policies, and solving personnel problems through "education." The unions' contractual role may diminish in importance with gradual implementation of domestic labor reforms issued in 1986 which require new workers to sign individual labor contracts with their employers. Implementation of this principle varies from place to place, with the unions continuing at least to participate in contract negotiations.[38]

National or local authorities also intervene in labor-management relations of foreign investment ventures through local government labor bureaus. For joint ventures, these are official sources of recruitment assistance in a restricted labor market, although ventures can try to hire independently. They are the initial place of appeal for workers or unions with grievances regarding disciplinary measures. In the Special Economic Zones, local labor bureaus collect the 25 per cent "service charge" for each foreign investment venture employee hired (see above).

Local labor agencies truly come into their own when "assisting" foreign companies with no mainland Chinese management participation (e.g., representative offices) to obtain essential labor. Agencies such as Beijing's Foreign Enterprise Service Company (FESCO), which is under the authority of the city's foreign affairs office, obtain workers for offices of foreign companies. These local government agencies specialize in supplying secretarial, translating, and other office staff for which they charge as much as ten times the going local wage. In 1983 the lowest-paid FESCO worker cost his employer 4,000 to 6,000 yuan per year--when the average annual urban wage was 850 yuan.[39] FESCO also makes the foreign employer pay for legal holidays; overtime; 15-day annual home leaves plus round-trip travel (a perk no other ordinary Chinese worker has); annual bonuses equal to one month's wage; up to one month sick leave per year, in addition to two weeks of "compassionate leave;" as well as disability payments normally covered by premium payments to the state monopoly People's Insurance Company of China. FESCO, not the individual worker, receives all of the wage payments and extracts a surplus of 60-80 per cent which goes to the government of Beijing. The smaller balance goes from FESCO to the worker as basic wage plus food and rent subsidies, all only marginally higher than he would get working for a Chinese enterprise. The foreign company is not informed how much money its workers are being paid by the labor agency. Local labor agencies thus put a buffer between some foreign enterprises and the domestic labor market.

In sum, foreign investors' labor management rights are limited and hedged with qualifications. In some cases, restrictions have become more severe rather than relaxing. Changes in the wording of regulations suggest that extra-local hiring as part of a search for qualified employees is frowned on. Discipline and dismissal decisions are subject to various approvals, not least of the Chinese equity partner. The state is unwilling to relinquish its middleman role in the payment of wages, generally extracting the largest cut for itself to distribute as welfare subsidies, leaving even highly skilled Chinese workers with the smaller proportion. The local labor bureaus also play a middleman role in hiring, although joint ventures can often do without them.

The intrusion of the state into labor management prevents exploitation and forestalls potentially disruptive inequalities among groups of Chinese workers. Chinese policy is not egalitarian, however. Wage differences among workers in the same enterprise (not to mention housing and transportation perks for Party cadres) are tolerated. Rather, it is the growth of a special privileged group working specifically for foreign capital that the government has prevented. However, those bearing the burden of this policy are not just foreign investors who want to hire without restriction, but also their employees, whose real incomes are severely diminished. This policy dispels tensions that might arise between groups of workers, and at the same time reasserts the state as master of the economy and disposer of Chinese labor.

Profits from Foreign Investment: Law and Policy

After the hiring of Chinese labor by foreign capitalist ventures, the most sensitive issue concerning foreign investment is how freely foreigners can produce and sell goods in the domestic market and take the net profits out. The issue is wider than repatriation of profits: it includes what rights the foreign investor has to purchase domestic raw materials; to market and sell his output; to retain and transmit profits and earnings in either nonconvertible renminbi, semi-convertible foreign exchange certificates, or convertible foreign currency; and what tax obligations the investor faces. All of these affect the real profits a foreign company may earn in compensation for the risk and cost of its initial investments of time, hard currency, personnel, technology or equipment and training.

Start with basic production inputs. As on many other points, the Chinese regulations have two sides regarding purchase of required equipment, materials, fuel, parts, transportation, etc. On the one hand, they permit joint ventures to import essential supplies duty-free. On the other, these enterprises are encouraged in written provisions of 1983 to purchase as much as possible inside China.[40] The purpose of these provisions is to get joint ventures to spend currency buying Chinese goods and thus turn convertible earnings over to state enterprises (which have exclusive rights to supply those basic goods that are under planned distribution). To encourage purchase of Chinese equipment and raw materials, joint ventures are allowed to purchase them using renminbi at the same prices as domestic manufacturers.[41] But foreign investors that need to obtain supplies of all kinds on the domestic market lack knowledge and back-door connections essential to accomplishing transactions in China. This increases their dependence on the Chinese enterprise acting as their partner, just as they are usually dependent on the partner to obtain most Chinese workers.

To import production inputs can also be problematic. Additional regulations issued April, 1984 specified which goods could be imported duty free: the original capital contributions of each side; equipment, machinery, or parts that "can not be procured in China;" and raw materials, parts, and packaging used for export production. That left open the issues of which Chinese supplies could be "guaranteed;" how broadly to define "original" investment; and how the decision whether to lift customs duties would be made.[42]

If the laws have been ambiguous about letting joint ventures spend earnings abroad on imported equipment and materials, they more clearly discourage foreign investment ventures from selling products on the domestic market. Yet this is the dream of nearly all foreign investors, who seek to use inexpensive Chinese labor to assemble consumer goods such as televisions which can then be sold to Chinese purchasers. The government urges and pressures foreign investors to help develop China's export production, and thus to enhance the state's hard currency resources. The increasing emphasis given to export orientation indicates that initial results were not satisfactory to Beijing. If even Shenzhen, next to Hong Kong, was selling 70 per cent of its output in the internal market, what were joint ventures situated in the interior likely to be trying?

The government's dilemma was built in to the basic Joint Venture Law of July, 1979. It "encouraged" ventures to export their products, but at the same time promised: "Products of the joint venture may also be distributed in the Chinese market."[43] This ambiguity allowed joint venture contracts to be signed even when the Chinese and foreign partners had conflicting aims. When American Motors Corporation joined Beijing Automotive Works to open the Beijing Jeep Corporation in 1983, AMC intended to produce up to 40,000 jeep vehicles annually for domestic sale, while the Chinese already had their sights set on highly competitive Asian export markets.[44] And when the Chinese government in the same year ordered the Fujian Hitachi Television joint venture to export half its production to protect local Chinese competitors, this demand proved so disruptive that the venture nearly halted production altogether.[45]

The 1979 Law's provisions allowing domestic sales were never revoked, but both law and policy from 1983 on established limitations. The Joint Venture Implementing Regulations of September, 1983, stated their newly restrictive scope: only "Products produced by joint ventures that China urgently needs or that China needs to import may be mainly sold on the Chinese domestic market."[46] The Regulations further specified that products normally under planned or centralized distribution should be sold to state materials or commercial departments to act as sales middlemen. This was quite a change from the 1979 Law's allowing domestic sales, period. Now, central bureaucrats could exclude a product by ruling that it was not "needed." The joint venture would then be legally obliged to export. To underscore the point, the 1983 Regulations also gave joint ventures the "right" to export their products or to entrust state Foreign Trade Corporations to do it.[47]

Chinese policy has been to encourage the export solution wherever possible. Since foreign investors can earn convertible currency only from exports, but pay some of their local expenditures in renminbi, they have realized that the key to a good joint venture contract is planning to export just enough to provide for import expenditures plus a hard currency profit.[48] Some Chinese commentary continued to assure that domestic sales could be "suitably expanded" provided products met domestic needs.[49] One source described how joint venture output would be sold domestically, where permitted: major equipment items, by state distribution units according to central plans; normal consumer goods and textiles, by state or provincial commercial units; minor consumer items, on the market through Chinese connections that the venture itself could make.[50] Since this last category hardly comprises "urgent needs," however, such sales would violate the 1983 Regulations. Therefore, the net effect of the laws and distribution policy was that the few joint venture products that could be sold domestically must be distributed by state enterprises.

The final stage in the winnowing down of foreign investors' domestic sales rights came in 1985-6, with such rights now offered as an explicit trade-off for introducing advanced technology into production. This was announced as policy a year before it became law. In January, 1985, a Mofert official explained that joint venture contracts could allow a portion of production to be sold in the domestic market provided the foreign investor supplies particularly advanced technology; or that the product is very useful in advancing domestic production; or that it can replace an item already being imported in large quantity[51] (the import substitution principle again). This was, of course, a sign of dissatisfaction with the level of technology so far obtained through foreign investment. The government now began to insist that it would not approve low-tech assembly ventures.[52]

One year after repeated official pronouncements made the "technology for market" trade-off a well established policy principle, it became law. On January 15, 1986, the State Council issued new Regulations on Joint Venture Foreign Exchange Balance, of which Article 4 stated:

> Highly sophisticated products produced with advanced technology or key technology provided by a foreign joint-venture party, or top quality products competitive in the international market, if badly in need domestically, may be given preferential treatment in the areas of the ratio of domestic sales and the time limit of domestic sales, after being determined to be up to standard by competent departments, and after being approved in accordance with examination and approval jurisdictions and examination and approval procedures stipulated by the State. Such domestic sales should be specified in contracts between producers and purchasers.[53]

In October, the State Council in the new "Provisions for the Encouragement of Foreign Investment"[54] reiterated "special preferences" that would be given foreign investment ventures whose products were mainly for export or which introduced advanced technology. These preferences included diminished land fees, priority in obtaining essential supplies, loan priority from the Bank of China, tax reductions, and others. But this time, the "technology for market" trade-off was not repeated. The government preferred to attract investors with incentives other than the domestic market.

Briefly put, access to the domestic market for joint ventures diminished from a legal right, to a limited right, to a reward granted only for introducing technology, to perhaps nothing. Of course, some shrewd venturers would find ways to dodge law and policy. Nonetheless, this policy development illustrates the rapidity with which the Chinese government attempted to respond to its realization that the domestic market was being penetrated.

An even more complicated and equally important issue was pricing of goods produced using foreign investment. Joint ventures that export their products can set their own prices; but if they sell in the interior, they are caught in the mesh of state-administered pricing. A key variable in setting prices is quality. But prices are also assigned at different stages of the distribution process. As a Chinese source summarizes: "An [industrial] product is usually assigned a factory price, an allocation price, a wholesale price, and a retail price."[55] Prices set for joint venture products must follow domestic Chinese price-setting procedures unless specifically exempted from doing so by the state Price Administration Office authorities.[56] This means that whatever portion of output is finally allowed into the domestic market usually has the most crucial variable affecting its sales--price--determined by government agencies rather than by the venture itself. The state will decide whether the venture can charge a market price. A more effective lever of influence over domestic sales could not be imagined.

The greatest hindrance to penetration of the Chinese market by foreign investment ventures, however, is neither importing inputs, nor pricing goods, nor even finding ways to sell in the domestic market. The most crucial barrier is currency nonconvertibility, which blocks the removal of most profits earned inside the country.

Repatriation of foreign investment profits is a clearly stated privilege under the Joint Venture Law of 1979 and later legislation. Article 10 of the Law states:

> The net profit that a foreign joint venture receives after fulfilling its obligations under the laws and the agreement and the contract, the funds it receives at the time of the joint venture's scheduled expiration or early termination, and its other funds may be remitted abroad through the Bank of China *in accordance with the foreign exchange regulations* and in the currency specified in the joint venture contract.
>
> A foreign joint venture shall be encouraged to deposit in the Bank of China foreign exchange that it is entitled to remit abroad.[57]

The key words are those I have underlined above. That provision was in essence repeated in the Interim Foreign Exchange Regulations issued December 18, 1980,[58] which added a requirement that joint venture foreign exchange remittances must be approved by the State General Administration of Exchange Control (or its branch office). This established the procedure as a formal and routine matter.

In the earliest foreign investment legislation, then, was embedded the "foreign exchange balance requirement," as it later became known: foreign exchange expenses must be paid for out of foreign exchange earnings, because the domestic currency (renminbi) is nonconvertible. Renminbi profits in the domestic market can not be converted into foreign exchange to be repatriated, except by special and rarely granted permission. But many foreign investment ventures which have to bring in foreign technology, staff, and workers have been unable to earn sufficient foreign exchange from export sales to cover hard currency expenses. They run foreign exchange deficits which cannot be rectified using renminbi profits.

Regulations issued in 1983 reemphasized the foreign exchange balance requirement. They made the requirement explicit but allowed that in certain cases, if a joint venture contract allowed domestic sales, its foreign exchange needs could be met by local or provincial subsidies. If not in the contract, Mofert and the State Planning Commission must approve these foreign exchange subsidies.[59] Such approvals have been rare.

It is true that goods for Chinese consumption produced by foreign investment ventures that substitute for imports can earn hard currency payment. But they have to be competitive with imported foreign goods in terms of price and quality, which is just as difficult as producing competitive export goods--due to the same restrictions of infrastructure, input supplies, labor recruitment, etc. In any case, government regulations envision import substitution as only a temporary means of relieving the foreign exchange burden of joint ventures.[60] Approval of the procedure is far from automatic.[61]

Another possible method for foreign investment ventures to raise foreign exchange is to use their domestic renminbi earnings to purchase Chinese export goods for overseas sale. This method, allowed only as a temporary relief to some noncommercial ventures since 1986, is also unlikely to solve the problem. It has several limitations.[62] If a Chinese export product is truly competitive, its producer or supervising bureaucrats may well resist selling it to a foreign investor for mere domestic currency. Furthermore, for such deals it is often necessary to find an export product from the same locality and organization as the foreign investment enterprise itself. And the export product involved may be one in which the foreign investor has no sales expertise. In effect, a wise foreign investor has to plan the feasibility of such an arrangement before he completes joint venture negotiations. And advance planning of foreign exchange earnings and expenditures (as a Chinese analysis noted[63]) has proven very difficult.

The Chinese government became aware as early as 1983 that joint ventures were not doing much to increase either the country's export sales[64] or their own hard currency purchasing capabilities. Still the government held firm: even such an important joint venture as AMC-Beijing Jeep was only allowed to repatriate the small proportion of profits that came from export sales. AMC accepted this condition despite intending to aim sales at the domestic market. Its local earnings could only be reinvested to increase the AMC equity stake up to 40 per cent, or used to buy exportable Chinese goods in barter.[65]

In 1986 another ostensible government concession distracted from the firmly restated foreign exchange balance requirement. During January of that year the State Council issued more rules intended (as Beijing's *China Daily* put it) to "beat the currency problem."[66] The State Council's solution could be described as robbing Peter to pay Paul. The new measures allowed five methods to alleviate foreign investors' shortage of convertible currency:

1. Chinese national or local bureaus could draw on reserves of joint ventures with foreign currency surpluses to compensate deficits of other ventures under their jurisdictions. (Problem: there were too few surplus-earning joint ventures to draw from.)

2. Joint ventures could sell production (not consumer) goods to Chinese units as import substitutes, and be remunerated in foreign exchange--provided local or national authorities approved. (Problem: at the time these rules were issued, Chinese units were under strict limits in spending foreign exchange that had shrunk too rapidly.)

3. Joint ventures that bring in "high technology" (not defined in the regulations) might get higher quotas of domestic sales "with the ap proval of the authorities concerned." (Problem: such domestic sales would not relieve their foreign exchange shortage.)

4. Joint ventures could trade renminbi earnings with Chinese units for exportable goods that could earn hard currency. (Problem: requires the foreign investor to have sales expertise in a product different from what he produces in China. Makes foreign investor act as a trading company.)

5. Foreign investors could establish two or more joint ventures to pool their foreign exchange resources and meet expenses.

The fifth solution requires at least one joint venture to earn such a surplus of foreign exchange profits that it can subsidize others. This means that profitable ventures should share their only usable net earnings among unrelated, unprofitable ventures. The problem here is that there have not been enough profitable ventures, especially outside the tourist and commercial sectors. These sectors are susceptible both to changes in demand and to shifts in government policy towards nonindustrial foreign investment.

Above all, why should the few profitable ventures share their hard currency surpluses with other ones that are in deficit, unless they are compensated with a financial premium? And indeed, beginning in 1986 some Chinese localities began to allow currency trading at rates different from those legally established in Beijing. During that year foreign exchange buyers and sellers (at first including only domestic, but later some foreign investors) could meet at an official "Foreign Exchange Adjustment Center" and trade renminbi for dollars at rates up to Rmb 4.2:US $1. When traders were reluctant to sell foreign exchange even with this premium, the ceiling was raised to Rmb 5:US $1 (versus the official rate of Rmb 3.71:US $1) in July, 1986.[67] In November, Shanghai followed suit. Its Center of the same name was run by the State Administration of Exchange Control, rather than the People's Bank of China as in Shenzhen. The Shanghai Center only allowed local foreign investment ventures to trade, once a week. It set a ceiling of Rmb 4.72:US $1.[68] These Centers, of course, could not avoid maintaining the high price of hard currency. They allowed market forces to push exchange rates close to those in the black markets. A manufacturer with domestic currency would face an added cost of 25 to 50 per cent or more for any purchases that required hard currency. Clearly the new foreign exchange markets would only work if the profitable joint ventures were paid a substantial premium for sharing their hard currency surpluses--or if these ventures faced government pressure to do so.

As for obtaining state foreign exchange subsidies by special permission, a Mofert publication summed up the prospects: "The Chinese Government will usually not provide foreign exchange subsidies."[69] The October, 1986 "Provisions to Encourage Foreign Investment" made no major change in the foreign exchange balance requirement. By that time, most manufacturing joint ventures in the major coastal cities of China were running foreign exchange deficits.[70]

In effect, then, the foreign investor's right to repatriate profits from domestic sales applies only to sales in a small part of the domestic market: namely to those Chinese enterprises and units with hard currency, who are authorized to spend it. The 1986 regulations imply that Chinese enterprises will be allowed to spend hard currency on joint venture products only if doing so diminishes the volume of their otherwise imported equipment purchases. Currency nonconvertibility goes hand in hand with the import substitution policy.

In case the foreign exchange balance requirement and other hindrances to profit repatriation are insufficient deterrents to foreign investors trying to penetrate the domestic market, most foreign investment ventures must pay a ten per cent tax on all goods they sell in China. This is the Consolidated Industrial and Commercial Tax, an internal Chinese transfer tax first introduced in 1958.[71] It is a domestic sales tax paid by the seller.

If the foreign partner of an investment project does despite all of the above seek to remit profits from any of his operations (including exports) out of China, he must first submit profit distribution and tax records to the Bank of China. Often, he must then pay a 10 per cent remittance tax to the Chinese government (see exceptions below).[72] One wonders how much revenue could possibly be derived from this particular tax, given that by 1988 only one third of all foreign investment ventures were making profits.[73]

Table 8-1

Tax Rates for Foreign Investment Projects by Type of Zone, 1985

	Standard Rate	Coastal Cities & Coastal Economic Zones	Coastal City Development Zones	SEZs
Income Tax	30% (joint ventures) 20-40% (foreign companies)	24%*	15%	15%
Local Income Tax	10% of above	10% of above	10% of above	exempt
Ind. & Commercial Consolidated Tax	10% (on domestic sales) exempt (on exports)	no change	no change	no change
Repatriation Tax	10%	10%	exempt	exempt

*Subject to approval of Ministry of Finance, de facto 24% rate on most industrial projects, as well as agriculture, aquaculture, forestry, and related processing industries.

SOURCE: *Intertrade Supplement*, Nov., 1985, 28.

A brief look at other tax terms faced by foreign investors in China reveals that the state is using tax policy as a bargaining chip to try to obtain productive industrial and technological investment, especially for showcase zones such as Shenzhen. Foreign investors are liable for taxes in the following categories: Consolidated Industrial and Commercial Tax; income tax on joint venture profits; individual income taxes; real estate taxes; car and vessel taxes; income tax on non-joint venture foreign enterprises; and customs duties on any goods not part of joint venture investment.[74] However, some rate reductions are offered to joint ventures. For example, income taxes are exempted or reduced for "high-tech" or export-oriented operations (see table below). The problem is that those investments China most wants are the least likely to be attractive to the foreign side, since they involve heavy commitments without promise of success in earning hard currency. Therefore, such tax breaks may mean little. And there is always the tendency to take a little more in taxes. For example, several welfare subsidy contributions required of joint ventures are not deducted from their incomes before calculating profit taxes.[75] This undercuts the effect of reduced tax rates. The special tax reductions to foreign investment enterprises in effect since 1985 indicate the government's priorities for types of projects. Table 8-1 presents a summary of rates by type of zone. Tax reductions similar to those originally offered by the prominent Special Economic Zones have been granted to the kinds of ventures China most wants to attract:[76]

Type of Enterprise	Tax Concession
low-profit industries, at least 10 year venture (farming, forestry, deep coal mining)	tax exemption, first profitable year 50% tax reduction, second profitable year possible 15-30% reduction up to 10 years (Min. of Finance approves)
enterprises exporting 70% or more of products by value	income tax reduced by one half after exemption period
"technologically advanced enterprises"	income tax reduced by one half for three years after exemption period
export and high-tech enterprises; enterprises in open city development areas and SEZs	exemption from profit repatriation tax
projects in open cities with over US $30 million in investment *and* advanced technology that need long time to recoup investment	15% state income tax rate
projects in open cities that develop key industries (e.g., machine building, electronics, metallurgy)	20% discount off state income tax rates
all enterprises in open cities (including development areas) and SEZs	reduction or exemption from local income tax (city government decides)
enterprises in open city development areas	15% state income tax; up to two years' tax exemption and

	three years' 50% reduction of income tax after that (city tax bureau approves)
SEZ enterprises in sectors other than tourism and commerce, over 10 years' duration	up to two-year income tax exemption; three-year 50% reduction after then (local tax bureau approves)
SEZ enterprises in service trades with over US $5 million investment planned for over ten years	up to one-year income tax exemption; two-year 50% reduction after that (local tax bureau approves)

Tax concessions are concentrated in development zones and the SEZs; and are granted to projects involving high technology, large industrial development, or export production.

The tax treatment varies also among types of foreign investment projects. Contractual joint ventures pay taxes separately based on profits distributed to the two partners, and pay no repatriation tax. Equity joint ventures, on the other hand, pay the taxes listed above based on income to the project as a whole entity.[77] For other types of foreign investment ventures, such as compensation trade, a variety of tax regimes and conditions apply. These depend on such variables as whether the venture is classified as a resident "establishment" (therefore liable to income tax rates similar to those listed above); the location; length of operation; and whether or not products are exported, and production is "high tech".[78]

An independent joint venture would seek to minimize its tax burden, and this could be a source of differences between Chinese and foreign equity partners. The former are state enterprises ostensibly dedicated to maximizing state income. However, this type of dispute seems not to have arisen. Apparently the Chinese partners quite agree to avoid their country's taxes where legal--and this is one reason why they are typically suspected by supervising Chinese authorities of putting the joint venture's interests ahead of those of the state.[79]

The fundamental principles of foreign investment regulation described above apply throughout China. Regional differences that became more pronounced after 1983 concerned mostly speed of approvals, administrative will and ability to carry out commitments to back up joint ventures, and of course local economic conditions. The variations among areas are important, but should not obscure basic conditions established by national law and policy.

The legal provisions of the relatively liberal Special Economic Zones, for example, are not fundamentally different from the rest of the country with regard to foreign exchange balance, profit repatriation, and related issues. Tax terms in the Zones are relatively generous, with income taxes for foreign investment enterprises set at 15 per cent, and profit repatriation taxes waived. (These terms have been extended to some other coastal city development zones[80]). On the other hand, Shenzhen's regulations are relatively strict on some points, such as the possibility of relying on international arbitration to resolve disputes.[81]

Chinese foreign investment laws reserve clear roles for state enterprises and thereby guarantee them lucrative business. Under the 1980 Exchange Control Regulations,[82] foreign investment ventures must deposit domestic and foreign hard currency earnings into the state-run Bank of China. By 1983 they were allowed to keep some hard currency deposits in foreign banks, with state permission. Still, they must apply to the Bank of China to remit any net profits abroad.[83] To require dealings with the state bank builds up its experience, assets, and future capacity to compete with foreign banks. (The state Bank of China handles foreign exchange deposit accounts and loans; not to be confused with the People's Bank of China which is the financial regulator, issuer of currencies and central bank.)[84]

A prominent regulatory role in these matters is assigned to the State General Administration on Exchange Control.[85] All foreign investment ventures must submit to it regular foreign exchange account reports; apply to it to transfer capital assets (as opposed to net profits) abroad; and must ultimately wind up operations and phase out foreign capital involvement under its supervision.[86] The Exchange Control Administration's roles therefore go beyond foreign exchange control and enforcement of official exchange rates and currency nonconvertiblity. In carrying out its regulatory duties, the Administration is under State Council authority, though it also has close ties with the Bank of China.[87]

* * *

Knowing all the restrictions, why do foreign investors come to China? Some earn nonconvertible currency with the hope of building long-term market share in a less restrictive environment in the future. Others set up joint ventures in hopes of developing goodwill and thus promoting sales to China, though they would scarcely admit this motivation. The most prudent foreign investors are those who identify a specific market niche for export products that can be assembled by a low-skilled labor force using foreign equipment, semi-finished components and local raw materials. The shrewdest simply try to avoid the regulations, particularly in the grey markets of the greater Hong Kong region. All foreign investment in China depends on hope that the environment will improve.

From the Chinese perspective, currency nonconvertibility has three relevant advantages. First, it protects Chinese sovereignty over the domestic market, preventing an accelerating erosion of the stability associated with state economic controls. Second, the foreign exchange balance requirement, by deterring or preventing foreign investors from penetrating the domestic market, protects existing state industries whether developing or simply inefficient from potentially devastating competition of foreign-run operations. Third, the government with the various limitations on domestic sales and operations keeps the right to compromise, in effect giving itself a set of invaluable bargaining chips to deal with capitalists who are often willing to bend when tempted with the China market. A restrictive policy is therefore preferable to Beijing even when the government knows that some major potential investors are shying away from China altogether in favor of other countries.

The familiar issue underlying the thorny question of foreign exchange balance is whether a foreign investor can sell goods he produces inside China for profits he can send home. Undoubtedly, some foreign investors have found ways to do so, whether by special exception, hard bargaining, offering goods in return, or evasion. But the nonconvertibility of the renminbi has remained a formidable barrier for most. Complemented by qualifications, restrictions, and administrative loopholes in most of the enacted laws, it gives the state formidable bargaining leverage in extracting productive goods from its capitalist suitors. However, the signs of disappointingly limited technology transfer occurring through foreign investment indicate that the government may have gone too far. Its concern with sovereign control has hampered attraction of the kinds of investment it most sought. State interests, including those of state enterprises, have been well protected--but China's rapid productive development may have suffered.

Notes

1. *China Daily*, Oct. 14, 1986, 2.
2. *Quarterly Economic Review of China, Hong Kong, North Korea*, fourth quarter, 1980, 14; *Quarterly Economic Review of China, North Korea*, second quarter, 1983, 17.
3. *China Daily*, Oct. 14, 1986, 2.
4. *Quarterly Economic Review of China, North Korea*, first quarter, 1984, 19; Ji Chongwei, State Council Economic Research Institute, interview, March 5, 1987.
5. *Renmin Ribao*, April 17, 1985, 2; Chu Baotai, *Foreign Investment in China, Questions and Answers* (Beijing: Foreign Languages Press, 1986), 41-2.
6. *Quarterly Economic Review of China, North Korea*, second quarter, 1983, 16-17; *Intertrade*, Jan., 1986, 16; *Intertrade Supplement*, May 1986, 11.
7. Chu Baotai, *Questions and Answers*, 8.

8. *Ibid.*, 119-120.

9. *China's Foreign Economic Legislation, Vol. 1* (Beijing: Foreign Languages Press, 1982), 21.

10. Michael J. Moser, "Foreign Investment in China: The Legal Framework," in Moser, ed., *Foreign Trade, Investment, and the Law in the PRC* (Hong Kong: Oxford University Press, 1984), 128.

11. *China Daily*, Oct. 14, 1986, 2.

12. *Intertrade Supplement* (translated from Beijing *Guoji Maoyi*), Nov., 1985, 13.

13. Jamie P. Horsely, "The Chinese Workforce," *China Business Review*, May-June, 1988, 51.

14. Lois Tretiak, Vice President, Business International/ Asia Pacific; interview, April 14, 1987.

15. Robert Taylor, Consul, US Consulate, Hong Kong; interview, April 3, 1987.

16. Robert Steinseifer, AMC-Beijing Jeep; interview, Jan. 21, 1987. AMC executive quoted in Bruce Cumings, "The Political Economy of China's Turn Outward," in Samuel S. Kim, ed., *China and the World* (Boulder and London: Westview, 1984), 247.

17. *Guoji Jingjifa Yanjiu*, No. 4, 1987, 32-33.

18. Moser, "Foreign Investment," 126.

19. Wang Yihe and others, *Zhongwai Hezi Jingying Qiye* (Shanghai: Social Science Academy Publishers, 1984), 302-4.

20. *China's Foreign Economic Legislation, Vol. 1*, 20.

21. *Ibid.*, 23. See also Moser, "Foreign Investment in China," 128.

22. Moser, "Foreign Investment," 127.

23. *China Business Review*, Sept.-Oct., 1983, 27.

24. Jamie P. Horsely, "Chinese Labor," in *China Business Review*, May-June, 1984, 24.

25. *Ibid.* More recent regulations repeat these provisions. See State Council Provisions on Foreign Investment promulgated Oct. 11, 1986. *China Daily*, Oct. 14, 1986, 2.

26. See SEZ Interim Labor and Wage Management Provisions, promulgated Dec. 24, 1981. *Foreign Economic Legislation*, 223-4, 226-7.

27. Robert Steinseifer, AMC-Beijing Jeep; interview, Jan. 21, 1987.

28. *Shijie Jingji Daobao*, July 20, 1987, 2.

29. China International Economic Consultants, *The China Investment Guide 1984/85* (London: Longman, 1984), 393.

30. *Foreign Economic Legislation*, 22.

31. Horsely, "Chinese Labor," 18-19.

32. *Ibid.* See also Horsely, "The Chinese Workforce," 54-55.

33. *China Business Review*, Sept.-Oct., 1983, 27.

34. Horsely, "Chinese Labor," 19-21.

35. China International Economic Consultants, *The China Investment Guide* (London: Longman, 1984), 394.

36. *Ibid.,* 521-2.

37. Horsely, "Chinese Labor," 23.

38. Horsely, "The Chinese Workforce," 50.

39. Horsely, "Chinese Labor," 22.

40. See *China Investment Guide,* 389.

41. Chu Baotai and Dong Weiyuan, *Zenyang Juban Zhongwai Hezi Jingying Qiye* (Beijing: Zhishi Chubanshe, 1986), 244-5.

42. *China Investment Guide,* 476.

43. Articles 8 and 9. *Foreign Economic Legislation,* 5.

44. *Quarterly Economic Review of China, North Korea,* No. 2, 1983, 16.

45. *Ibid.,* 16-17.

46. Article 61. *China Investment Guide,* 389.

47. *Ibid.,* 389-390.

48. *China Business Review,* Sept.-Oct., 1983, 28.

49. Wang Yihe, *Zhongwai Hezi Qiye,* 119-120.

50. *Ibid.,* 265-6.

51. Wei Yuming of Foreign Investment Department, Mofert, interview in *Guoji Maoyi* No. 37 (Jan., 1985), 7.

52. Wu Chao, Deputy Head of the State Council Foreign Economic Research Group, *Intertrade Supplement,* May, 1986, 11.

53. Effective Feb. 1, 1986. *Shenzhen Tequ Bao,* Jan. 27, 1986, 1.

54. Promulgated Oct. 11, 1986. *China Daily,* Oct. 14, 1986, 2.

55. Dong Shizhong in *Intertrade Supplement,* Nov., 1985, 10.

56. Chu Baotai and Dong Weiyuan, *Zenyang Ban,* 188.

57. *Foreign Economic Legislation,* 5-6.

58. *Ibid.,* 126.

59. *China Investment Guide,* 391-2.

60. Lucille A. Baralle, "China's Investment Implementing Regulations," *China Business Review,* March-April, 1988, 22-23.

61. Note the pleas by the Chinese manager of a motorcycle manufacturing joint venture reported in *Guoji Maoyi,* No. 4, 1987, 42.

62. John Frisbie, "Balancing Foreign Exchange," *China Business Review,* March-April, 1988, 28. See also *Guoji Maoyi,* No. 4, 1987, 33-37.

63. *Guoji Maoyi,* No. 11, 1987, 25-27.

64. *China Business Review,* Sept.-Oct., 1983, 28.

65. *Quarterly Economic Review of China, North Korea,* No. 2, 1983, 16-17.

66. *China Daily,* Jan. 21, 1986, 1.

67. *Business China,* Aug. 25, 1986, 121-2.

68. *Business China,* Nov. 24, 1986, 171-174.

69. Dong Shizhong in *Guoji Maoyi*; trans. *Intertrade Supplement*, Nov., 1985, 11.

70. Chu Baotai of Mofert in *Guoji Maoyi*; trans. *Intertrade*, March, 1986, 46. See "Provisions" in *China Daily*, Oct. 14, 1986, 2.

71. Hu Zhixin, Director, Treaty and Law Department, Ministry of Finance, in *Guoji Maoyi*; trans. *Intertrade Supplement*, Nov., 1985, 36. Another Chinese authority, Dong Shizhong, says the tax was introduced only by January 1, 1973. *Ibid.*, 8.

72. *Ibid.*, 28, 32.

73. *FEER*, March 24, 1988, 78.

74. Chu Baotai, *Questions and Answers*, 62-66.

75. Dong Shizhong, *Intertrade Supplement*, Nov., 1985, 9.

76. *Ibid.*, 33-37; *China Daily*, Oct. 14, 1986, 2.

77. Moser, "Foreign Investment in China," 114.

78. For a detailed but slightly dated legal description, see Timothy A. Gelatt and Richard D. Pomp, "China's Tax System: An Overview and Transactional Analysis," in Moser, ed., *Foreign Trade, Investment and the Law*, 36-83.

79. *Shijie Jingji Daobao*, July 20, 1987, 2.

80. *Intertrade Supplement*, Nov., 1985, 28.

81. *China Investment Guide*, 537-8.

82. PRC Provisional Exchange Control Regulations, promulgated Dec. 18, 1980, Article 22; *China Investment Guide*, 491-2.

83. Article 24, *Ibid.*

84. For a very clear explanation see Franklin D. Chu, "Banking and Finance in the China Trade," in Moser, ed., *Foreign Trade, Investment and the Law*, 229-266.

85. See *China Investment Guide*, 489-511 passim; esp. 491-2.

86. PRC Provisional Exchange Control Regulations, Articles 22, 24, 26; *Ibid.*, 491-2.

87. Chu, "Banking and Finance," 240.

9

Economic Results of Foreign Investment Policy

The Chinese government has used policy and law to bargain and bluff foreign investors into providing contract terms favorable to China's interests. But the interests so promoted are those of the Chinese state, not always Chinese workers. Some Chinese workers and managers benefit from foreign investment, others do not. Neither workers as a whole nor those employed by foreign investment ventures have a complete correspondence of interests with the state as it tries to build up its stock of capital and technology. Workers in China's poorer regions fall further behind, relatively, as the government promotes investment in already built-up coastal cities. Workers in foreign investment ventures have potential incomes reduced by state wage restrictions and de facto labor taxes.

The study of policy and law in the previous chapter suggests these points, but they cannot be demonstrated without a look at economic results. Unfortunately, a definitive analysis is out of the question at present for three reasons. First, China's foreign investment policy is only a decade old and is constantly changing. Conclusions about economic results are therefore premature. Second, many Chinese statistics are unreliable. Sources such as foreign trade almanacs are typically compilations of reporting by provincial and local trade officials trying to throw a rosy light on results. There is no independent verification, only that by central officials. For example, the provinces boast of their "pledged" investment, and one has to scrutinize their reports carefully to find the much lower level of real foreign investment--if it is reported at all.

The third problem with looking at economic results is one of method. Since Hobson and Lenin, Western academics have been debating whether the effects of foreign investment on underdeveloped host countries are benign or harmful. However, as Thomas Biersteker noticed in his summary of issues in this debate,[1] each side depends partly on arguing what would have been the case if foreign investment had not been there. Proponents argue that the alternative is inefficient socialism, or unde-

veloped productive capacity. Critics insist that instead of foreign investment, national or local control of production would ensure wider distribution of benefits, more indigenous development, and better integration of
economic sectors. Of course, no one can prove what "would have"
happened in China with different policies.

For these reasons, the conclusions of this chapter on the economic
results of foreign investment in China cannot be definitive. Still, the
evidence presented here does allow some significant observations. The
results of foreign investment in China indicate that many of the fears of
Western Marxist critics of multinational corporations do not apply there,
because the state has effectively intervened to protect perceived national
interests. However, by some economic indicators such as the overall
direction of capital investment and the extent of technology transfer, the
net benefits to China have been ambiguous. This is because foreign investors have limited incentive to make major commitments in China; and
when they do invest, restrictive policies and red tape hinder efficient
production of export goods that could earn the hard currency profits both
sides desire. That remained true even during phases of relatively relaxed
central government control.

Foreign Investment: Volume, Distribution, Quality

The volume of investment attracted to China has been considerable. From 1979 through 1987, China received about $8.47 billion from
direct foreign investment in more than 4,000 joint ventures of various
kinds.[2] Considering the underdeveloped state of China's economy, in per
capita terms one of the poorest in the world, this was an achievement.
China became a full-fledged competitor with its neighbors for foreign
capital:

Table 9-1

Direct Foreign Investment, 1985

	Total, of which:	Manufacturing
China	US $ 1.96 bn	(unavailable)
Hong Kong	$ 3.21 bn	$ 1.52 bn
Taiwan	$ 701 m	$ 439 m

SOURCE: *Almanac of China's Foreign Economic Relations and Trade,
1986*, 702, 743, 1212.

China has not only attained a volume of foreign investment that makes it a major competitor with other Asian states, it has also diversified its sources of foreign capital. Although China still depends most on Hong Kong, it has also obtained substantial capital investment from the United States, Japan and Western Europe. In 1986 the proportions stood as indicated in Table 9-2.

Table 9-2

Sources of Real Direct Foreign Investment, 1986

Real	Proportion of Investment	Year's Total
Hong Kong	US $1,132 m	60 %
United States	$ 315 m	17 %
Japan	$ 201 m	11 %
Britain	$ 27 m	1.4%
France	$ 42 m	2.3%
West Germany	$ 19 m	1.0%

SOURCE: *Almanac of China's Foreign Economic Relations and Trade, 1987*, 619. Percentages rounded.

To have a number of competing bidders works to the advantage of China, which can play them off against one another and sometimes obtain bargains. An unusual but classic case in point was when in 1985 the British rock group "Wham" paid the Chinese government 300,000 pounds ($362,000) cash to give a concert in Beijing. "Wham's concert [was] described as a 'coup' by the group's promoters because they beat other groups to it."[3] "Wham" never returned. Although foreign investors may not be as charitable, they are under similar pressures to precede their competitors into China (and they face much higher costs to operate there). Potential investors now include the Soviet Union. Officials in Mofert observe that Russia possesses technical strength in industries such as energy, transport, and raw materials production which are priorities for renovation in China.[4] Soviet-Chinese industrial joint ventures would be welcomed by Beijing.[5]

Now let us turn from the volume and sources of foreign investment to its quality and usefulness to China. Does foreign investment displace potential indigenous production, as Western neo-Marxists charge?[6] According to scholars critical of capitalist investment in poor countries, multinational corporations typically buy out local enterprises, especially import-substituting ones; use their superiority in scale and technology to compete with local production; and attract skilled workers and managers away from local firms by offering them higher wage scales. These alleged tendencies would stunt local entrepreneurism and weaken the potential economic capacities of the host state for indigenous development.

If these effects were present in China, one would certainly expect Chinese spokesmen to join the chorus of denunciation. They are, after all, ostensibly Marxists and have written explicit enumerations of the dangers of capitalism. However, displacement of Chinese entrepreneurship and productivity is not an issue they have raised about the foreign investment China has accepted.

On the contrary, spokesmen for the state's industrial ministries vie with each other in their optimistic plans for beneficial use of foreign capital. In the oil industry, "the whole industry from exploration to refining is being technologically upgraded," largely through foreign investment, with expectations of rapidly increasing output and income.[7] In the chemical industry, China is seeking American investment and patent sales to build up "underdeveloped" areas of production for export.[8] In machine building, the state is concentrating on technology transfer, software, and imports of key instruments and equipment, as well as co-production agreements--all intended to foster growth in export industries.[9] In energy production, the Chinese have already obtained or are seeking American, Swiss, and Soviet involvement in large projects in at least seven provinces.[10] And in another crucial sector: "China's Ministry of Metallurgical Industry has worked out a plan to use foreign funds to transform China's iron and steel enterprises."[11] These plans hardly reflect fear that foreign capitalism will displace local production. Even the Ministry of Railroads is hoping to attract foreign investment to extend and develop the nation's heavily overburdened railroad network.[12]

Such are the plans for the future. The reality is more mixed. One could find examples of productive capacity being greatly enhanced by foreign investment. The $650 million Pingshuo project in Shaanxi Province, a joint venture with Occidental Petroleum Corporation of the United States, promises to become one of the world's largest coal mines.[13] Foreign investment up to 1988 helped to construct electricity generation projects with a total capacity of 7.6 million kilowatts.[14] On the other hand, the three automobile production joint ventures set up by 1985 fell far short of China's announced output needs, and negotiations over further ventures were complicated by demands to increase local parts content.[15] Then there are the assembly operations, especially in Shenzhen and other parts of Guangdong Province, which mainly take advantage of cheap Chinese labor and often attempt to penetrate the domestic market. Yet even in these ventures, Chinese workers get useful experience working in enterprises sensitive to costs and profits, which emphasize labor productivity. And wealth and local jobs are created.

Neo-Marxist concerns about displacement of indigenous production are mostly irrelevant to the Chinese case. For example, the danger of multinational corporations buying out local firms, a key point for the critical school, does not exist there. The state prohibits it. Competition with domestic production, no matter what some foreign investors might wish, is certainly under control. The government has not allowed any state enterprises to be seriously threatened by such competition. Rather, foreign investment ventures that do sell in the domestic market are usually providing badly-needed consumer goods otherwise in short supply, or import substitutes. To the extent they put indirect competitive pressure on state enterprises, it might benefit them by reducing their notorious inefficiency.

As for hiring skilled workers and managers away from local firms, this is prevented by state regulations that severely constrain labor mobility. State hiring quotas for educated and skilled workers restrict joint ventures from attracting the "cream of the crop" with high wages--and wage differentials are also limited in order to forestall resentment of workers employed by foreign capital.

Another critical assertion about multinational corporations in poor countries is that they aggravate real income disparities of several kinds: between relatively skilled workers they hire, and the majority they do not employ; between urban and rural areas; and between developing and undeveloped regions. Foreign capitalism, goes the argument, uses its superior resources to offer high wages and make investment in relatively developed areas. This contributes to growth in one limited sector which becomes increasingly detached from the nation as a whole. Such a result hinders integrated economic development.

Foreign investment in China justifies some of these critical observations. The most dramatic evidence of unequal distribution concerns differences in investment levels among China's regions. These were highly unequal to start with. In 1982, according to the World Bank,[16] six of China's provinces and state municipalities had a per capita net material product of 553 to 2,490 yuan, while the bottom six all fell between zero and 314 yuan per year. Shanghai's ratio of output to population in 1982 was over eight times the level in most of China's provinces, and about three times the level of other key cities. In 1985, Gu Mu noted in *People's Daily* that the "fourteen coastal cities" have only 8 per cent of China's population but account for 23 per cent of the national volume of production.[17] This is evidence that China's industrial capacity is unequally distributed, as it always has been, especially between coast and interior.

Table 9-3

Distribution of Direct Foreign Investment by Province

US $ million

	Direct Foreign Investment Contracts:			
	1983	1984	1985	1985 per capita
Beijing Municipality	29.3 m	119 m	379 m	40.0
Tianjin Municipality	2.14 m	106 m	68.5 m	8.57
Hebei	2.58 m	11.2 m	46.2 m	0.84
Shanxi	--- .	1.11 m	2.68 m	0.10
Inner Mongolia	2.98 m	2.99 m	5.14 m	0.26
Liaoning	17.6 m	44.1 m	254 m	6.95
Jilin	0.75 m	1.37 m	18.1 m	0.79
Heilongjiang	---	5.23 m	30.1 m	0.91
Shanghai Municipality	46.0 m	431 m	771 m	64.00
Jiangsu	3.41 m	56.5 m	118 m	1.91
Zhejiang	7.39 m	31.5 m	45.4 m	1.14
Anhui	---	3.55 m	19.4 m	0.38
Fujian	39.2 m	236 m	377 m	14.10
Jiangxi	---	6.92 m	32.7 m	0.96
Shandong	21.9 m	105 m	100 m	1.31
Henan	0.05 m	5.97 m	70.7 m	0.92
Hubei	---	9.86 m	27.0 m	0.55
Hunan	---	34.6 m	26.0 m	0.47
Guangdong	581 m	1409 m	2198 m	35.65
Guangxi	16.2 m	26.7 m	226 m	5.94
Sichuan	4.57 m	28.9 m	55.7 m	0.55
Guizhou	---	2.88 m	9.78 m	0.33
Yunnan	---	1.51 m	17.5 m	0.52
Shaanxi	10.25 m	1.59 m	407 m	13.72
Gansu	---	0.32 m	4.31 m	0.21
Qinghai	---	23.5 m	0.18 m	0.04
Ningxia	---	3.0 m	2.81 m	0.69
Xinjiang	---	3.29 m	56.45 m	4.20

NOTE: In most provinces actual investment falls short of "contracted" investment provided in these Chinese government statistics. Therefore this table is useful only for comparing relative levels in provinces, not for absolute figures.

SOURCES: *Almanac of China's Foreign Economic Relations and Trade*, 1984, 1097-8; *Ibid.*, 1985, 1071; *Ibid.*, 1986, 702, 1216-1217; *Statistical Yearbook of China*, 1985, 188, 617.

It is not surprising that most foreign investment is going to China's relatively developed regions. Industrial and service ventures require infrastructure and skilled labor simply unavailable in some parts of the country. The data for a typical year in the right-hand column of Table 9-3 confirm that distribution of contracted foreign investment among China's regions is hugely unequal. (Actual investment falls short of the amount supposedly "contracted" for, but similarly so across regions. Therefore the conclusion remains.[18]) Whatever the contribution of foreign capital to Chinese productive capacity, it is adding large quantities of investment onto a regional inequality of productive capability, and aggravating it.

What about urban-rural inequality? According to World Bank estimates,[19] rural per capita income in 1982 was less than half of urban per capita income, on average. In some provinces the disparity was four to one: "Large differences in average incomes remain between urban and rural areas, especially in poorer regions."[20] Most foreign investment has occurred in cities. Of 134 US-Chinese joint ventures listed by the American Embassy in Beijing in early 1986, over 100 were located in major cities.[21] Since foreign investors have complained that infrastructure and facilities are inadequate even in the cities, they would certainly avoid rural areas except when the nature of a project requires locating there. In most cases, therefore, rural areas benefit only from an indirect "trickle down" from foreign investment after it benefits the whole economy. Meanwhile, much Chinese state investment and the growth it fosters is concentrated in the cities to match foreign capital contributions and develop necessary infrastructure.

As for inequality among workers, it is revealing what the government allows and what it does not. In the period covered in this study, it did not generally allow joint ventures and other foreign investors to pay Chinese workers a cash wage more than 50 per cent above comparable Chinese wages. On the other hand, the government left joint ventures free to determine relative wage scales within their enterprises. This permitted wide intra-firm income disparities between higher and lower level workers. Such a policy matches the situation in Chinese state enterprises, in which special privileges such as automobiles for personal use and more comfortable and spacious housing are provided managers and officials, vastly multiplying their real incomes. The government's wage policies tolerate wide differences in wage and benefit income, so long as those working in foreign investment ventures are not doing conspicuously better than other workers.

How does one assess the extent of technology and technical training provided China by corporate foreign investment? On this question the data problem becomes more serious: What is "high" technology and when is it "appropriate" for China? In addition there recurs the problem of hypothesizing: what kind of technology transfer would have been possible under different policies? The bases for serious conclusions are not now available.

Published official statistics are of little help. China has issued breakdowns of foreign investment by category,[22] which for example indicate that 37.6 per cent of 1985 foreign investment contracts by value were for industrial projects. But this does not tell us what kind of industry. There are lists of joint ventures and of technology transfer contracts, yet many of the items beg questions. Asahi Breweries provided "technological cooperation for improvement of barley quality for beer and other uses."[23] Just how is the barley changed and how much does that improve Chinese beer? Atsugi Nylon provided technology for production of pantyhose to the Shanghai Petroleum Corporation.[24] Was this technology "appropriate to China's needs" as the law requires? More tellingly, Chinese figures reveal that only 45 percent of all joint ventures approved through 1985 were "productive type" (versus hotels and other commercial ventures).[25] In 1986 that proportion increased to 76 percent but total new investment had dropped by half, so the real volume of industrial and agricultural-oriented productive direct foreign investment in fact shrank also.

Reports on foreign investment in China have mixed implications about the extent and appropriateness of technology transfer. Chinese economists have been aware since the early 1980s that some foreign investment was failing to provide much technology, but merely giving foreign companies a potential bridge to the domestic market.[26] However, other projects did expose Chinese workers and managers to advanced technology. The Shanghai Aviation Industry Corporation in early 1985 signed a licensing agreement with McDonnell Douglas to build MD-82 passenger aircraft for the Chinese state airline beginning in 1987. The planes would be assembled from kits for domestic sale rather than export, but Chinese workers and technicians would get valuable training from working on the project.[27]

There have been some clear successes for China, technological and financial. On Daya Bay near Hong Kong, China arranged for construction of a double-reactor 300 megawatt nuclear power plant by Framatome of France and Britain's General Electric. To support financing of the $3.5 billion project, the French government provided for export credits to be repaid "over 12-15 years after a six-year grace period," reported *The Economist*.[28] And the price the British finally obtained was made an official secret by London.[29] The Chinese have also cultivated potential West German and Japanese nuclear power suppliers.

Overall, however, technological results were not spectacular. During the Sixth Five-Year Plan period (1981-85), Beijing Municipality signed 276 foreign investment contracts, yet in 1986 municipal authorities could certify only twelve as "technologically advanced." Shanghai signed 354 foreign investment contracts in the same period, but in 1986 gave only 26 projects such certification.[30] Those certified become eligible for preferential treatment under 1986 regulations. (Nearly half of the projects certified in each case were United States joint ventures.) These results are not necessarily all negative for China. If the level of technology brought in is too advanced or capital intensive, the labor force and economic structure will not be able to adapt to it. An unusually frank assessment that appeared in *Shijie Jingji Daobao* in August, 1982, admitted as much: "Utilization of foreign capital and the import of technology must be in line with the rationalization of our industrial and production structure."[31] A country's ability to absorb foreign technology, the article pointed out, depends on its supporting facilities and management capabilities--not on "subjective wishes." Some Chinese realize that technology transfer must be a slow process.

Turning to the net flow of capital in or out of China as a result of foreign investment--another theme of critics who allege that capital drain is nearly inevitable--here too evidence is mixed. Foreign investors are generally cagey about profit levels in China, but few projects have been stunningly lucrative. Companies that have decided to locate in China complain of exorbitant costs. According to a survey in 1985, 86 per cent of 115 companies operating in Beijing were convinced that they were treated as if "to exact the maximum amount of money in the shortest possible time."[32] Businessmen operating in Beijing have had to live in hotels or segregated apartment blocks, paying up to $72,000 per year for an apartment (utilities extra).[33]

Even more serious for foreign investment ventures was the effect of Chinese currency nonconvertibility. Most manufacturing joint ventures through 1985 ran foreign exchange deficits.[34] A well-known case was AMC's Beijing Jeep joint venture. After two years of operation, it faced a hard currency crisis in 1985. Only after the problem was widely publicized and became the subject of high level discussions between China and the United States did the Chinese government reportedly agree to make an exception and provide US $6.9 million in exchange for domestic currency that had been earned by the company, and increase hard currency payment for future domestic sales.[35] This would cover payments for imported kits. Recognizing that similar measures might well be necessary in other cases, the government in January, 1986 issued regulations authorizing such steps when necessary.

One tendency in Chinese policy has been to take a generous approach to such hard currency shortfalls, sharing the burden where necessary in order to attract investment. This could lead to production improvements and greater export income in the long run. The other, contrary tendency has been to seek quick gains through exorbitant fees and service charges on foreign companies. Some Chinese who are not specialists in economics have thought that "...there are plentiful idle funds in all parts of the world...,"[36] and have been slow to realize that China competes with other countries for foreign capital. The fact that foreign investment rose steadily until 1986 despite all the exorbitant charges encouraged such misperceptions.

At the same time, there have been signs of a capital drain from China related to its foreign investment policies. As discussed in Chapter Three, Chinese capital has flowed to Shenzhen in response to commercial opportunities; many of the profits in Shenzhen went to Hong Kong entrepreneurs. By the nature of joint ventures, China also had to match most foreign investment contributions in other locations, predominantly in the coastal cities. This is not such a problem to the extent China's investments bring returns in hard currency. But, although detailed data are unavailable, many manufacturing ventures instead drained foreign exchange.[37]

Meanwhile, mainland Chinese investment in Hong Kong grew rapidly, with both commercial and political purposes. China became involved in major commercial, property, and infrastructure projects there, in some cases apparently sacrificing profits to build Hong Kong market share.[38]

The Hong Kong investments are indirectly related to China's domestic foreign investment policy. China still needs to reassure its business partners that their interests will be protected within the People's Republic. As China takes on greater influence in the capitalist British colony prior to assuming control in 1997, the continuing prosperity of Hong Kong becomes an obvious index of confidence in Chinese policy towards business. China's growing external investments underpin economic stability in Hong Kong and also help maintain a favorable climate of opinion about doing business with China itself. But the immediate result is a further drain of capital out of China. If this aspect is included, then there quite possibly has been a net flow of capital from state revenues not only to a few development centers but out of the country altogether.

These economic consequences are more serious for China than the social effects of foreign investment. The fears of neo-Marxist scholars that multinational corporations foster a local elite in the host country while manipulating broader consumer tastes as well, have little foundation in China--even after $8 billion in direct foreign investment. Wage differentials among enterprises are limited, but more importantly the percentage of Chinese workers hired by foreign capital remains small. According to Chinese employment statistics,[39] the total number of Chinese employees of joint ventures of all kinds has remained far below one-half of one percent of the urban workforce. These workers receive take-home pay only a fraction higher than their state enterprise counterparts. The government is aware of the envy that could be caused by allowing this difference to grow, and therefore maintains wage as well as mobility restrictions.

Foreign investors are prevented from freely hiring skilled workers and college graduates, but must apply to obtain annual quotas of them. The proportion of such workers who end up employed by foreign companies is too miniscule to form an indigenous pro-foreign elite. They are

anyway nearly all employed by Chinese-foreign joint ventures, not directly by foreign companies. There is thus little danger of skilled nationals
directly absorbing a foreign cultural perspective from their employers, as
critics of foreign investment charge.[40] It is well known that the Communist Party has run campaigns against "spiritual pollution" and "bourgeois
liberalization," which seem to reflect fears of growing foreign influence.
But these targets are diffuse political and cultural trends rather than any
ethos transmitted by multinational corporations. If anything, the Party
since 1979 has expressed admiration for capitalist work habits suggested
by its slogan "Time is Money."

    China, in sum, does not face direct threats to its social harmony, or
to the national identification of its skilled elites, from multinational corporate investment. The effective state restrictions on activities of foreign
business prevent this. The state does, however, face economic costs of
regional inequality, concentration of both domestic and foreign capital in
urban commerical sectors, and a possible net outflow of capital. In these
respects what the critics say about direct foreign investment could apply
to China.

    The costs, however, must be weighed against economic benefits to
the state. These are as yet unmeasurable. They include increased productive capacity in various sectors of the economy including mining and
manufacturing. Foreign investment has achieved some technology transfer, as the certification of ventures and expansion of the country's export
production attest. As joint ventures become increasingly export-oriented,
they will add further to the state's hard currency income and its capacity
to buy production goods. Above all, foreign investment has developed
China's human resources, as workers and hundreds of managers (albeit a
small minority) are exposed to cost- and profit-consciousness, an emphasis on efficiency, and more modern equipment. Training of at least a part
of the workforce, making adaptation to new techniques easier and faster,
is an urgent economic need for China.

Decentralization, Regionalism, and Foreign Investment in the Late 1980s

    The benefits to be had from attracting foreign investment encour-
aged the venerable Chinese tendency, already noted in Chapter Six, for
each province and locality to pursue its own advantage through *tu zhengce*
or "indigenous policies" under the leadership of its own all-powerful officials. This trend became evident during a phase of relatively relaxed
central control in 1987 and early 1988. However, even during that period,
the most important restrictions foreign investors face in China remained
intact. And furthermore, other economic conditions spawned by the
loosening of control proved unacceptable to the central government,
leading to an increasingly severe austerity program that recentralized

some controls and worsened the investment environment even before the 1989 Beijing massacre.

One sign of relaxed control was that the central government began to tolerate open competition among provinces and cities to offer themselves as partners to foreign capitalism. This is how the Deputy Mayor of the Municipality of Tianjin described several alternative locations to some potential foreign investors:

> Tianjin enjoys various advantages over other areas. Dalian, of course, is an oil center, but it suffers from chronic water shortage. The northwest region is far inland, and supplies from abroad have to come through Tianjin anyway. Shanghai's facilities are already overloaded, it has no more undeveloped industrial land nearby, and the quality of water from the Huangpu River is far from good. As regards Guangdong and Fujian, Japanese investors [the audience] may not mix too well with the large number of overseas Chinese and Hong Kong entrepreneurs already there. Water from the Pearl River is not good and transportation in inland Fujian is difficult.
> By contrast, Tianjin...[etc.][41]

The central government allowed various provinces to compete with each other not only in words but also in practical measures designed to appeal to foreign businessmen. Hebei Province, for example, enacted preferential policies to entice foreign investors to a new "Bohai Bay Open Economic Zone." There, foreigners would be allowed to "directly manage the enterprises in which they invest," and would even be permitted to "run, lease, or purchase existing state-owned or collectively owned industrial and commercial enterprises in the province."[42] Five cities in Hebei would henceforth be allowed to approve foreign investment projects valued up to US $30 million. After the setback of June 1989 it is impossible to tell what such provincial initiatives might have meant. Taken at face value, they would seem to permit businessmen from Taiwan (for example) to purchase and manage the local facilities of state enterprises for profit, in some cases without Beijing's approval. Liaoning Province announced measures nearly as sweeping for its Peninsula Economic Development Zone in 1988: new tax incentives, tariff reductions, local authority to approve many foreign investments, and 50-year land leases.[43] Other new "open" zones were established or under consideration, as discussed in Chapter Four. Here one sees the possibility of a further widening of the opening up policy (some other provinces would surely follow suit), to an extent unprecedented in the history of the PRC, *if* China's rulers in the post-Deng era embrace accelerated economic reform. The inevitable outcome would be further differentiation among the provinces in their foreign trade and investment policies.

It was precisely the increasingly obvious differences of interest and policy among provinces to which Prime Minister Li Peng was responding when he declared in September, 1988: "we must firmly do away with economic overheating....Orders must be obeyed and prohibitions observed....The principle of subordinating partial and local interests to overall interests must be followed without hesitation."[44] Few listened.

By contrast with Premier Li's call for recentralization, Party leader Zhao Ziyang three months later took the relaxation of central government controls a significant step further by abruptly announcing that wholly foreign owned enterprises should be "encouraged".[45] (Previously they had been allowed, but not particularly encouraged). The unstated reason for the change is easy to infer: during the domestic fiscal tightening that was already underway, wholly foreign investments could bring in capital and technology without requiring matching Chinese contributions. This policy experiment, however, fell victim to the tanks of Tiananmen Square in June, 1989. Its promoter, Zhao, was dismissed from his position by Deng Xiaoping, and all new foreign investment was certain to drop sharply in the aftermath of the turmoil. Still, if a reformist regime should emerge after Deng's death, this initiative could well be revived, and it would be another significant extension of China's economic opening policy.

The accelerating tendency for regions or localities to go their own ways as guided by provincial or local leaders complicated implementation of Beijing's post-1988 austerity policy, because provincial and local cadres have ties to local branches of state enterprises that want to pursue unhindered growth. These enterprises receive much of their funding from a large and increasingly well organized system of private foreign exchange traders and moneylenders over which China's central bank retains little control.[46] That, together with foreign investment has brought some spectacular results. The South Manchurian Peninsula of Liaoning Province, for example, experienced a doubling of its rate of new foreign investment contracts in the first half of 1988.[47] The province claimed to have imported technologies worth over $3.1 billion since 1979,[48] which suggests impressive achievements even when one allows for exaggeration. But it is Guangdong Province, the hinterland of Hong Kong, that is in the vanguard of these trends. Some 60 per cent of all foreign investment in China has been in that province, a fact which has helped it achieve explosive growth rates, some of the highest living standards in China, and export production roughly one fifth of China's total.[49] Residents and Party leaders in neighboring shortage-ridden provinces are resentful of the wealth and purchasing power Guangdong has developed, feeling that some special advantage must be involved other than having Hong Kong cousins and an ability to outwit bureaucrats from Beijing. Guangdong officials respond humbly that "We started from a low base, so a 30-40 per cent growth [rate] is quite normal."[50] In this heady atmosphere, the appeal of doing business with coastal China reached across the ideological barrier to Taiwan, whose businessmen in 1988 made investments of some $200 million in Guangdong and Fujian Provinces--an impressive figure in the mainland even though it was much less than Taiwanese were investing in each of four Southeast Asian countries.[51]

The extreme case of regional autonomy is Hong Kong as it prepares to return to China in 1997. It is Hong Kong's separateness and economic success under capitalism that have allowed it to become the major stimulus of regional development in neighboring Guangdong Province, and the largest foreign investor in China. Meanwhile, mainland Chinese enterprises enjoy Hong Kong's free economic atmosphere as much as ever. Their investment there, concentrated in the property market, has been estimated at US $10 billion[52]--far more than the total of all Hong Kong investment in China. Beijing is apparently incapable of exercising much discipline over the operations of its own state enterprises in Hong Kong, and probably does not even know the precise extent of their assets there.[53] In fact, mainland-controlled enterprises are the source of some one-fifth of Hong Kong's "foreign" investment into China.[54]

Despite the partial decentralization of control over the domestic economy, however, foreign investors were not able to manipulate local conditions greatly to their advantage and realize more exploitive relations with the host country. Most of the hindrances to their activity described in previous chapters remained, whether created by objective conditions or government policy. While the physical shortcomings of Chinese infrastructure and the frequent power cuts (for which no compensation is offered) hinder efficient operations, labor management remains the biggest problem. Foreign businessmen attracted by labor costs lower than those in Taiwan or South Korea discover that their biggest problem is the shortage of available skilled labor. It is difficult to recruit trained employees because they are usually already tied into the social welfare and subsidized housing system of state enterprises. Foreign investors report having to make payoffs of up to 10,000 yuan to hire such employees.[55] Regarding the attitudes of workers, there are reports of poor morale, incompetence, and leaving the job to attend lengthy but pointless meetings.[56] The Chinese vice president of one Sino-Japanese joint venture took enough time off from his duties to attend college courses and obtain a university degree.[57]

Even at the peak of decentralization, foreign invested enterprises were not given managerial autonomy in their hiring of labor. There is often pressure from the Chinese partner to cater to networks of traditional *guanxi* (interpersonal "connections") among the workers. According to one Chinese description, "...if you hire a man, you have to hire a woman [his wife or girlfriend]; if you hire the husband you have to hire the wife and even [others such as] their son, daughter-in-law, daughter, son-in-law, and his brother- and sister-in-law.... These additional people have poor vocational skills but they demand excessively high wages and benefits....

what's even worse is that there are some Chinese personnel who if they're not perfectly satisfied [that the above demands are met], just won't cooperate, and they even resist by counteracting [the factory's efforts], which makes the foreign investment project difficult to keep going."[58] Even where such pressures to hire relatives can be avoided, state labor management policies ensure that technically proficient Chinese managers in foreign invested enterprises are "[as precious and rare as] phoenix feathers and unicorn bones."[59] And if qualified managers are found, their supervisors in the Chinese bureaucracy often fail to give them operational autonomy.[60] Having unskilled workers and managers on the payroll complicates assimilation of imported production technology. According to a local official, for example, only three per cent of the equipment and technology actually brought in to Canton from abroad by mid-1987 could be "assimilated and digested." [61]

Most foreign investors believe that being able to dismiss the minority of unproductive workers would improve overall productivity, but this has not become easier to do. According to the account of a local Chinese official, when one Sino-American joint venture in Tianjin did relocate 200 of its 2,500 workers elsewhere, the venture's output actually doubled.[62] Chinese officials generally recognize this situation but remain reluctant to countenance firing workers or even to accept the use of individual labor contracts.[63]

Chinese joint venture partners that do agree to dismiss unproductive workers usually transfer them back to the partner's original operations. This is convenient because most joint ventures (especially large industrial ones) are located adjacent to or near a much older factory belonging to the Chinese partner. This type of arrangement is what Chinese and foreign pundits, in a funny play on Deng Xiaoping's "one country, two systems" slogan for Hong Kong, refer to as "one plant, two systems." Part of the humor in this expression is the hope it expresses that the relatively modern joint venture will enliven the older all-Chinese factory with its exemplary productivity. In fact, that is difficult when the latter must take on the least able and dedicated workers, pay them lower wages and provide fewer perks than the joint venture, and work with far inferior equipment. The "two systems" remain very separate and feelings between them are often far from friendly.[64]

Nor did foreign investors find that decentralization provided relief from the difficulty of earning sufficient hard currency to pay for imported inputs, as government policy requires. Alleviating this by increasing local content is hindered by the substandard quality or unavailability of locally manufactured parts, and by rapidly rising costs associated with domestic inflation. The Chinese government has also reiterated its suggestion that products of foreign investment enterprises could be sold into the domestic market as import substitutes, and be paid for in convertible or semi-convertible currency. In order to do so, however, the products must be competitive with previously purchased imported goods in terms of price

and quality--a difficult feat when the joint venture is hindered from obtaining reliable supplies of inputs. The other methods that the central
government continues to propose in order to alleviate the foreign exchange squeeze also have serious drawbacks. To use a venture's domestic
currency earnings to purchase unrelated export products forces the foreign
parent company into the role of international sales agent for items in
which it may have no expertise or sales outlets. To try to earn foreign
currency directly inside China (as opposed to making import substitute
arrangements) requires selling to the small foreign community there, most
of whose dollars go into the service sector.[65]

One indication of the extent of difficulties is that some joint ventures have found themselves dependent on--of all things--high-level
government intervention to help them survive. Special "emergency assistance" to foreign investment enterprises has sometimes been provided
when ventures seem in danger of failing altogether, in the form of temporary and modest relief from the "foreign exchange balance requirement."
Since this practice erodes the nonconvertibility of the renminbi, however,
it remains unusual. The other "emergency assistance" the state has provided consists mostly of smoothing minor inconveniences such as exit and
reentry formalities for foreign executives.[66]

Normally, foreign investors cannot expect "emergency assistance"
to alleviate the shortage of foreign exchange that afflicts most of them as a
result of lagging export sales. And that problem is widespread. Fewer
than ten percent of the industrial foreign invested enterprises in China as
of June, 1987 exported more than half of their products; only 30 per cent
of these could balance their foreign exchange.[67] The prevalence of
projects aimed at producing for the domestic market instead of for export
is particularly great in the poor interior provinces, due to their lack of
infrastructure and experience.[68]

In large part because it has failed to create a hospitable environment for foreign investment, China remains disappointed with the prevalence of tourist-related, commercial, and light assembly projects foreigners have brought in, instead of the hoped-for large industrial projects.[69]
China has also experienced frustration in its attempt to obtain up-to-date
production technology. Foreign investors often skimp where possible on
their capital contributions to minimize potential losses in what appears to
them a harsh environment for any kind of profitable activity.[70]

In cases where disputes between Chinese and their foreign investment partners reach the point of going into arbitration, however, the
Chinese have managed to keep conditions stacked effectively in their
favor without regard to phases of decentralization. To start with, the
Chinese side normally insists during joint venture negotiations that any
serious contract dispute be resolved through arbitration conducted in
Beijing, at the state Foreign Economic and Trade Arbitration Commission, rather than in a third country. Some foreigners report satisfaction
with the Commission's actions. In several cases, however, Chinese courts

have failed to enforce arbitration settlements.[71] And in one case, the Commission refused to order compensation to the foreign insurer of a defective shipment of export products because it could not be determined whether the Chinese manufacturer or the Chinese shipper was at fault.[72] Whether a Chinese state agency is capable of making impartial decisions to resolve disputes between state enterprises and their foreign partners is more than a matter of academic interest: by 1988, no fewer than 200 such arbitration cases were pending before the commission in Beijing.[73]

All in all, the prospects for foreign investors in China even under slightly relaxed central control were not encouraging. In any case, unbalanced growth under the semi-reformed economic system generated new problems by late 1988 which made the investment environment even less appealing. Not only did price inflation accelerate. Many factories, unable to afford the increased cost of inputs, had to shut down part time. Everywhere, corruption flourished among those with special access to sought-after goods or resources. The partial decentralization of economic controls allowed the richer or more experienced provinces and localities to pursue their own growth booms with little regard to national impact. Macroeconomic levers of control the central government might use to impose some restraint on economic growth, such as raising interest rates or enterprise taxes, did not work because government subsidies to state enterprises reimbursed such expenses. The central government's demands that cities such as Canton freeze growth in their fixed investment (in buildings, equipment and durable production goods) meant, with the rapid price inflation already existing, a sharp cut in funds available for public infrastructure development.[74]

Further austerity measures after mid-1988 made conditions worse for foreign investment projects. First, tightened controls on the People's Bank of China made borrowing from the state bank much more difficult for joint ventures. Second, the provincial economic development zones which had only recently been announced now found it all but impossible to obtain the finance for necessary infrastructure development that could help attract foreign investment.[75] And third, Beijing began discouraging or requiring central approval of twelve types of foreign investment that the government concluded had not brought in sufficient technology or export earnings: hotels, shopping arcades, cotton spinning, low level consumer good assembly, automobile assembly, film development, and others.[76]

Under the new austerity policy international technology transfer contracts are also subject to more stringent guidelines. The number of contracts approved by central government authorities has been cut back. For those that are approved, the government in 1988 announced a new set of rules governing their administration. The new rules make clear that protection of intellectual property will only be assured for the life of a technology transfer contract (generally less than ten years), after which

China may continue to use the technology in question unless the contract specifies otherwise.[77]

Foreign reactions to these developments were mixed. Two groups of potential foreign investors remained cautious: the Japanese and the Germans. Japanese investment in China (generously estimated at some $2 billion) during the five years through March, 1989 amounted to only one-sixteenth of all Japanese foreign direct investment in Asia during that period.[78] West German companies had altogether directly invested only somewhat more than $100 million in China by 1989.[79] Yet many American businessmen remained hopeful--perhaps influenced by the optimistic slant in some business publications. Just two months before the turmoil began, *Fortune* magazine ran a prominent article entitled "Why There's Still Promise in China".[80] The article--ostensibly based on interviews with dozens of experts--argued that despite inflation, austerity, and tightening of credit, the central government's attitude toward foreign management of joint ventures was becoming increasingly flexible. And even more radical economic reforms were under discussion. Therefore "Western executives...agree that it's no time to let up their efforts in China."[81] There was one problem, however, that *Fortune*'s article failed even to mention: political risk. After Tiananmen, that factor would no longer be overlooked.

Most of the illusions about investing in China that still remained were destroyed by the government's military invasion of Beijing in June, 1989, together with the dismissal of reformist Party Secretary Zhao Ziyang and purge of his followers. The subsequent attempt to whitewash the actions of the Chinese Army against unarmed civilians, and to claim they were in self-defense, shattered foreigners' illusions about the legal development and institutionalization that some supposed had occurred under Deng Xiaoping. Ten years' worth of patiently built up trust was lost.

Besides losing the trust of foreign investors, the Chinese government suddenly found itself saddled with a cutback in Western economic aid in response to worldwide shock at its brutality. Even the relatively cautious Japanese government, hesitant to inflame the Chinese Communist leadership and endanger long-term economic relations, suspended a set of foreign aid loans to China to support 42 projects with a total value of US $5.59 billion that were scheduled to commence in early 1990.[82] In the United States, President Bush (after the massacre and the first stages of repression) announced a temporary suspension of high level contacts with Chinese officials, and a US vote to postpone multilateral concessionary loans to the Chinese government. Under pressure from the US and its allies, the World Bank froze seven pending development loans which would have been worth $780.2 million, for which final approval has been pending. (Other Bank loan commitments to China of some $8 billion, much of which had already been disbursed, would continue to be paid as planned.) The postponed projects included rehabilitation of the Nanjing-

Shanghai highway, a coal-burning power plant in Henan Province, and a large industrial development project in Shanghai.[83] China would find the cost of further long-term bond issues in foreign markets rising due to foreign awareness of potential instability there. The delays and costs would further tighten the government's fiscal crisis, worsen inflation, and intensify China's domestic political dilemmas.

The austerity program, the political turmoil of 1989, and the struggle over Deng's succession that would follow, cut short the gradual decentralization of authority that had been hastening wider differentiation among China's provinces. Thus the ultimate outcome of that experiment will not be known until and unless it is resumed under a reformist leader after Deng's departure. From the relatively relaxed phase of the late 1980s, however, two conclusions are possible. Local and provincial interests are, as in earlier periods of Chinese history, becoming increasingly influential, shaping implementation of policy as well as its results (often in illicit ways through the connections of powerful local officials who can in one way or another sell access to the protected domestic market). But at the same time, the temporary phase of relaxed central control did not much improve conditions for foreign investors in most parts of the country--or change the fact that state-imposed restrictions on many aspects of their activity remained effective.

Overall Conclusions on Foreign Investment Policy

China's foreign investment policies since 1979 effectively uphold Chinese interests as Beijing sees them. It is true that China has relaxed the limits on foreign equity control more than several other Asian countries, including South Korea; and that laws such as China's on patent protection may be comparable to those elsewhere in Asia.[84] It is also true that a foreign investor in China can, to a limited degree, sell in the domestic market. But the restrictions and red tape involved are formidable. The foreign investor cannot freely and flexibly make local business connections; hire, pay, and promote workers directly; or repatriate profits earned in the national currency. Such policies prevent most foreign businesses from penetrating the domestic market and threatening established state enterprises with competition. The central government normally allows profit repatriation from domestic sales by foreign investment ventures only when the product is an import substitute--when it competes with foreign products, not Chinese.

From the central government's point of view, all of this is necessary and desirable. Officials observe that joint ventures get more preferential treatment than state enterprises, which continue to have to make "back door" deals despite government promises of autonomy. Spokesmen stress that China has strenuously responded to complaints and problems of foreign investors. The government is unlikely to give way on the fundamental issues of currency convertibility, direct access to the labor market, or domestic sales rights.

   To give foreign investors both opportunities and constraints has advantages for China. Foreign investment proceeds in some accord with other state policies and priorities. Foreign business cannot develop a strong domestic constituency among workers (because its employees are too few), among Chinese business partners (which remain state enterprises with distinct interests), or among consumers (who cannot purchase most joint venture products because of currency restrictions). Neither the local employees of foreign capitalism, nor the production in which it is involved, have been allowed to develop into a privileged or elite pro-foreign sector, detached from the rest of the economy and draining its best resources. And the policies are easy to justify, since state controls on labor mobility, on access to production supplies, on the structure and duration of operations, and a host of other variables apply to state enterprise activities as well as to joint ventures. It is not as though foreign investors are singled out for especially harsh treatment.

   Moreover, by some more positive measures China's opening to foreign investment has been a success. New hotels, factories, and resource extraction facilities have been set up rapidly and in large numbers. Although the amount of advanced technology brought in is limited, an increasing proportion of operations began achieving export sales by 1986.[85] Chinese sources claim foreign investment ventures exported US $480 million of products in that year, an increase from $320 million in 1985.[86] Export operations will also benefit more widely from a better trained and more experienced labor force, and this will enhance future income in foreign trade.

   Most important from the government's standpoint, its foreign investment policies have not threatened China's political and social structure. State control of the economy and guidance of major enterprises, albeit partially decentralized, remains firmly in place. No privileged group of workers and managers threatens to become a disruptive pro-foreign pressure center. Foreign investment has not created any direct threat to political rule by the Communist Party. And the state has produced a growing body of laws which enshrine general rights granted to foreign investors, while serving as flexible and effective negotiating tools in bargaining for their capital contributions.

   Yet despite the successes of the policy, there have been costs to China. These include not only the concentration of investment in a few regions, and the possible net outflows of capital. Equally serious, many foreign investments that China has sought--large plants for export production in the chemical industry, to take one example--have not been forthcoming. Technology transfer has by any account been limited. Foreign investors consistently cite the investment environment as the reason. By that they mean the quality of infrastructure and locally available inputs, as well as policy restrictions of the kind discussed in this chapter. Because of the limited potential profitability of investing in China, the quality and quantity of investment have suffered. Japanese commitments, for example, have been a mere fraction of their investment level in eight other Asian countries.[87] American investment has also lagged behind its level in other Asian countries. In 1986, China received only $199 million in US direct investment, as compared with Hong Kong, $3.58 billion; Taiwan, $860 million; South Korea, $792 million; the Philippines, $1.11 billion; Singapore, $2.29 billion; and Thailand, $1.04 billion.[88]

The additional concessions offered by Beijing after 1986 proved inadequate. In fact, the total volume of contracted foreign investment, which dropped by half in 1986, recovered only slightly in 1987.[89] A full resumption of growth after the 1989 disaster depends on a more flexible policy approach in Beijing, gradual improvement of the Chinese industrial infrastructure, and sustained interest on the part of potential investment partners such as Japan and South Korea. That will take at least several years.

Chinese officials realize some of the costs of their policies. One might ask, why has the government drawn the limitations as it has? It is not out of concern about growing inequality: Chinese policy encourages investment to concentrate in already wealthy areas, and allows enterprises to expand wage differentials among grades of workers. Nor can the policy be ascribed to Marxist reservations. Nothing in Marx justifies "one country, two systems," Deng Xiaoping's idea of making capitalism a long-term participant in the peaceful development of socialism.

Rather, the opening to foreign investment has been insistent on maintaining Chinese state control over inputs to the productive process, over most of the production that occurs in China itself, and over the national market. This is the consistent principle underlying policies that otherwise waver between flexibility and firmness in different cases according to the market value of projects under negotiation. How the state maintains a predominant influence over ventures with foreign participation is complicated; that it has largely succeeded in this aim is the unavoidable conclusion from studying Chinese law and policy.

Table 9-4

Direct Foreign Investment by Type of Contract

US $ m=million
bn=billion

	1982		1983		1984		1985		1986	
Direct Foreign Investment (total)	649	m	916	m	1.42 bn		1.96 bn		2.19 bn	
1. Joint Ventures (equity type)	34.3 m		73.6 m		255	m	580	m	804	m
2. Contractual Joint Ventures	178	m	227	m	465	m	585	m	794	m
3. Joint Exploration	179	m	291	m	523	m	481	m	260	m
4. Wholly Foreign-Owned Firms	39.3 m		42.8 m		14.9	m	12.9	m	16.3	m
5. Compensation Trade	122	m	197	m	98.4	m	169	m	181	m
6. Other	97	m	83.5 m		62.8	m	129	m	140	m

NOTE: Most of "other" category refers to processing and assembly contracts.

SOURCES: *Almanac of China's Foreign Economic Relations and Trade*, 1984, 1095; *Ibid.*, 1986, 1212; *Ibid.*, 1987,618.

Notes

1. Thomas J. Biersteker, *Distortion or Development? Contending Perspectives on the Multinational Corporation* (Cambridge, Mass.: MIT Press, 1978), 1-48.

2. *Beijing Review*, Feb. 8, 1989, 30.

3. *FEER*, April 25, 1985, 115.

4. See Li Yuanzheng, Mofert, in *Intertrade*, Jan., 1987, 12-13.

5. Ji Chongwei, Economic, Technological, and Social Research Institute, Chinese State Council, interview, March 5, 1987.

6. See Biersteker, *Distortion or Development?*, 7-9.

7. Fu Zhida, Ministry of Petroleum, in *Intertrade*, June, 1986, 16-17.

8. Zhang Gengxing, Ministry of Chemical Industry, in *Ibid.*, 17-18.

9. Fan Hongcai, Ministry of Machine Building, in *Ibid.*, 18-20.

10. *Beijing Review*, Feb. 8, 1989, 30-31.

11. *Beijing Review*, June 29, 1988, 24.

12. See Li Chunsheng in *Beijing Yanjiu*; summarized in *FEER*, June 13, 1985, 120; and *Beijing Review*, June 6, 1988, 42.

13. *FEER*, July 11, 1985, 66-68.

14. *Beijing Review*, Feb. 8, 1989, 30-31.

15. *The Economist*, Dec. 14, 1985, 76-77; and April 16, 1988, 81-82.

16. The World Bank, *China, Long-Term Development Issues and Options* (Baltimore: Johns Hopkins University Press, 1985), 74-75.

17. *Renmin Ribao*, Jan. 18, 1985, 2.

18. See *Shijie Jingji Daobao*, Nov. 9, 1987, 15.

19. The World Bank, *China*, 87.

20. *Ibid.*

21. "U.S.-P.R.C. Joint Ventures in China," Beijing, US Embassy xeroxed list, January, 1986.

22. *Almanac of China's Foreign Economic Relations and Trade, 1986* (Hong Kong: China Resources Advertising Company, 1987), 1221.

23. See "Technology Transfer" listing in each issue of *JETRO China Newsletter* (Tokyo).

24. Both items, *Ibid.*, Sept.-Oct., 1986, 20.

25. *Guoji Maoyi*, No. 8, 1987, 5. See also No. 4, 1987, 33-37; and No. 11, 1987, 25-27.

26. See *Guoji Maoyi Wenti*, Sept., 1980; trans. JPRS 76913, Dec. 2, 1980, 32-5.

27. *China Daily*, April 16, 1985, 2.

28. *The Economist*, Jan. 11, 1986, 61-4.

29. *Ibid.*

30. *Almanac of China's Foreign Economic Relations and Trade, 1986*, 660, 721; *China Business Review*, Jan.- Feb., 1987, 17.

31. Trans. JPRS, Nov. 9, 1982, 42-49.
32. Quotation from survey by Nigel Campbell of the University of Manchester; see summary in *FEER*, Aug. 14, 1986, 103.
33. *International Herald Tribune*, March 25, 1985, 4.
34. Chu Baotai, Mofert, in *Intertrade*, March, 1986, 46.
35. See *JETRO China Newsletter*, Jan.-Feb., 1987, 15-16.
36. *Jiefangjun Bao*, July 21, 1979; trans. FBIS, July 23, 1979, L17-21.
37. *The Economist*, Feb. 8, 1986, 65.
38. E.g., see *The New York Times*, March 24, 1987, B1, 30.
39. *China Quarterly*, No. 111 (Sept., 1987), 521; and Chu Baotai and Dong Weiyuan, *Zenyang Juban Zhongwai Hezi Jingying Qiye* (Beijing: Zhishi Chubanshe, 1986), 3.
40. Peter Evans, *National Autonomy and Economic Development*, quoted in Thomas Biersteker, *Distortion or Development?*, 19.
41. Tianjin Deputy Mayor Zhang Zhaoruo in *JETRO China Newsletter* No. 77 (Nov. 1988), 17. For a similar statement boosting Dalian, see *Beijing Review*, Jan. 25, 1988, 42.
42. *Beijing Review*, June 29, 1988, 24.
43. *Beijing Review*, August 15, 1988, 14-16.
44. *FEER*, Oct. 13, 1988, 42.
45. *Beijing Review*, December 19, 1988, 5.
46. *FEER*, Nov. 24, 1988, 74.
47. *Beijing Review*, August 15, 1988, 17.
48. *Ibid.*, 14.
49. *New York Times*, June 28, 1989, 4.
50. *FEER*, Dec. 8, 1988, 60-61.
51. *The Economist*, March 25, 1989, 79-80.
52. *FEER*, June 23, 1988, 64-65.
53. *Ibid.*
54. *FEER*, Nov. 17, 1988, 91.
55. *China Business Review*, May 1988, 51.
56. See *JETRO China Newsletter* No. 74 (May, 1988), 17-23.
57. *JETRO China Newsletter* No. 79 (March, 1989), 12.
58. Xia Bing, "Xiying Waizi bixu Xiangying Gaishan 'Ruan Huanjing'," *Guoji Maoyi Wenti*, Aug., 1988, 43.
59. Yan Zheng, "Lun Touzi Huanjing," *Kai Fa*, Jan., 1988, 28.
60. Wang Yongjun, "Woguo xishou Waiguo Zhijie Touzi de Xianzhuang he Wenti," *Guoji Maoyi Wenti*, June, 1988, 47.
61. Xie Houying, "Fazhan Waixiangxing Jingji yao heli Liyong Waizi," *Guangzhou Yanjiu*, No. 10, 1987, 18.
62. *JETRO China Newsletter* No. 77 (Nov., 1988), 19.
63. *JETRO China Newsletter* No. 74 (May, 1988), 23; and *China Business Review*, May, 1988, 50.

64. For discussions and examples of this, see *China Business Review*, July, 1988, 10; *Beijing Review*, August 15, 1988, 18; and *JETRO China Newsletter*, No. 76 (Sept., 1988), 12-13, and No. 77 (Nov., 1988), 18-19.

65. See *China Business Review*, March, 1988, 24-28.

66. *JETRO China Newsletter*, No. 75 (July, 1988), 17-18.

67. Ren Huizhong, "Zhengque Yindao Waizi de Touxiang," *Jingji Kexue*, No. 2, 1988, 28-30. See also Huang Jianping, "Duiwai Maoyi, Liyong Waizi yu Guomin Jingji Fazhan," *Guoji Maoyi Wenti*, May, 1988, 9.

68. Song Hai, "Xibei diqu Liyong Waizi Cunzai de Wenti, Yuanyin Ji Duice," *Guoji Maoyi Wenti*, April, 1988, 26-30.

69. *Beijing Review*, March 6, 1989, 23-24.

70. For example, see *Beijing Review*, Feb. 29, 1988, 21-22.

71. Thomas Peele and Marsha A. Cohen, "Dispute Resolution in China," *China Business Review*, Sept. 1988, 46-47.

72. *Ibid.*, 47.

73. *Ibid.*, 46.

74. Xie Houying, "Fazhan Waixiangxing Jingji yao heli Liyong Waizi," *Guangzhou Yanjiu*, No. 10, 1987, 15.

75. *Beijing Review*, Jan. 2, 1989, 29-30.

76. *FEER*, March 2, 1989, 59.

77. *China Business Review*, July-August, 1988, 35-36.

78. *Japan Economic Institute Report* No. 31A (Aug. 11, 1989), 3. Only 12.4 per cent of foreign investment by value in Shanghai until June, 1987 came from Japan. See Chu Yukun, "Shanghai Fazhan Waixiangxing Jingji de Ruogan Silu," *Guoji Maoyi Wenti*, May, 1988, 23.

79. *FEER*, July 13, 1989, 40.

80. Ford S. Worthy, "Why There's Still Promise in China," *Fortune*, CXIX:5 (Feb. 27, 1989), 95-100.

81. *Ibid.*, 100.

82. *Wall Street Journal*, June 22, 1989, A10.

83. *FEER*, July 6, 1989, 69-70.

84. Genevieve Dean, "Investment Incentives Throughout Asia," *China Business Review*, March-April, 1988, 49.

85. Robert Taylor, Consul, Economics Section, US Consulate, Hong Kong; interview, April 3, 1987.

86. *Shijie Jingji Daobao*, Nov. 9, 1987, 15.

87. *Japan Economic Institute Report*, Feb. 5, 1988, Appendix, Table 1.

88. Genevieve Dean, "Investment Incentives," 50.

89. *The Economist*, March 12, 1988, 61.

10

Conclusion

"The purpose of socialism is to make the country rich and strong."

--Deng Xiaoping, 1980[1]

China's opening to the outside world had its origins in the political choices of its leaders, responding to economic circumstances rather than any ideology. Deng Xiaoping and the Communist Party decided beginning in 1978 that foreign interests, especially capitalist multinational corporations, could play a constructive long-term role in the development of Chinese socialism. They were confident that the state could promote China's interests effectively and prevent exploitation by foreigners. In theory, the opening policies meant a rejection of domestic and international class struggle, the essential principle of Marxism that was "discovered" by Marx himself. In practice, these policies went far beyond any then existing Communist precedent. China now embraced international cooperation as a means of fostering national economic capacity under more flexible and thus revitalized state control.

Why did the ruling Communist Party turn China's back on principles that it had consistently for decades declared fundamental? One could enumerate incentives the country faced to open up: the prospect of obtaining foreign capital investment in support of national modernization; the economic and political costs of falling ever farther behind Japan, South Korea, Taiwan and Hong Kong in rates of growth and development; and the fact that those same competitors offered models of some economic policies China itself could adopt. Yet these factors were incentives, not compelling circumstances, and they had all existed many years before 1978. If the rulers of the country had been more flexible in deciding economic strategy, the growth of China's economic strength and stature that has recently occurred might have come at a different time: nineteen years earlier, for example, when the break with the Soviet Union ended

China's opening to that country. Then, Mao's ideological rigidity vis-a-vis capitalism hampered the improvement of foreign relations that would have been necessary for a wider opening. When Deng finally did break away from class struggle as a guiding principle after 1978, his allusions to Marx and Mao only barely concealed the economic nationalist assumptions of his new foreign economic policy.

Despite references to "objective laws of development"--a Marxist code for necessary caution in setting the pace of economic reform--Chinese policy discussions evince deep confidence that an admittedly poor country has the political resources to promote national economic interests. They reject fear of exploitation and vulnerability. The primary sources of their confidence are national sovereignty and the ubiquitous intervention of the state.

Published Chinese analysis of the opening policies accords the state a crucial role as benign protector of national interests. From foreign investment, the state obtains capital (hard currency, equipment, and technology) and develops economic capacity with its equity control and eventual ownership of joint ventures. Through foreign trade, the state can develop hard currency earnings while restraining deficits by means of state planning, management, encouragement of exports, and import protectionism. The periodic campaigns against foreign influence (spiritual pollution, bourgeois liberalization, etc.), including reiterations that news media must remain mouthpieces of the Communist Party, rely on the state to control the side-effects of China's opening up. In the long term, state economic intervention and control will remain. Reform and partial decentralization of authority will (Chinese officials believe) make state control more flexible and effective. The goal of opening up enunciated by Chinese leaders and commentators is neither class transformation nor laissez-faire global interdependence. It is national economic strengthening that will eventually allow diminished dependence on world markets, foreign management, and outside equity ownership.

After the violent repression of June, 1989, some Chinese scholars (particularly those abroad in the West) began to engage in a fundamental rethinking of the goals of reform. Some say privately that now, instead of promoting market-oriented measures disguised with such meaningless labels as the "primary stage of socialism"--the sort of theoretical activity pursued by Party leader Zhao Ziyang's followers before his purge--they will advocate an out-and-out restoration of capitalism when reformers return to power after the death of Deng Xiaoping. If sufficiently widespread, this rethinking could open new possibilities for China.

Before one jumps to the conclusion that economic liberalism will or even could prevail in China, however, one should bear a few facts in mind. To start with, the rethinking that is undoubtedly also taking place on the mainland is no doubt less radical in its challenge to neomercantilist assumptions than are the debates taking place among Chinese intellectuals and students abroad. Within China, the long-term influence persists of official propaganda which uses the same word (*guojia*) for "state" and "country," and makes it difficult for most people to distinguish clearly between the central government's interests and those of their country. Even many pro-reform Chinese intellectuals share in some form Deng Xiaoping's fear of the disorder that might result from a serious weakening of the central government's powers that true economic liberalism presupposes. Indeed, a decade of reform has made all too clear China's lack of an alternative structure of power which tolerates loosened control and decentralization yet preserves stability. The political system is so dependent on central domination that any sustained relaxation of control always seems to threaten collapse. To the extent people still identify freedom with disorder, they will hesitate to rally to its cause.

Despite these obstacles to liberalization, the central government has been willing to make remarkable concessions to attract capitalist involvement. These include setting aside Shenzhen and three other Special Economic Zones for capitalist-led development, to which Hainan Island was added later. In its gung-ho attempt to promote models of Chinese-foreign cooperation and at the same time reassure capitalist Hong Kong about its future under China, the government provided Shenzhen huge construction subsidies. These, combined with the apparent eagerness of Chinese enterprises from the interior to invest in lucrative commercial operations in Shenzhen, led to a drain of national capital resources that forced the central government to clarify and reassert its original objectives.

In response to the mixed success of its experiment in Shenzhen, Beijing tried to redirect the Zone to serve national rather than only local development needs. It cut down state subsidies of capital and manpower. It pressured foreign investors to contribute technology and export-oriented production facilities that would add to national capital resources. The same principles were applied to the other Special Economic Zones, including the fifth one (Hainan Island) which was established in 1988.

In this way, Beijing responded to imbalances in the growth of national economic capacity caused by Shenzhen's rapid development. This was an issue of national, rather than class interest, and the response to it reaffirmed the neomercantilist conception of the opening policies stated by Chinese officials.

China's opening to foreign trade after 1978 revealed even more clearly the nature of its objectives. Some outside observers were misled by the sharp increases in trade volume to believe that the country was embracing free trade liberalism. This misimpression was strengthened when China's imports twice went out of control in response to pressing domestic demand for imported equipment and consumer goods. Suddenly, many Chinese found themselves able to buy Japanese color televisions and motorcycles. But demand far exceeded permitted supply, encouraging smugglers to take advantage of domestic versus external price differentials, and by their activities add to the outward drain on national hard currency reserves. Such trends were exacerbated by the reemerging tendency of provincial and local Chinese officials to operate the areas under their control as "independent kingdoms," in pursuit of their own interests--and in competition with other regions.

Except for two brief periods of ineffective central control, China's opening up to trade included import protectionism as an integral element. This mitigated the economic readjustments that higher levels of trade would make necessary, and helped China defend its broadening base of industries from foreign competition. Each time this policy was violated, Chinese demand for imported goods caused huge trade deficits. These had to be cut back not only for financial reasons, but because of the vocal political reaction they spawned among domestic protectionist elements.

Above all, Beijing's priority in trade affairs was to secure productive capital, not to meet consumer demand. The central government found that for this purpose, levers of control mostly developed in the 1950s were sufficient. Such methods included foreign exchange controls, trade licensing, quotas, tax adjustments, frequently revised customs tariffs, and state import pricing. As China prepared for further growth of trade volume, the central government was learning from new experience how to intervene and regulate foreign trade more effectively. State protectionism, however, also helped inefficient domestic industries avoid market competition that the World Bank and other observers thought necessary to improve productive efficiency.

State intervention was equally central to China's policy after 1979 of welcoming foreign capitalist investment. The declared goals of the policy were the same as in foreign trade: to acquire productive equipment and technology, and develop the state's foreign exchange income from export production. Here, regulation was qualitative. The central government emphasized control of a majority stake in most joint ventures, while developing elaborate tax, domestic sales, and labor management regulations. These put a distance between the foreign capitalist and whatever means of production were available in China--with state or local bureaucratic agencies usually in the middleman role.

Although foreign investment did not manifest the wild fluctuations experienced in foreign trade, unforeseen problems did develop. The quality of foreign investment was disappointing to Beijing. Much of it was commercial rather than industrial in nature; or (what the central government disliked even more) was aimed at selling products in the Chinese market. This again threatened to drain hard currency and capital resources. Yet the central government understood that a crackdown in response would jeopardize future foreign investment in China and business confidence in capitalist Hong Kong.

The state's reaction to undesired aspects of foreign investment consisted of reaffirming investors' legal opportunities while trying to pressure foreign business into higher-technology, export oriented capital contributions. This involved a mixture of carrot, stick, and bluff. Extra tax and favorable treatment incentives were granted to foreign investment ventures that matched the government's long-term objectives. At the same time, the government tightened domestic market access and reiterated the policies that prevented repatriation of domestic renminbi profits. It also became clear that approval of commercial or tourist-oriented operations would be more difficult.

Subsequent regulations and announcements proclaimed new concessions to foreign investors, but many of them were merely repackagings of existing arrangements. The announcements helped distract businessmen from restrictions on labor management and currency conversion. Nonetheless, in 1986 foreign investment dropped off by half. For this there were two separate reasons. One was that government eagerness to obtain short-term income from fees and high prices, while allowing only limited market access, raised the cost of operating in China and deterred some foreign companies from investing. The other was that the treatment of foreign investment revealed an insistence that it develop national capital resources and revitalize key state industries. To push it in this direction, the central government was willing to tighten regulations to the point of slowing growth in some sectors. Such actions, too, confirmed the economic nationalist principles proclaimed by the government since 1979. Of course, foreign investment dropped off further after 1988, in response first to the central government's austerity program, and then to its violent crackdown on popular protest.

* * *

Economic and political conditions in China limited the pace at which the goals of the opening up policies could be realized, regardless of the intentions of national leaders. The most fundamental problem was the physical capacity of the country in its current state of development to absorb new capital and technology and put them to work in a geographically balanced manner. Regional differences in levels of development have the effect of concentrating new growth in relatively advanced cities that already have the best infrastructure and service capacity. The government recognizes that this inequality is inevitable, and has made only limited efforts to diminish it.

The new and partly experimental foreign economic policies have largely followed market forces, rather than any program or plan. This has made regional and sectoral imbalances more difficult for the central government to control. Enthusiastic participation by Chinese enterprises discovering new profit opportunities has led to local growth of unexpected scale. To the central government, some of this growth is actually undesirable if it drains the state's capital resources away from planned priorities. This occurred in both the Shenzhen Special Economic Zone and in foreign trade. Tangible benefits to some key cities masked hard currency drains and deficits faced by the nation. In its responses, the central government never found an easy compromise between relaxation of controls and orderly balanced growth.

Beijing's dilemma was that any backtracking on its policy initia- tives would threaten tangible present and future benefits. From foreign investment China was getting new factories (which after set periods it would own and control), training for managers and workers, new goods produced for use or export, hard cash, new commercial and tourist facilities, and some production technology. These benefits drew attention away from the pronounced gap between the areas that were getting most of the benefits, and the rest of the country.

Two other factors mitigated the inequalities permitted by the opening up policies. One was that agricultural reforms, which dismantled Mao's collectives and restored private family farming, were proceeding at the same time. These fostered a recovery of rural productivity and a jump in living standards that compensated in part for continued urban-rural disparities. The other mitigating factor was state wage regulation, which prevented too wide a difference in take-home pay between ordinary workers and those employed in foreign investment enterprises. This prevented the rise of an elite pro-foreign class as described in neo-Marxist accounts of foreign investment.

As the economic reform process continued, the central government's primary concerns were about regional and enterprise autonomy, rather than inequality. Discussion of problems often centered on growing domestic economic competition. The idea that it could stimulate more efficient use of resources escaped many Chinese economists. On the contrary, they constantly warned that duplicate import orders would drain foreign exchange. Competition among export producers would lead to self-destructive price cutting. To avoid waste, they generally prescribed unified state planning, production, and distribution. Concerning technology transfer, they seemed to assume that wide diffusion would be possible after very limited purchases--an assumption that flew in the face of Chinese experience and of supposed government protection of patents and other intellectual property.

Chinese policy is explicitly directed against another kind of competition, that between Chinese and foreign products in the domestic market. Chinese economists assume that foreign competition would threaten development of a broad base of Chinese industries. To judge from delegates' speeches in the 1985 National People's Congress summarized in Chapter Four, there is widespread demand for even tougher protectionist measures. Fears about competition, foreign and domestic, add to political pressure to put limitations on the opening up policies.

Such concerns tend to reinforce another broad tendency that hinders structural change: the widespread habit of resorting to higher authority to resolve emerging problems. Thirty years of obedience to central

commands were not good training for Party officials supposed to implement a gradual introduction of market forces after 1978. Habit had bred
authoritarianism among superiors, and passivity among subordinates.
Since each new step in the opening up had little precedent in state socialist
experience, each meant preparing for unknown results. As development
proceeded, some individuals (including many officials) adapted quickly to
take personal advantage of new opportunities, while others called for
renewal of central controls to prevent abuses and diminish economic
uncertainties. In foreign trade, imports threatened to undercut existing
industries and this added to calls for protectionism. Exporting enterprises
engaged in cut-price selling to earn foreign exchange, prompting numerous calls for strengthened central supervision of their subsidized purchases and sales practices. In Shenzhen, vigorous trading activity (often
illegal) undermined state distribution systems and led to public questions
about the faults of the Special Economic Zone experiment. In one form or
another, demands to return to orderly, predictable central control arose
regularly. Within the Party, even reformers have been unwilling or unable
to challenge too sharply the habit of obedience to dictates from above.
During the crisis of May-June, 1989, the hopes of Chinese reformers were
pinned on the possible emergence of a reformist top leadership--not on a
transformation of the structure of state and Party power.

Concerns about competition and dependence on central authority
help explain the complexity of China's opening up process. Despite the
importance of granting increased discretion to local authorities, there was
no period when administration was simply and in all respects being decentralized. There was frequent reemphasis on central controls. For example, in mid-1985 the central government reduced the number of import
goods requiring its approval. Local authorities could now approve more
trade deals. During that same period, however, higher customs duties and
a new import regulatory tax imposed from the center made the same
imports more costly to provincial enterprises (see Chapter Four). Such
contradictions do not mean that the opening up was mere deception. It
was, however, qualified and complex, with tendencies to revert to central
controls in the face of uncertainty about emerging results.

The central government's abilities to react flexibly to ongoing
developments have benefited from its turn away from Marxist ideology.
The quotation at the outset of this chapter reflects that socialist slogans
justify rather than guide policy. In China as it opens up, Marxism is less
than an ideology, as Marx himself understood the concept: a system of
fundamental assumptions about the world. Of course, some elements of
Marxism-Leninism remain in China. Its institutional legacy is largely
preserved, in government by a Party with a dictatorial structure and a
monopoly of state, media, and educational control.

Yet every chapter in this study has found government policies
antithetical to the essential principle of Marxism, class struggle. To make
capitalism a long term participant in national development as a prelude to

"one country, two systems" is a reversal of the historical sequence of development Marxists claim is inevitable. This remains true regardless of whether "reformers" or "hardliners" hold the balance of political power.

Then what is left of Marxist ideology in China? First, it contributes to nationalist self-confidence that a poor "proletarian" country is destined to assume great power in the world. One popular and durable feature of Marxism has been the hopeful conviction of inevitable victory it provides to those who identify themselves as proletarian--a conviction which in China has outlasted interest in class struggle and revolution. Second, the influence of Marxism persists in frequently expressed doubts about capitalism, even while researchers under the State Council are studying policies of Taiwan and South Korea for possible emulation.[2] Chinese commentary frequently expresses fear that capitalism, if allowed in unchecked, could penetrate and monopolize the domestic market. Capitalist interests would ignore local development needs and pollute the environment, according to these views. Some Party officials at all levels also dislike perceived social influences of foreign capitalism, as the campaigns against spiritual pollution and bourgeois liberalization attest. These doubts and in some cases opposition put a drag on the pace at which top level officials can pursue the opening up reforms.

In addition to instilling confidence in progress and doubts about capitalism, Marxism continues to give the government a basis of legitimacy. Prominent leaders who once were nationalist revolutionaries can claim that the political structures they later rule "serve the people" and that theirs is a "Liberation" army. This logic is difficult to challenge and is most unlikely to be attacked by the leaders who benefit from it. Marxism as justifier of political rule therefore has great staying power. Nevertheless, the opening up policies provide abundant evidence that Marxism no longer guides either strategic or tactical aspects of economic policy. That has remained true even in the bleak aftermath of Tiananmen: those Chinese leaders who supported the slaughter did so not to promote Marxian class conflict, but to protect the special privileges represented by the Mercedes-Benzes in which they are driven through the streets of Beijing.

* * *

The decision of China's leaders after 1978 to replace class conflict with national economic strengthening provided a new justification for the exercise of centralized state power. Divisive domestic issues of inequality were downplayed or ignored. Instead, the most potent ideological element of Marxism in practice--nationalism--became the standard theme of official propaganda supporting the new policies. The government claimed that the opening up would benefit economic modernization of the whole nation.

With that concrete and measurable goal, the central government needed to develop more sophisticated methods of administration and economic control. Despite the importance of regional powerholders in making policy, the center did not succumb to creeping decentralization and laissez-faire trade. The central government pursued national interests (as it perceived them) with considerable success. It confronted shortcomings in the composition of new trade and investment: both tended to be commercial and consumer oriented (and pointed at China's domestic markets) rather than devoted to manufacturing and export production, as Beijing would prefer. The forms of central intervention included holding equity control of production, limiting approval of joint ventures, restricting access to means of production, preventing repatriation of domestic currency profits, and maintaining trade controls. By the same means, the state prevented direct exploitation of Chinese labor and natural resources by foreign capitalism.

The protectionist features of China's foreign economic policy have been maintained despite a great deal of well-meaning US and Western advice and assistance which some allege to be an attempt to "enmesh" China in the world market system.[3] If China had truly become "enmeshed" in international capitalism, one would expect foreign businessmen to be enthralled about their opportunities there, yet most of them remain at best cautious about their prospects in China--and few are willing to work there for more than a few years.[4] The considerable aid and advice granted by the World Bank has *not* drawn China into the world capitalist system (which in any case is not one system but several, none of them fully open). Rather, it is China itself that has decided to make a partial entry, and to reap the benefits from doing so--in particular, to receive the benefit of the doubt from Western governments and some of their advisers who believed (at least until June, 1989) that liberal treatment of China would bring liberalizing policies in return. But China has in fact shown itself quite capable of continuing to put limits on both economic and political liberalization, rather than submitting to an inexorable process of integration with outside capitalism. China has ignored most of the gently presented policy suggestions of the World Bank, described in Chapter Six, about foreign economic policy, and the government has continued to intervene in transnational economic matters to its advantage.

This is not to say that state power was unlimited or its actions always successful. After ten years of opening up it was not clear whether development would assume the orientation central government officials desired. Beginning in 1986, the volume of foreign investment dropped more than was compensated by the increased proportion of manufacturing joint ventures. Regional disparities in the distribution of investment continued to grow. On the other hand, income differences between individuals hired by foreign investment projects and others were held in check to forestall complaints from those who might be left behind. And while some localities were flourishing commercially, national policy ensured that much new development was under the control of state industries and that their capacity was growing. This prevented an erosion of economic power and initiative away from central government-run institutions.

The effectiveness of state intervention into China's economic relations invalidates the "dependent development" model as a description of multinational corporate investment in Communist countries. The model of multinational trade and investment relations described by Peter Evans,[5] for example, draws on his research in Brazil to amend neo-Marxist dependency theory. Evans acknowledges that considerable industrial development takes place in the developing country that is host to multinational corporations. In fact, three distinct elements all promote local industry: state-run enterprises, host country businesses, and multinational corporations.

The results include industrial growth in the host developing country, but it is unbalanced and perpetuates dependency. On the one hand, cooperation between multinational corporations and some local businesses facilitates penetration of the domestic market by foreign capital. On the other hand, because of the superior technological and capital resources available to the multinationals, they dominate higher technology production where limited availability of such resources creates barriers to entry. They do not share production technologies with local or host country firms until after the methods are already becoming outdated. This inhibits local development of export industries. Meanwhile, growth fostered in the host country is unbalanced between a small elite benefiting from the presence of multinationals, and the great majority of people who are only the objects of intensified consumer advertising.

China under the opening policies has exhibited some tendencies in these directions, but that is all. There has been a growth of consumerism; host country and foreign capital have cooperated to form joint ventures; regional inequality has grown; foreign companies have tried to penetrate the domestic market.

However, there are crucial dissimilarities between China and the dependent development model. As Chapter Five has shown in detail, multinational corporations are prevented from repatriating profits earned from selling in the domestic market. Regarding technology transfer, Chinese complaints belie the fact that state negotiators have insisted with increasing stringency on obtaining relatively advanced equipment. Economic development in China has not been allowed to foster a pro-foreign economic elite. Finally, the joint venture partners of multinational corporations are not local private businesses that must cooperate with them in order to survive, but state enterprises with equity control that assume full ownership after set and agreed periods of time. They are anything but subservient to foreign capital. Indeed, in Guangdong, the province most dependent on foreign investment, local entrepreneurism has been greatly stimulated rather than quashed by the presence of foreign business (mostly from Hong Kong).

The Chinese case demonstrates why none of the Communist countries is likely to fit the dependent development model. (By Communist I simply mean a country governed continuously by a Communist Party that professes Marxism-Leninism.) All of these countries possess the strong state apparatus that can intervene in trade and investment relations to influence the quality of capital and goods supplied. All have currency convertibility restrictions that hamper profit repatriation by foreign capitalist firms. All are likely to insist (as the Soviet Union does in its new joint venture law[6]) that the host country retain equity control over most joint ventures. These and similar methods of intervention will give Communist states bargaining strength to avoid the pattern of dependent development.

Very well, a neo-Marxist might respond: dependency is avoided by socialism. Here is the solution that has eluded developing states like Brazil that allow their business classes to collaborate with foreign multinationals. But when we take a closer look at this socialist solution, what kinds of interests are at stake and which prevail?

To describe the divergence of interests involved in foreign investment in China, there are better ways than following the "dependent development" model. Even its proponents would probably concede that it does not apply in this case--and hence has only limited validity. Rather than using an inappropriate distinction between state and private domestic capital, one can adopt a perspective suggested by Chu Baotai of Mofert's Foreign Investment Bureau in Beijing.[7] Leaving aside those not involved directly in foreign investment projects (e.g. most ordinary Chinese workers), Chu observes three distinct interests: foreign businesses; the Chinese state and its state-run enterprises; and workers hired by foreign investment ventures. Of course, all three wish for the success of ventures in which they have a stake. Beyond that, their interests differ.

The three-way divergence of interests is clearest on labor management questions, especially wages. The state insists on acting as middleman and taking out a portion of wage payments to cover labor subsidies and other national expenses. The foreign investor would prefer to pay Chinese workers and managers directly so that his incentive wage structure will have more immediate impact. Many Chinese workers hired with foreign capital (as Chu notes) are completely in agreement with the foreign capitalist's viewpoint on this. Why, they ask, should most of their wage be appropriated by the state so that they never see it? This "misunderstanding" (Chu's word) is particularly widespread among Chinese managers in joint ventures, who are allowed to take home as little as ten per cent or less of their wages.

The possibility of other such "misunderstandings" prompts the government to hold joint venture wages low. As Chu notes, the central government is worried about resentment of joint venture (or any foreign investment) employees by other workers. The existing wage gap between the two is limited to 50 per cent, that difference justified by joint ventures' demands for higher productivity and quality work.

In the division of interests in foreign investment ventures, which side has the upper hand in bargaining? Subject to the limited supply of possible investments, the state has held its own. It has successfully negotiated its wage policy with multinational corporations. As for Chinese workers, there is no sign that their reported wish to have less of their wages appropriated by the state has affected policy. Bonus and real wage payments to joint venture workers remain at a fixed proportion above ordinary, low Chinese wages.

The state takes on the ostensible role of defending all workers' interests, and in doing so promotes its own. Its middleman role in labor management and its earnings from per capita labor taxes add to its capacity to act as benign industrial planner. The state restricts the opportunities of some workers for the supposed benefit of all. This became apparent again in 1987, when the central government rejected programs that would have allowed workers to purchase equity shares in state enterprises.[8] This too might well lead to divergences of interests among workers. The government's decision had the effect of preventing such "contradictions," and at the same time forestalled dilution of state control of key industries.

The three-way division of interests just described is not just over labor management. The state's strength in bargaining on this issue is matched in arrangements regarding other factors of production. Of these, labor is only the most sensitive issue: workers' complaints could be disruptive, and they have a special claim to attention according to the state's professed ideology. Yet there is no question that the state can use "national interest" as a justification to compromise the interests of particular groups of workers. In bargaining about land use fees, equity control, and sales rights, the state has equally proved its capabilities to defend its interests effectively. On all these issues it has held its own against potential domestic political pressures, as well as the demands of multinational corporations. At the same time it has assured itself a pivotal role in the management of new production made possible by foreign investment.

*   *   *

This study has not attempted to identify individual political leaders other than Deng Xiaoping who have been associated with one or another aspect of foreign economic policy. That question is secondary to the main issues here: the overall aims of the reforms as generally agreed on, and the dynamics they set in motion. However, two observations about the relations between domestic politics and foreign economic policy are in order. The first is that amid the complexity of the Chinese political environment, one should not overestimate the extent to which centralized political control has been eroded during the course of the reform process. In the area of political reform, it was conventional wisdom among foreign China scholars in the late 1980s that significant progress had been made in the direction of institutionalization, legal reform, and a consultative style of policymaking.[9] This optimism faded quietly after the bloodshed of June, 1989. In the area of foreign economic relations, the periodic slippage of central control should not obscure the response that always followed that development, namely effective central government interventions into trade and investment matters.

The second observation is that in foreign economic policy, as in all other areas of Chinese politics during the 1980s, Deng Xiaoping himself remained the key decision-maker, the individual who either formulated or at least approved every major aspect of the opening up reforms: the Special Economic Zones; foreign investment policy; "one country, two systems;" and so on. It is quite conceivable that Deng's successor might use similar authority to advance the reforms further than Deng would have; or, on the contrary, to retreat. However, a radical change is unlikely, because Chinese leaders all share the goal of economic modernization and that will require a continued and growing interchange with the advanced capitalist countries. They also all share the nationalism that underpins the restrictions attached to the opening up policies.

Yet the possibility of systemic political change in China remains present and unpredictable. Opening up to the outside world has brought in Western managers, teachers, coworkers, and Chinese students returned from abroad. Many of these people have established relationships that cut across Communist Party-dominated networks of authority and foster the spread of Western ideas of freedom and individual autonomy, making an unmeasurable but significant contribution to the yearning of educated Chinese for a more "democratic" or consultative style of government. In 1989, of course, such demands produced only repression and the downfall of Party leader and former Premier Zhao Ziyang, who had been something of a champion of the opening up reforms. In the longer run, however, Zhao and fellow reformers will be vindicated because of the benefits these policies have brought to many parts of China.

*   *   *

China's opening up to foreign trade and investment allowed the country to obtain the maximum possible benefits from its independent foreign policy. At the end of the 1970s, an acceleration of foreign trade and investment was made possible by normalization of relations with the United States and EEC countries. Some hindrances to trade, such as US export controls on most high technology items, were relaxed in the early to mid-1980s. Others continued, notably US restraints on some textile imports and Chinese protectionism against consumer goods.

On the Chinese side, the remaining restrictions served economic nationalist rather than ideological purposes. Trade barriers were meant to protect certain industries, not to express revulsion against capitalism. Once Mao's concern about class struggle was discarded as a guide to foreign policy, China's political independence allowed it to encourage competition among trade and investment partners of all kinds.

During the period of Deng Xiaoping's rule, China increasingly stressed its independence in foreign policy, and a subtle shift occurred. Initially after 1978, China seemed to lean towards the West, which encouraged American hopes that China was beginning to engage in liberalization and perhaps join the US in strategic cooperation. China joined America in antagonism toward the socialist regime Beijing had previously championed in Vietnam. In 1979, Deng approved an invasion of Vietnam that proved a costly failure. Hanoi's Soviet-backed army withstood the pressure and continued its occupation of Cambodia, to Chinese and American opposition.

After 1982, however, Sino-American relations cooled somewhat for several reasons. The Reagan Administration tended to perceive China as a regional rather than a global power, and downplayed possibilities of strategic cooperation. Furthermore, the two sides failed to resolve the Taiwan issue to Beijing's satisfaction. And finally, there began a subtle shift in the global balance of power in favor of the US relative to the Soviet Union, a trend which encouraged China to redefine its posture vis-a-vis the superpowers as one of equidistance rather than tacit cooperation with the US.

China responded by renewing cultural and economic ties with the Soviet Union. By the mid-1980s trade with that country, though far lower than with the West, was growing more rapidly. China welcomed this and invited the Soviets to repair and develop some of the industrial projects they had abandoned in 1960. All of this while the Soviets and their allies were still "encircling" China in Vietnam, Afghanistan, and Outer Mongolia.

Did this mean that China's desire to admit one more competing trade partner would outweigh foreign policy considerations? Not at all. China was not succumbing to economic convenience. It calculated that it could keep political pressure on the Soviets and at the same time benefit from trading with them (as America did in the Reagan years). Rapidly expanding trade would remind the Soviets of what they could gain from peaceful behavior and full normalization of relations with China. By 1988 this strategy seemed to be effective, without substantial Chinese concessions, in encouraging the Soviets to withdraw from Afghanistan and to pressure Vietnam to retreat (policies the Soviets had other good reasons to adopt as well). Progress on these issues and reduced Sino-Soviet border tensions allowed further improvement in relations.

The People's Republic would find advantages in these developments. The Russians could refurbish some factories. They could sell or
supply industrial equipment which, though not the most advanced in the
world, would be useful to Chinese state enterprises. To trade with the
Soviet Union gives China a more diversified set of partners, and therefore
makes the country less vulnerable to fluctuating conditions in any one of
them. It adds an export market and another import supplier willing to
compete with others on price. For these reasons, Beijing decided in the
mid-1980s to separate trade from foreign policy issues--again underscoring its political independence from the West.

Americans need not be concerned, however, that China will begin
to substitute political and economic relations with the Soviet Union for the
ties with the West that it developed during the 1970s and 1980s. Only the
West has the capital and technology that China needs in order to modernize. It is true, as Nicholas Lardy has pointed out,[10] that the Soviets and
East Europeans are supplying some needed commodities and basic industrial equipment to China. However, an economy that cannot provide
sufficient soap for consumers in Moscow, its own capital, will hardly be
capable of furnishing the means to modernize China. And besides the
well known economic liabilities of the socialist countries, Soviet leader
Gorbachev and his principle of *glasnost* are politically dangerous for the
Chinese Communist Party. He is the embodiment of the kinds of changes
Chinese students were unsuccessfully demanding with their hunger strike
during his May, 1989 visit to Beijing. The turmoil that followed that visit
makes it clear that the Chinese Communists will have to maintain political
distance between themselves and Gorbachev until they are prepared to
allow *glasnost* at home.

Nor will China be able to turn to the Third World as the principal
focus of its foreign relations, as it attempted to do during the late 1960s.
Other Third World countries lack the markets for most of the goods China
will be exporting in larger numbers, and have even less of the capital and
technology China needs. Furthermore, China's aim of leaving the Third
World altogether by making itself wealthier and becoming a major power
widens the political gap between Beijing and other Third World regimes.
As a perceptive observer has commented: "[China's] call for South-South
cooperation is designed to blunt and disguise the competitive edge of
Sino-Third World relations."[11] China has used its membership of international organizations such as the World Bank to pursue national advantage
rather than Third World solidarity--an elusive ideal which China knows to
have few economic benefits.

The fact that China's foreign economic relations, if they are to
flourish, must be predominantly with the West, explains why China
cannot credibly threaten a severe curtailment of its opening up to the
outside world. The Chinese government has not, for example, linked
continuation of major aspects of its opening up policy to other bilateral
issues to try and gain concessions from the United States. To make such

linkages would have meant jeopardizing the very considerable benefits China has realized from a decade of engagement in foreign economic relations.

*   *   *

The case of the Chinese opening up policies presents other Communist governments with a blueprint for reform of their foreign economic policies. The benefits to a reforming state make it likely others will follow China's path in some respects, especially after the political openings in Eastern Europe in late 1989. By promoting regulated trade, China has shown how a socialist state can earn hard currency income for its production ministries and state-run enterprises which they can apply to their capital development needs. With foreign investment the state gets both productive capital and enhanced export production capacity. Special Economic (investment) Zones attract more capital, can be used as testing grounds for reform experiments (such as socialist equity stocks in Shenzhen), and publicize the country's tolerance of economic diversity. The economic drawbacks and problems discussed in this study are minor compared with these advantages to national productivity and economic strength--which can be easily embraced given the climate of rapid change in Eastern Europe.

Certain conditions were necessary, however, before China could welcome long-term participation of foreign capitalism in its economic development. The most fundamental was a weakening of the rulership's Marxist ideology. According to Marx, socialism would arise only after the self-destruction of capitalism. The idea of private corporations cooperating with socialist construction denies both class struggle and Marx's analysis of doomed capitalism. Only when a government's leaders doubt Marx (though they may not admit it) can they permit "one country, two systems." Since the governing ideology in other Communist states is a mixture of Marxism and nationalism, one cannot predict when the latter will prevail and alter national policy in the direction of neomercantilism. This transition means rejecting some of the beliefs on which government and politics have for decades been based. It also means sacrificing part of the justification of Communist Party rule (its supposed destiny as vanguard of the triumphant proletariat). Only stark economic and political failures could provide sufficient impetus for a Communist Party to institute these changes, and even then they have depended on extraordinary leaders such as Deng and Gorbachev.

The socialist government attempting an "opening up" must make substantial concessions to foreign business and must do so credibly. In China, whatever the restrictions on joint ventures, foreign partners know it is government policy not to let most operations become so costly that they fail. Business partners of the Soviet Union will require similar assurances. Credibility will depend on major laws and policies in support of joint ventures, backed up in practice. Some accompanying changes in domestic policy, such as increased autonomy for enterprises, are also necessary to persuade foreigners that reform reflects a genuine change of attitude in the government. Further, the country's foreign relations with at least some capitalist powers have to be adequate to permit substantial expansion of economic exchanges, particularly if technology transfer from the West is a major object.

The apparent success of China's opening up policies according to a variety of criteria has no doubt encouraged other Communist governments to try to emulate them. So far, it seems that China's trade and investment policies have been successful in obtaining hard currency earnings and productive capital contributions from foreign business partners. However, only incomplete data are available on the net flow of capital between China and its largest foreign investment partner, Hong Kong. This factor will qualify the results for China, as will the substandard quality of some equipment it has accepted. Furthermore, huge trade deficits arose when Chinese consumer demand for imports was unleashed. These indicate that protectionist barriers on consumer goods will have to be maintained by Communist governments unwilling to permit foreign competition against state-run industries. Whether or not the new non-Communist regimes in Eastern Europe will try to protect state industries remains unclear at this writing.

With regard to political issues of concern to the ruling elite, the first decade of opening up in China was a success. Contrary to some American predictions, it did not produce a snowballing political liberalization. To the contrary: the Communist Party retained the means of control (though they were ineptly handled). Regarding the possibility of a free press, for example, even the late Party leader Hu Yaobang (considered a hero by some Chinese students after his dismissal in early 1987) repeatedly emphasized that all newspapers must be mouthpieces of the Party. As noted previously, the Chinese government did not succumb to creeping liberalization. However, the opening up process did entail an expansion of contact, actively discouraged by the Chinese government, between Chinese and foreigners which spread knowledge of the outside world and fed demands for political reform. Whether these demands will prove successful, and what form the outcome will take, no one can predict. But the logic of the opening up process so far is suggestive about its future direction.

From the Chinese experience to date with several different aspects of opening up, one can identify several stages likely to be faced by any Communist country that initiates similar reforms in its foreign economic relations. These stages have appeared in the implementation of each of the policies examined in this study.

When China began its sweeping changes in foreign trade and investment policy in 1979, it was entering the unknown. There was no precedent or example to call on for guidance on how to replace central government fiats with macroeconomic intervention and partially decentralized authority. Previously, foreign trade deals were negotiated by the central government with strict quotas on import and export goods; now, specialized industries and provincial authorities could play more of a role while pricing and permits replaced rigid quotas. A parallel change was taking place in foreign investment--heretofore banned--while nothing reflected the new impulse toward decentralization more clearly than the creation of Special Economic Zones which relied on local initiative and foreign investment as the motors of growth. The methods of regulating and limiting these activities were not yet developed. The change in China's foreign economic posture necessitated broad compromises with foreign capitalism which had unforeseen economic consequences.

The first stage of development after that initial step into the unknown is a burst of economic growth. It is led by foreign capital moving to fill previously unavailable market niches, and by the increasingly profit-oriented activity of enterprises belonging to the state socialist economy itself. Initially, all looks favorable to the host country: cooperation with capitalists, who seem willing to subordinate themselves to "socialist" rules, begins. National growth accelerates, led by conspicuous commercial and tourist development in key cities (which are also the most frequently visited by foreigners, leading to more favorable publicity abroad). Host country consumers are getting more goods to purchase, and industry is getting more equipment.

The second stage begins two to four years later when the central government begins to scrutinize the quality of the invigorating new growth. Broad, dramatic openings that offer across-the-board concessions to foreign interests create unintended opportunities. In the Chinese case, relaxation of trade regulations led to buying sprees by enterprises seeking imported equipment, and by domestic consumers--with massive trade deficits the result. Also, the creation of Special Economic Zones gave some outside businessmen the means to penetrate the domestic market. This created an outflow of wealth that diminished the benefits of foreign capital contributions--which anyway contained less technology than initially hoped. It took several years for the central government to realize that to attain its goals would require influencing the quality of trade and investment flows crossing the border in both directions. This discovery was followed by central government action.

The third stage that occurs as the state socialist economy opens up is the reaction to initial economic results. The timing of this response depends on how quickly the government assesses the problems that have emerged. The Chinese government reacted within one year to its discovery of unsatisfactory results, with interventions in trade and investment; new protectionist controls on imports; strengthened restrictions on foreign investors' sales in the domestic market; and a cutoff of state subsidies to the Special Economic Zones.

Each central government action was accompanied by attempts to persuade foreign business partners that their privileges were being expanded, while in fact the contrary was true. The new rules limited some of their most profitable opportunities. The government tried to compensate for its intervention with renewed efforts to keep foreign business interested, such as offering joint ventures the right to trade convertible and nonconvertible profits among each other. In time, however, the inevitable result of reduced opportunities, all else being equal, is a drop in trade or investment. For example, to restrict joint ventures' sales rights diminishes their profitability and raises net costs. This causes some potential investors to reduce their capital commitments--even allowing for goodwill, propaganda, and other independent factors. The host country then has to readjust to the result: a diminished level of growth in some localities or sectors, though overall quality of growth is closer to the government's priorities.

After that, the process begins again with action and reaction. The host government enacts new measures designed to increase the amount of investment coming in while also continuing to try to influence its quality. Foreign businessmen seek remaining opportunities for profit, aware of both the need to maintain good relations with the host government (which tends to keep them in), and the fact that other countries may offer them better prospects. The ongoing results will fluctuate continually, not only because of the action-reaction cycle in the host country, but also because each side is affected by other fluctuating opportunities and constraints (including other economic conditions in the host country such as inflation, control of which may well take priority over further opening up).

Three outcomes are possible in the continuing interaction of political decisions and economic results. To examine them will show why the neomercantilist character of China's opening to the outside world is unlikely to change. Let us consider the less likely possibilities first.

One possible outcome is a reversion to the Marxist-Leninist political and ideological system that has already been partly repudiated. This would occur during one of the phases of retrenchment just described. Two conditions would make this outcome likely. First, if economic results remain unsatisfactory to the central government of the host country: for example, foreign investors persist in threatening domestic producers with competition in their home markets. Second, if government attempts to improve regulation of economic activity fail to accomplish their purposes. In the Chinese case, the effort to pressure foreign investment to develop export-oriented industries may only produce a drop in incoming capital. Or (as has actually happened) domestic price reform causes inflation which drives up costs of production and threatens to diminish the competitiveness of Chinese exports and enlarge trade deficits. Then, a "conservative" or hardline statist faction could with success call for a return to previously established policies, with foreign trade under strict central control and foreign investment kept to a minimum. This might be justified as cutting expensive losses.

The results to date indicate that such a reversal of the overall direction of policy is unlikely in China. The events of 1989 demonstrated that the hardliners are still there; indeed they are temporarily in the ascendant. But so far their grounds for complaint about foreign economic policy have been limited by the evident success of the opening up in stimulating growth and enlivening the domestic economy. By no standard have the problems outweighed these benefits.

There are several reasons why a sharp reversal of China's opening up reforms is very unlikely. To start with, the hardliners in government have not called for an outright ban on foreign investment, but only for tighter rules on its intrusion into the domestic economy. Furthermore, various state and provincial institutions have developed an interest in maintaining the policies that have developed, and they can point out the damage to China's international credibility if "basic" (since 1979) policies are reversed. Finally, in China, another factor supports continuation of the opening policies: the desire to emulate the stunning accomplishments of other East Asian states in rapid economic development. This is more and more explicitly reflected in published Chinese commentary about foreign economic policy and related topics, and has remained an important factor even in the repressive post-massacre environment.

There is, however, a second possibility for the eventual outcome of opening up by a state socialist economy: a true economic liberalization. This would mean a fundamental decentralization of authority over economic matters, to the point of acknowledging that international market forces could exert substantial influence on the allocation of goods in the domestic economy. It would lead to competition with home industries on both price and quality of goods, forcing some into bankruptcy or closure. Such an outcome is prevented in China by restrictions on domestic market access.

Yet there are tendencies toward economic liberalization: the eagerness of foreign business, whether by sales or investment, to penetrate the domestic market, and of some Chinese enterprises to further the growth of domestic commerce. Some Chinese economists are advocating further relaxation of central controls. Were they to be successful, the benefits of trade and investment to some cities might become so great that political demands for further opening up without restraint would arise. If some Chinese industries became truly export-competitive, they could begin to resent central oversight of their activities (e.g., hiring of labor), and policies that interfere with their obtaining of production inputs.

This second possibility, of initial opening up leading to self-sustaining decentralization and free trade, is only likely under certain circumstances. First, the initial results of policy would have to be successful in both quantity and quality of capital obtained through foreign economic cooperation (as was not true in China). This would undercut demands to slow down the pace of further opening up. Second, there would have to be clear prospects for substantial further growth in foreign trade and investment (the latter questionable in China until internal conditions and infrastructure improve). This would provide an incentive for further change. Third, the domestic economy has to be sufficiently diverse in geography or level of development that some sectors develop a strong association with and interest in promoting foreign economic relations. China does meet this condition. Finally and not least, decentralization in a Communist state would require overcoming the vested interests of central authorities in maintaining their grip on the economy. These necessary conditions make true economic liberalization of a state socialist economy highly unlikely.

The stunning decline of Communism in Eastern Europe after 1989 suggests another way in which economic liberalism *might* arise. If a Communist-dominated government is replaced in power by a non-Communist or even non-socialist coalition, the new regime could encourage a degree of opening up of the domestic economy to foreign competition that previously would have been anathema. However, such an outcome is unlikely in China, where the Communist Party has a strong indigenous base and even the illegal opposition has not been able to articulate a coherent vision of an alternative government.

Furthermore, even where Communism is toppled politically, the new government may not embrace economic liberalism wholeheartedly-- for much the same reasons just described. The new regime may not welcome economic forces that threaten state industries, which some perceive to be the economic base of state power. To the extent a weakening or rejection of Communism sparks a resurgence of nationalist fervor, such as that expressed with such passion by student-led demonstrators in April and May of 1989, renewed restrictions on foreign capitalist penetration are likely to be part of the end result--liberal rhetoric notwithstanding.

It is improbable that China's opening up will collapse into either restored Marxist-Leninist state control or economic liberalization as it is understood in the West. Rather, the process of adjustment described above is likely to continue indefinitely into the future. The domestic economy will continue to grow, in part under the stimulus of increasing economic exchanges with the outside world. The kinds of incentives and obstacles facing foreign business partners will probably not experience radical change. Investors and traders will always be attracted to the proverbial domestic market of one billion people, no matter what its level of openness and real wealth--and regardless of the lack of basic human rights the Chinese government has granted its people.

The central government will continue to have reasons for upholding its restrictions and protectionism that are part of the opening up policy. The resulting process of opening up, growth, and restoration of central control coincides with the fundamental aims of China's opening to the outside world clearly enunciated by national leaders.

The opening was a dramatic break with previous Marxist practice, intended to foster the growth of national productive capacity with a broad industrial basis. It logically treats all foreign countries as competing potential partners in a world in which China must also compete. In the People's Republic itself, nationalism, always the most potent factor in modern Chinese politics, has become the motivating force of foreign economic policy. Rather than transforming China into a pacific, liberal state, the opening to the outside world promises to make the nation a more formidable competitor, with a growing base of economic--and thus political--strength.

Notes

1. Quoted by the *New York Times*, Dec. 30, 1980; as cited by Maurice Meisner.

2. Ji Chongwei, Economic, Social, and Technological Research Institute, State Council; interview, Beijing, March 5, 1987.

3. Bruce Cumings, "The Political Economy of China's Turn Outward," in Samuel S. Kim, ed., *China and the World* (Boulder and London: Westview, 1984), 249-261.

4. Murray E. Bovarnick, "Human Resources Policies for Transnational Corporations in China," in Weizao Teng and N.T. Wang, eds., *Transnational Corporations and China's Open Door Policy* (Lexington, MA: Lexington Books, 1988), 233-250.

5. Peter Evans, *Dependent Development* (Princeton: Princeton University Press, 1979).

6. *The Economist*, Dec. 20, 1986, 93.

7. Chu Baotai, *Foreign Investment in China, Questions and Answers* (Beijing: Foreign Languages Press, 1986), 90-91; and *Zenyang Juban Zhongwai Hezi Jingying Qiye* (Beijing: Zhishi Chubanshe, 1986), 175-8.

8. *Los Angeles Times*, April 27, 1987, Business section, 1.

9. See for example Harry Harding, *China's Second Revolution* (Washington, DC: Brookings, 1987), Chapter 7.

10. Nicholas R. Lardy, *China's Entry Into the World Economy* (Lanham, MD: University Press of America, 1987), 19.

11. Samuel S. Kim, "China and the Third World: In Search of A Neorealist World Policy," in Kim, ed., *China and the World*, 207.

Selected Bibliography ⎯⎯⎯⎯⎯⎯⎯⎯⎯⎯⎯

This study relied primarily on English and Chinese language periodicals. The most important sources are indicated below. For a complete list of citations from the primary sources, please consult the footnotes.

PERIODICALS

Beijing Review
Caimao Jingji [Finance and Trade Economics]
The China Business Review
China Daily
The China Quarterly
Chinese Economic Studies
Daily Report, People's Republic of China (US Government, Foreign
    Broadcast Information Service)
The Economist
Far Eastern Economic Review
Guangzhou Yanjiu [Canton Research]
Guoji Jingjifa Yanjiu [Research on International Economic Law]
Guoji Maoyi [International Trade]
Guoji Maoyi Wenti [International Trade Problems]
Intertrade
JETRO China Newsletter
Jingji Yanjiu [Economic Research]
New York Times
Quarterly Economic Review of China, Hong Kong, North Korea
Quarterly Economic Review of China, North Korea
Renmin Ribao [People's Daily]
Shenzhen Tequ Bao [Shenzhen Special Economic Zone Report]
Shijie Jingji Daobao [World Economic Herald]

Summary of World Broadcasts, Part 3, The Far East (British Broadcasting Corporation, UK)
Survey of People's Republic of China Press (US Department of Commerce, Hong Kong)
Translations on the People's Republic of China (US Joint Publications Research Service)
Wall Street Journal
Weilai yu Fazhan [Future and Development]

BOOKS AND ARTICLES

Barnett, A. Doak, *China's Economy in Global Perspective*. Washington, DC: Brookings, 1981.
Biersteker, Thomas J., *Distortion or Development? Contending Perspectives on the Multinational Corporation*. Cambridge, MA: MIT Press, 1978.
China International Economic Consultants, *The China Investment Guide*. London: Longman, 1984.
China's Foreign Economic Legislation, Vol. 1. Beijing: Foreign Languages Press, 1982.
Chu Baotai, *Foreign Investment in China, Questions and Answers*. Beijing: Foreign Languages Press, 1986.
Chu Baotai and Dong Weiyuan, *Zenyang Juban Zhongwai Jingying Hezi Qiye* [How to Conduct Chinese-Foreign Equity Joint Venture Enterprises]. Beijing: Zhishi Chubanshe, 1986.
Chu, David K. Y. and Kwan-yiu Wong, eds., *Modernization in China, The Case of the Shenzhen Special Economic Zone*. Hong Kong: Oxford University Press, 1985.
Delfs, Robert, and others, eds., *China*. London: Euromoney Publications, 1986.
Deng Xiaoping, *Selected Works (1975-1982)*. Beijing: Foreign Languages Publishing House, 1984.
Evans, Peter, *Dependent Development*. Princeton: Princeton University Press, 1979.
Fang Sheng, ed., *Shenzhen Tequ Jingji Kaocha* [Economic Investigation of Shenzhen Special Economic Zone]. Shenzhen: Shenzhen University Press, 1984.
Gilpin, Robert, *U. S. Power and the Multinational Corporation*. New York: Basic Books, 1975.
Guojia Tongji Ju, *Zhongguo Tongji Nianjian, 1986* [Statistical Almanac of China, 1986]. Beijing: Zhongguo Tongji Chubanshe, 1986.
Guoyuyuan Jingji Jishu Shehui Fazhan Yanjiu Zhongxin, *Zhongguo Jingji Nianjian, 1986* [Almanac of China's Economy, 1986]. Beijing: Jingji Guanli Chubanshe, 1986.

Gu Shutang, ed., *Shenzhen Jingji Tequ Diaocha he Jingji Kaifaqu Yanjiu* [Investigation of Shenzhen Special Economic Zone and Research on Open Economic Zones]. Tianjin: Nankai University Press, 1984.

Harding, Harry, ed., *China's Foreign Relations in the 1980s*. New Haven, CT: Yale University Press, 1984.

Harding, Harry, *China's Second Revolution*. Washington, DC: Brookings, 1987.

Herzstein, Robert E., "China and the GATT: Legal and Policy Issues Raised by China's Participation in the General Agreement on Tariffs and Trade," *Law and Policy in International Business* XVIII:2 (1986), 371-415.

Ho, Samuel P. S. and Ralph W. Huenemann, *China's Open Door Policy: the Quest for Foreign Technology and Capital*. Vancouver: University of British Columbia Press, 1984.

Hu Changnuan, *Jiagexue* [The Study of Prices]. Beijing: Renmin Daxue Chubanshe, 1982.

Jao, Y. C. and K. C. Leung, eds., *China's Special Economic Zones*. Hong Kong: Oxford University Press, 1986.

Kim, Samuel S., ed., *China and the World*. Boulder and London: Westview, 1984.

Kleinberg, Robert, "The Spirit of Chinese Socialist Bureaucracy," in Christopher Hamilton and Jaroslaw Piekalkiewicz, eds., *The Theory of Socialist Public Bureaucracy*. London: Berg, 1990.

Lardy, Nicholas R., *China's Entry into the World Economy*. Lanham, MD: University Press of America, 1987.

Lenin, V. I., *State and Revolution*. New York: International Publishers, 1932.

Ma Hong and Sun Shangqing, eds., *Zhongguo Jingji Jiegou Wenti Yanjiu* [Research on Problems of China's Economic Structure], 2 Vols. Beijing: Renmin Chubanshe, 1983.

Mao Tsetung, *Selected Works*, Vol. 5. Beijing: Foreign Languages Press, 1977.

McDonnell, J. E. D., "China's Move to Rejoin the GATT System: An Epic Transition," *The World Economy* X:3 (Sept., 1987), 331-350.

Ministry of Foreign Economic Relations and Trade (Beijing), ed., *1984 Almanac of China's Foreign Economic Relations and Trade*. Hong Kong: China Resources Trade Consultancy, 1985.

Moser, Michael J., *Foreign Trade, Investment and the Law in the People's Republic of China*. Hong Kong: Oxford University, Press, 1987.

The Official Chinese Customs Guide, 1985/86. London: Longman 1985.

Qian Jiaju, ed., *Tequ Jingji Lilun Wenti Lunwenji* [Collected Articles on the Theoretical Problems of Special Economic Zones]. Beijing: Renmin Chubanshe, 1984.

Riskin, Carl, *China's Political Economy*. New York: Oxford University Press, 1987.

Scalapino, Robert and others, eds., *Asian Economic Development--Present and Future*. Berkeley: Institute of East Asian Studies, 1985.

Schwartz, Benjamin, *Chinese Communism and the Rise of Mao*. Cambridge, MA: Harvard University Press, 1979.

Shenzhen Municipal Party Committee, *Qianjinzhong de Shenzhen* [Advancing Shenzhen]. Beijing: Hongqi Chubanshe, 1984.

Stoltenberg, Clyde D., "China's Special Economic Zones," *Asian Survey* XXIV:6 (June, 1984), 637-54.

Teng Weizao and N. T. Wang, eds., *Transnational Corporations and China's Open Door Policy*. Lexington, MA: Lexington Books, 1988.

Tsao, James T. H., *China's Economic Development Strategies and Foreign Trade*. Lexington, MA: Heath, 1987.

Wang Yihe and others, *Zhongwai Hezi Jingying Qiye* [Chinese-Foreign Equity Joint Venture Enterprises]. Shanghai: Shehui Kexueyuan Chubanshe, 1984.

Wei Lin and Arnold Chao, *China's Economic Reforms*. Philadelphia: University of Pennsylvania Press, 1982.

The World Bank, *China, Economic Structure in International Perspective*. Washington, DC: World Bank, 1985.

The World Bank, *China, Long Term Development Issues and Options*. Baltimore: Johns Hopkins University Press, 1985.

Xu Dixin, ed., *China's Search for Economic Growth*. Beijing: New World Press, 1982.

Xue Muqiao, ed., *Almanac of China's Economy, 1986*. Hong Kong: Modern Cultural Company, 1987.

Youngson, A. J., *China and Hong Kong, the Economic Nexus*. Hong Kong: China Resources Advertising Company, 1988.

Yu Guangyuan, ed., *China's Socialist Modernization*. Beijing: Foreign Languages Press, 1984.

Zheng Tuobin and others, eds., *Almanac of China's Foreign Economic Relations and Trade, 1987*. Hong Kong: China Resources Advertising Company, 1988.

Zhou Taihe and others, eds., *Dangdai Zhongguo de Jingji Tizhi Gaige* [Reform of the Economic System in Contemporary China]. Beijing: Zhongguo Shehui Kexue Chubanshe, 1984.

Index